World of Wildlife

World of
Wildlife

Anthony and
Jacqueline Nayman

Facts On File ☑ **New York**

Editorial Coordinator: John Mason
Art Editor: Grahame Dudley
Design: Ann Dunn
Editor: Livia Wilde
Research: Frances Vargo

ISBN 0-87196-408-2
Library of Congress Catalog
Card No: 78-24711
© 1979 J.G. Ferguson Publishing Company
First published in the United States
by Facts on File, Inc.,
460 Park Avenue South,
New York, N.Y. 10016
Printed and bound in Hong Kong by Leefung-ASCO.

Introduction

This book is about the world's animals and where they live. Animals are found everywhere – in all climates and in all types of terrain from icy waters to burning deserts, from mountains to plains. In fact, the world has so many animals that it is not possible to count them. So far, scientists have classified or grouped almost a million kinds of fauna all over the globe, but each year hundreds of new kinds are discovered. The book is organized into chapters along the same lines that zoologists use to divide the world's animal life, which is into six regions or realms together with Antarctica and various islands and island groups scattered around the world. These zoogeographical regions are shown on the next two pages. Then, after a first chapter explaining how animals developed into their present forms, each chapter describes a region in detail. Using over 20 relief maps with clearly recognizable symbols to show where the various animals live, this volume takes the reader on a worldwide wildlife safari, from Africa to Antarctica and from Greenland to the Galápagos.

Contents

Overleaf: the map of the world showing
how wildlife is divided geographically.
Neither Antarctica nor certain islands
are considered part of the six
zoogeographical regions, Antarctica
because it can support only insects and
marine animals, and particular islands
because each one is different from the
other and also from the region nearest
to it.

How Zoologists Divide the World

40°

80°

120°

160°

80°

ARCTIC CIRCLE

O P E

A S I A

40°

TROPIC OF CANCER

C A

EQUATOR 0°

A U S T R A L I A

TROPIC OF CAPRICORN

40°

ANTARCTIC CIRCLE

A N T A R C T I C A

40°

80°

120°

160°

Chapter 1

Animal Distribution

Animals are not spread evenly and uniformly over the earth. Sometimes the fauna of one country is surprisingly similar to another, sometimes it is markedly different. Some people believe that this is because God created the different animals according to how well suited they were for the various countries. Others believe that all animals of a kind have evolved from the same simple forms over thousands of millions of years, according to the Theory of Evolution.

Then, why are kangaroos, pandas, or lions not found everywhere? Obviously climate has a great deal to do with it, and also the presence of oceans that prevent the spread of most animals from one continent to another. However, if we examine animal distribution closely we find that it is not quite as simple as that. If we believe that the arrangement of the continents on the world's surface has always been as it is today, peculiar distributions like that of the tapir, which is found both in Asia and South America but nowhere else, defy understanding. However, science has recently proved that for millions and millions of years the land masses have been moving slowly over the surface of the globe, grouping and regrouping themselves into different configurations. This helps explain the sometimes strange distribution of animals.

An African elephant assumes its characteristic threatening pose against an enemy. Unlike their Asian cousins, African elephants eat a large amount of bark and leaves as well as grass. They are so destructive in their methods of uprooting trees and have such huge appetites that they have contributed to endangering other wildlife of Africa.

Similarities and Differences

With very few exceptions all animals are capable of reproducing themselves, and unless each mating pair produces not more than two offspring during their lives, the number of animals must increase. Aside from humans, who can control the size of their family, all animals produce many more than two – in fact, some may give birth to several hundred at a time. Charles Darwin, who formulated the Theory of Evolution, calculated that, taking the slowest breeding species he knew of – the elephant – and starting with only one pair, there would be 19 million elephants alive after 750 years. All of these would be descended from that first pair. Darwin was not the first person to realize that animals have a geometric rate of increase, however. It was Thomas Malthus, a British economist who lived from 1766 to 1834. Alarmed by the increase in population that followed the Industrial Revolution, Malthus predicted doom for the human race on the basis that food production would not keep up with the rate of procreation.

As their numbers increase, animals tend to spread out in order to have enough living space and food. The logical end product of such movement is a worldwide distribution of all species. This does not work out in fact, of course. Many animals will not survive long enough to breed, having been killed by starvation or other animals. Predators have the effect of restricting the spread of their prey; in turn, the scarcity of prey will limit the numbers of predators and prevent them from spreading.

Direct competition with other species for space and food is another factor that limits the spread of animals. This kind of competition becomes clear when humans upset the balance between competing animals by introducing a new species. Sometimes the newcomer manages to survive better than indigenous animals. This happened on the introduction of rabbits into Australia, for example.

The distribution of animals is also influenced by climate, both directly and indirectly through the vegetation it produces. No one expects to find polar bears in the tropics or boa constrictors in the Arctic. They are each adapted to one of the two extremes of climate. Other animals are adapted to other extremes such as desert, marsh, or tropical jungle. But animals can be restricted to an even greater degree if they have become adapted to one special food. For example, the giant panda can only live in bamboo forests because it lives on bamboo shoots, and the koala only in Australia because it lives on eucalyptus leaves.

Physical barriers will also prevent animals from spreading. Deserts, mountains, and rivers present impassable obstacles to some species. The most efficient barrier of all is the sea, even though wide oceans have not stopped some animals from colonizing. The seas have not proved a total barrier to birds and bats which, therefore, tend to have a wide distribution, nor to salt water fish. Even some reptiles and land mammals have managed to journey to offshore islands. Tapirs and pigs are strong swimmers, and tortoises can float good distances in their boatlike carapaces. It is possible for small animals to be carried a long way on rafts of debris washed out to sea by flooding rivers. None of these animals could be expected to cover the vast distances between one continent and another, so most land species come to a

full stop on the coastline of the continent on which they live.

The fact that no continent has a unique fauna, and that the sharing of species among the continents is sometimes extraordinary is a problem that has only recently been largely resolved.

Left: the koala, which looks like a small bear but is closer to an opossum, is tied by a very restricted diet to living only in Australia. It feeds exclusively on tender eucalyptus shoots.

Below: an American saw-whet owl swoops on its prey swiftly and silently, usually catching it off guard. Owls are found all throughout the world in temperate, tropical, and subarctic areas.

The Theory of Evolution

In 1835 a 10-gun brig, the *Beagle*, sailed its way toward a low, black, lava-covered island. Its volcanic cones reminded the ship's naturalist, Charles Darwin, of the foundry chimneys of his native Staffordshire. The place was Chatham Island, their first landfall on the Galápagos Islands, whose wildlife filled Darwin's mind with speculation on the origin of animals.

"All the small birds that live on these lava-covered islands have short beaks, very thick at the base, like that of a bullfinch. This appears to be one of those admirable provisions of Infinite Wisdom by which each created thing is adapted to the place for which it was intended," commented the *Beagle's* captain, Robert Fitzroy. But Darwin looked a good deal closer and philosophized differently. He saw that, although they were remarkably alike in most other ways, several of the small dull finches had differently shaped beaks. Some had large beaks as the captain described, ideal for cracking nuts. Others had small neat beaks better for eating insects. Still others possessed a long beak for feeding on leaves and buds, while, finally, the extraordinary cactus finch used a cactus spine held in its strong beak to extract insects from vegetation. All these birds had similar bodies, all built the same sort of nests, and all laid four similarly colored eggs. What is more, all were practically identical to a finch from the coast of South America, though that was 300 miles away. Reasoning from these facts some 26 years later, Darwin theorized that all these birds had a common ancestor, that some of these ancestral birds must have been blown across from the mainland to the various islands, and that there they had developed in different ways over the centuries and had adapted to make the best use of their new habitats. This was one of the many hundreds of examples Darwin used to argue that animal species were not immutable but changed over millions of years. The logical conclusion was that human beings had evolved with the animals from simple primeval forms.

These ideas Darwin finally published in 1859 in a book, *The Origin of Species*. They were very shocking to some people. They seemed to disprove the biblical stories of Adam and Eve, of the earth's being created in six days, and of Noah and the flood, and they categorically denied that the world had been in existence for only 6000 years. Worse still, they seemed to replace divine guidance by a hit-or-miss system of chance based on the idea of the survival of the fittest. This holds that no two animals in any species are exactly alike, and that those with variations which help them to succeed – perhaps in getting more food than others of their kind – survive. Those not having these advantageous variations perish.

Even though publication of this work caused a great furore, the ideas that Darwin set forth were not entirely new. During the previous century geology had been established as a new science and James Hutton, known as the father of geology, had theorized in 1785 that the earth was far older than rigid believers in the Old Testament supposed. At the time of his death he was working on a book in which he expressed belief in evolution by natural selection. Hutton's book was not published and Darwin had no inkling of its existence, although he was familiar with the works of Charles Lyell, Hutton's disciple. Darwin must also have read the works of the French naturalists Georges-Louis Buffon and Jean-Baptiste Lamarck, and of his own grandfather, Erasmus Darwin, whose ideas on evolution were similar to Lamarck's and unorthodox for his day.

Above: different beaks of four Galápagos finches as studied by Darwin. The variations are adaptations by one species for feeding.

All these earlier writers had something to say about the evolution of animals from early simple forms and the relationship between living and dead forms, fossils of which were being dug up in Darwin's time. The 19th century was an age of intense scientific curiosity, in which inquiring minds were pursuing similar lines of thought. Therefore it is not too much of a coincidence that two men, Darwin and Alfred Russel Wallace, came to the same conclusion at the same time with a theory that evolution took place by natural selection.

In 1859 Wallace was studying the natural history of the East Indies and, while suffering from a bout of malaria, began to read Malthus. This reading triggered off very much the same ideas that Darwin had been pondering ever since his *Beagle* voyage. Wallace wrote out his "Theory of Evolution by Natural Selection" in two days and sent it for comment to the older Darwin, by then a well-established scientist, without knowing of Darwin's work on the subject. They published their theories jointly in the *Journal of the Linnaean Society* and quickly followed the first paper by "The Origin of Species."

Left: Darwin's tanager was named after the naturalist Charles Darwin, who made this drawing of the bird for his book *The Voyage of HMS Beagle*. The tanager is related to the finch, of which Darwin's close observation led to his theories on evolution.

Continental Drift

Wallace added to his work on evolution by plotting maps that showed the distribution of animals on the earth, and came to the conclusion that the world could be divided into six zoogeographical regions according to the types of animals living in each one. A former president of the Zoological Society of London had already produced such a zoogeographical division and, although he only used the distribution of birds as the criterion, his results were much the same as Wallace's. Of course, there are some animals found almost worldwide – the barn owl and osprey among birds for example – but by and large the animals of one region differ from those of another. The exception is in areas between the regions, which are known as transitional zones and where species tend to overlap.

The Theory of Evolution explained why animals within each region had evolved differently, but it did not explain how they had arrived there in the first place. In 1915 Alfred Wegener published a theory that made possible a logical explanation of animal distribution. Having pondered on how beautifully the coastlines of America and Africa would fit together if Africa were moved about 1000 miles to the west, he went on to formulate his theory of continental drift. According to this theory, until about 300 million years ago, when the forests that later became coal were growing on the earth, all the continents were united into a single supercontinent. This vast land mass began to break up gradually into the continents of today that proceeded to drift away from each other with infinite slowness. This slow pace of movement apart allowed the early evolution of animals and plants to occur along similar lines before the fragmentation of the single land mass. Once the separation had taken place, the animals evolved differently in response to different conditions.

Although subsequent scientific discoveries proved that Wegener was amazingly close to the truth, his theory of continental drift convinced few scientists at the time. So scientists had to find other explanations for the distribution of animals. One was that the seas have not always been at their present level, and that when they sank dramatically, they left land bridges between some of the continents. Certainly the Palaearctic and Nearctic regions have been joined across the Bering Strait at various times in the earth's history, and this explains why the wildlife of the two regions are so similar. Distribution of animals in two far-flung places, such as that of the tapirs, can also be explained in this way. Presumably the ancestors of present-day tapirs crossed the Bering Strait from Asia and spread throughout North and South America, and survived only at the farthest limits of their range: the Malayan Peninsula and South America. In the same way animals probably migrated to islands lying near continental coasts, but in order to account for the present distribution of all animals by this means, imaginary land bridges had to cross the oceans like highways in a spaghetti junction. How else explain that Australia shares pouched animals with South America? That Australia, South America, and Africa share various freshwater fish, turtles, and frogs? That these same three countries share flightless birds?

The land bridge theory also fell down when applied to fossils of a type of seed fern that had flourished in the Carboniferous period, that had long been known in Asia, Australia, and South America, and that were discovered in Antarctica by the Scott expedition. Only a theory that joined these continents at a latitude considerably warmer than the one on which Antarctica is now situated could make sense.

Confirmation of Wegener's theory came long after his death and from an unexpected source. The facts that really clinched his argument stemmed from a study of the magnetic properties of rocks.

Below: the royal albatross lives on the islands near New Zealand and the southern tip of South America. This bird, of which there are nine species, is one of the few animals to be found worldwide. Albatrosses build their nests on the cliff tops of remote islands, and this isolation makes them free of natural enemies.

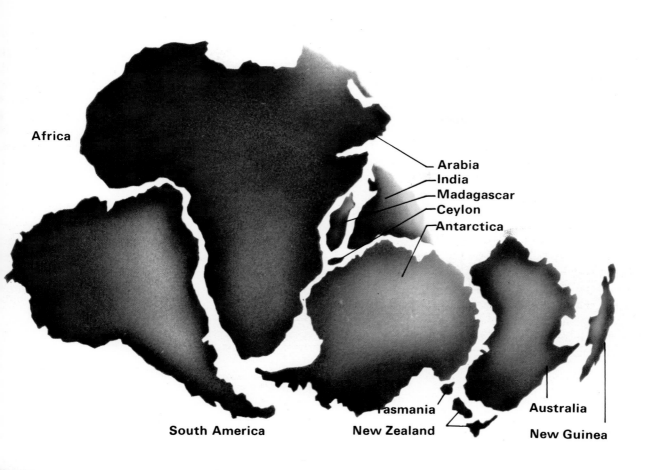

Africa

Arabia
India
Madagascar
Ceylon
Antarctica

South America

Tasmania
New Zealand

Australia

New Guinea

Above: a diagram showing how the continents and large islands of the southern hemisphere once fitted together into one big land mass or supercontinent. The theory that this supercontinent broke and drifted apart, as proposed by Alfred Wegener about 55 years ago, is now generally accepted.

Plates on the Move

When iron filings are sprinkled onto a piece of cardboard placed over a bar magnet, they immediately arrange themselves into a pattern showing the force field of the magnet. The earth on which we live behaves like a huge magnet and has a force field similar to that indicated by the iron filings on a bar magnet, except that instead of having two dimensions it has three. When new rocks are formed, the magnetic particles arrange themselves like the iron filings in the experiment and, as the rock hardens, they are frozen into position like tiny compass needles.

Ever since the 17th century it has been known that the magnetic field of the earth is slowly changing, with the magnetic north pole slowly changing its position around the earth's axis. The studies of earth magnetism that were conducted at the beginning of the 20th century showed something far more dramatic: at various times during the history of the earth, the polarity has actually reversed itself, the north and south poles swapping positions.

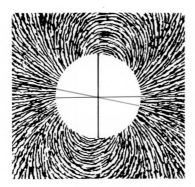

Above: this diagram shows how the lines of force of the earth's magnetic field are increasingly dipping toward the poles. The axis of the magnetic poles is in blue, the axis of the geographical poles is in red, and the line of the equator is in black.

This strange fact, which has never been satisfactorily explained, provided proof for the proponents of the theory of continental drift. In 1955 the floor of part of the Atlantic Ocean was mapped by dragging a magnetic detector over its surface and, amazingly, was discovered to be made of strips of alternating polarity. What is more, the pattern of the strips on one side of the Atlantic was found to be the opposite of those on the other side with the mid-Atlantic ridge – a mountain chain on the ocean floor – as its center. It has since been established by taking samples of rock from the sea floor that molten rock is constantly oozing out from this central ridge and is pouring down on either side. As it cools it becomes imprinted with the earth's polarity. In this way the Atlantic Ocean is growing at a rate of about two centimeters a year and has been doing so for approximately the last 200 million years.

All the oceans have underwater ridges that ooze out volcanic basalt from the earth's interior. Is the world expanding dramatically because of this extra sea floor? Geologists do not believe so, holding instead that it is probably being destroyed somewhere.

The concept of the spreading of the sea floor together with the theory of continental drift has given rise to the theory of plate tectonics, which in itself goes a long way to explain animal distribution and for which there is a good deal of proof. According to this theory, the lithosphere or outer shell of the earth is made up of a number of rigid plates which are in constant slow movement and which float on the molten or semimolten rock of the next layer called the asthenosphere. These plates may be made up of ocean crust only, which are often called oceanic plates, or of ocean floor with pieces of less dense continental

crust riding on them, which are referred to as continental plates. One of the explanations for plate movement is that it is due to hot molten rock which produces currents, known as convection currents, that rise vertically from the hotter lower layers beneath the earth's crust.

Whatever the reason, plates can move in any direction relative to each other. They may slide past each other, which is the kind of movement that takes place at the San Andreas Fault in California. They can move away from each other, as they are doing in the mid-Atlantic and which can be seen on opposite sides of the oceanic ridge. They can collide after moving toward one another.

When two plates collide, one of them overrides the other, the oceanic one has to dip down, and a trench is formed. If both plates are oceanic, the lower one descends into the molten asthenosphere and the ocean crust forming its outer layer melts in the increasing heat. Fused with other materials from the earth's interior, the crust is spewed onto the surface. This results in a chain of volcanoes that rise through

Above: earthquake activity in the United States is centered on California's San Andreas Fault where drainage patterns all along the fault have been disrupted, as this photograph shows. Horizontal jerking movements of continental plates cause earthquakes.

the sea near the trench in the form of a string of volcanic islands. There are several such trenches and island chains in the Pacific Ocean.

If an oceanic plate collides with a continental plate, the lower plate dips toward the center of the earth and a trench forms close to the coast of the continental plate. The melted crust that gushes up rises through earth in volcanic action that forms mountains. The Andean range of South America probably was and still is being formed in this way.

If two continental plates collide, neither can dip down. This means that the impact of their collision crumples the rock layers of the continents and forces up vast mountain chains. It is thought that the Himalayas were formed many millions of years ago by a collision of the plate carrying India with the plate carrying Asia.

Earthquakes and volcanic action occur when plates meet. If such seismic activities are plotted on a map of the world, they outline the tectonic plates.

Above: the coral-fringed island of Raiatea is one of the many mountainous islands pushed up in the Pacific Ocean by volcanic action. In fact, most of the world's major island chains occur on the rim of the Pacific Ocean, around the edge of the Pacific plate. The Carolines, Marianas, Ryukus, Kurils, and Aleutians all rise steeply from the sea and have underwater trenches near.

19

Earliest Animals

If it is accepted that the Atlantic sea floor is spreading slowly from its central ridges and has been doing so for eons, then it follows that the Americas must at one time have lain virtually next door to Europe and Africa or even were joined as Wegener suggested half a century ago. This theory is now generally believed. In fact, it is now currently thought that the continents have been on the move, riding on their rigid plates of

somewhat before that point that the plates had moved apart. For, it is argued, if animals live on a fairly uniform land mass, they have no reason to evolve differently. If, however, the world is made up of a large number of land masses, all with different climates that produce different habitats, the number of species that evolve will be correspondingly greater. A comparison of fossil changes with the make-up of the world's land masses therefore supports the argument that the plates have moved.

Here is a tentative account of what might have happened to the world in the last 2000 million years:

The ancient rocks of the earth's crust that are found in the shield regions of the continents, and

Left and below: two reconstructions of the ichthyostega, which was one of the earliest of the amphibians. Fossils of this vertebrate show that it still retained some characteristics of the fish from which it evolved, such as a small dorsal fin along the tail. The ichthyostega lived in the warm swamps that once covered Greenland in the late Devonian period, which started about 400 million years ago and lasted for about 55 million years.

earth crust, for more than 200 million years and possibly as long as 2000 million years. This movement created or closed oceans different from those existing today.

Two thousand million years is a very long time, and it is difficult to ascertain what was happening so long ago. However, by studying the rocks of the ocean floor and the continental crust, particularly those of mountain ranges that were thrown up when plates collided, scientists are able to make an informed guess. The study of fossils can also throw light on plate movement because fossils show at what point in time animals evolved differently, and it would be that are more than 2000 million years old, are not made up in the same way as the younger mountain chains and volcanic islands that we know are formed by the collision of the tectonic plates. It is therefore believed that the movement of the tectonic plates did not start until after 2000 million years ago.

About 700 million years ago in pre-Cambrian times, when the highest form of animal life was some kind of marine worm, it is thought that all the continental crust was joined into one supercontinent. This may not have been the very first arrangement of the land masses which, like today, may have been in the form of separate continents before, but it was the beginning of the split up into the slowly drifting rigid plates that form the earth's crust of the present.

In the Cambrian period about 570 million years ago, this supercontinent broke up into four land masses, incidentally forming three new oceans in the process. One land mass, called Gondwanaland, probably consisted of all the present-day continents of the southern hemisphere – Africa, Australia, Antarctica, and South America. The three other land masses consisted of what are now known as North America, Europe, and Asia, although Greenland and part of North America were probably part of the European mass.

This break-up was followed by a burst of evolutionary activity during which time the invertebrates began to diversify and form the forerunners of such present-day animals as clams, spiders, lobsters, and starfish. The marine animals bearing shells left fossils such as trilobites.

It was during the next 180 thousand years, as the North American and European continents slowly drew together, that the vertebrates first made an appearance. The early history of vertebrates is not as easy to study as that of their boneless relations because they evolved in fresh water and have left few fossils, but somewhere around 400 million years ago the first fish appeared

By the Devonian period 390 million years ago, two of the northern continents had come together to form Euramerica. The Caledonian mountain system of northern Scotland and northwest Scandinavia and the Appalachian system of Canada and the United States were thrown up in the process. It was on this continent that the vertebrates first crawled ashore. The earliest amphibian fossils are found in Greenland, which at that time was situated near the equator along with Euramerica. The Sahara Desert, on the other hand, was then covered by a polar icecap.

Further convergence of continents followed, and by the end of the Carboniferous era 280 million years ago, Euramerica had joined the vast southern continent of Gondwanaland. Some 55 million years later Asia collided with the other land mass, at which time the Ural Mountains were formed. All continental crust was once again joined to form one immense land mass known as *Pangaea* (all lands).

Left: an artist's impression of a forest in the Carboniferous period that began about 345 million years ago and lasted about 100 million years. Winged insects and reptiles developed during that period.

Below: dinosaurs and flying reptiles lived during the Cretaceous period that started about 135 million years ago. Pictured, a Tyrannosaurus attacks a Monoclonius in view of a Pteranodon.

The Age of the Dinosaurs

It was during the formation of Pangaea, when the continents crashed together obliterating seas and throwing up mountain chains, that the reptiles started to conquer the land and to largely replace the amphibia. The age of reptiles lasted more than 200 million years.

The fact that amphibia and reptiles were in existence at the time of the fusion of the land masses goes a long way to explain the distribution of their successors after the drift apart. For example, there is a primitive frog of New Zealand whose only close relation is found in the streams of North America. There is also one form of fossil reptile that has turned up in Antarctica, India, South Africa, and western China.

By the end of the Triassic era some 180 million years ago, Pangaea started to break up into northern and southern parts, separated by the Tethys Sea. The northern land mass, known as Laurasia, consisted of present-day Europe, North America, and Asia except for India. The southern block, called Gondwana, was composed of all the remaining continents.

This splitting up was accompanied by a great diversification of marine animals and by the development of the first small mammals, but the most spectacular animal to appear was the dinosaur. It has been suggested that the sundering of the continents caused both the development and extinction of these giant reptiles. This theory holds that the amount of

Above: the Triceratops was one of the armored dinosaurs of the Cretaceous period. It had long pointed horns over each eye, and these horns were an adaptation for feeding as well as for defense, being used to bend down small trees to reach its leaves.

carbon dioxide released into the air by volcanic action during fragmentation created a greenhouse condition, raising the world temperature to one suitable for such monsters. After the final fragmenta-

tion of Pangaea was complete, the theory goes, the amount of carbon dioxide in the atmosphere diminished, the temperature fell, and the creatures died.

In terms of the earth's history, Laurasia and Gondwana did not remain intact for very long. By the late Cretaceous period, about 70 million years ago, they were breaking up. Gondwana divided into five

Above: the Trachodon was a very large duck-billed dinosaur whose fossils have occurred fairly widely in North America, but it had close relations all over the world. Trachodons had webbed feet and probably went into the water when looking for escape.

segments. Of these, Africa and Indi
ward, obliterating the Tethys Sea. Ultimately they met and joined Asia, throwing up both the Alps and the Himalayas. Australia probably severed itself next. Then Antarctica and South America separated, the latter moving westward as the Atlantic Ocean opened up. This spread of the Atlantic sea floor also split up Laurasia, although it is possible that the separation took place after the opening up of the southern Atlantic. Finally, and very much later, North and South America united at the Isthmus of Panama, as they are today.

The dissolution of Pangaea into the present continents provided animals with a diversity of habitats. The response was a rapid acceleration of evolution which led to the enormous variety of animal forms of today. The comparatively new class of mammals adapted best and gained the ascendancy.

Shortly before the great break-up, two groups of mammals evolved. One group consisted of pouched animals, or marsupials, that produce relatively unformed babies which must finish their development in the mother's pouch. The other group, to which humans belong, gives birth to fully developed offspring. On most of the continents the pouched mammals soon became extinct, surviving only in South America and Australia.

The comparatively late separation of North America from Europe explains the very great similarity in the mammals of the two regions as well as the big difference between the wildlife of North and South America.

The Last Million Years

By the beginning of the Pleistocene epoch about one million years ago, the continents of the world were in much the same positions as they are today. However, two things happened to alter the distribution of animals. One was the occurrence of the Ice Ages, and the other was the emergence of the human.

Beginning about one million years ago, and advancing and retreating in four main cycles, ice covered most of the northern hemisphere. This had the effect of lowering the temperature all over the world and, because a large amount of sea water was turned into ice, of reducing the level of the oceans.

influence their distribution was the human being.

For thousands of years men remained hunters, but because they used primitive tools and because their number was comparatively small, the human impact on the animal world was not noticeably adverse. It might even have been beneficial, for in the same way that wolves and other predators weed out the weak and sickly specimens from the herbivorous herds on which they prey, so might people possibly have kept the numbers of deer, bison, and antelopes in check. There is no certainty of this, however. Hunting by early men has been put forward as an explanation of the rather sudden extinction of so many species at the end of the Ice Ages.

Once people began to cultivate the land – about

Below: this view of the mountains of the Antarctic Peninsula is a reminder of what much of the world looked like in the Ice Ages. Animals died out or retreated south before the glaciers.

As the Pleistocene ice spread south, many animals unable to survive the cold conditions either died out or were pushed even farther south, but this epoch also witnessed the evolution of a number of new giant animals. There were mammoth elephants, giant beavers, and giant moose in the north, giant sloths in South America, giant pigs in Africa, and even giant kangaroos in Australia. They may have become so large because it is easier for a big animal to conserve body heat than it is for a small one. Another adaptation to the cold was long hair, so that the now extinct relative of the elephant, for example, bore a wooly coat.

By the end of the Ice Ages the harsh conditions had had an effect on the variety and distribution of animals throughout the world. The cat known as the saber-toothed tiger, the mammoth, and other giant animals were extinct. Tapirs, rhinoceroses, monkeys, and camels which until then had roamed the northern hemisphere, were restricted to the south, although the camel still kept a foothold in the Palaearctic region. In fact, by the end of the last glaciation the world's animals had sorted themselves into the groups in which they now exist. The factor that was most to

10,000 years ago – it meant that they interfered with wild animals in a different way, because in order to grow crops they had to clear the land of its natural vegetation. This destroyed the habitats of large numbers of animals. With the rapid growth of the human race, it is cultivation of the land that has probably had the worst effect on wildlife.

The invention of the gun was another decisive influence on the animals of the world. Since it has made killing so easy and so comparatively safe for the hunter, humankind has exploited animals for fur and feathers as well as for food – and even fun. The animals most vulnerable to attack have been those living on islands where there is little chance of escape.

Even on the continents, however, some animals have become extinct as the direct result of adverse human conduct. People have grown aware of the dangers with which they threaten the animal kingdom belatedly, and have tried to reverse the situation with the establishment of reserves and parks.

Right: reconstruction of a woolly mammoth, an Ice Age mammal related to the elephant, based on remains found in the ice in Siberia. The long hair of this type of mammoth helped to protect it from the severe cold. It died out about 10,000 years ago.

Chapter 2

The Palaearctic Region

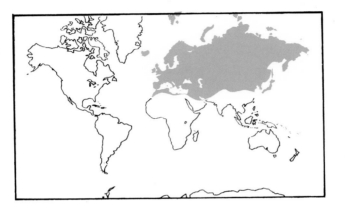

Of all the zoogeographical regions the Palaearctic is far and away the largest, covering more than half the earth's circumference. It is bounded on the east by the narrow Bering Strait which separates it from North America (part of the Nearctic Region), and on the west by the Denmark Strait between Iceland and Greenland. It stretches north to the Pole and south to an uneven line midway between the 40th parallel and the Tropic of Cancer. In the Arabian Peninsula, however, it dips farther and cuts across the Tropic of Cancer.

In so vast an area, the climate, vegetation, and terrain vary enormously. A person could freeze to death in the north of Siberia, or die of heatstroke in the Arabian deserts, for example. This diversity of conditions is matched by a diversity of wildlife, among which few of the animals are unique to the region.

The Siberian tiger has a thicker and longer coat than tigers that live in warmer climates. Siberia was the original home of this animal, which is one of the largest of the cats. During the Ice Ages, the tiger spread over most of Eurasia. Today, however, it is again found only in Asia, although its range has been extended as far south as the islands of Java and Bali.

Man's Impact

Because the Palaearctic region contains the most densely industrialized parts of the world, it is hardly surprising that its ecology has been greatly disturbed. The only areas of the Palaearctic that have escaped disruption are those that are too uncomfortable for human beings to occupy in any great numbers – such regions, for instance, as the frigid north, the high mountain ranges, and the deserts and semideserts. The deciduous and evergreen woodlands that once covered great tracts of central and southern Europe and parts of Asia have by now almost completely disappeared, sacrificed to cities, farms, and factories.

With the clearing of the woodlands came the destruction or dispersal of the many animals that lived within them. Northern China with its very dense human population is an extreme example of this. In 1872 the French missionary and naturalist Père Armand David (1826–1900), who spent a great deal of time in China, wrote: "I have often wondered what leads the Chinese to destroy the woods of their vast empire so completely." He concluded that their motivation was fear of the wild animals of the forest. "To comprehend the sacrifices made to procure tranquility and security, one must have lived as I did in these houses near thickets haunted by some of these terrible beasts." No doubt the thick woodland

was a frightening place, especially when one might meet wolves, bears, wild boar, tigers, and leopards. In any case, by the end of the 19th century these animals had either been killed or driven from most of their original haunts into the mountains or northward into the harsh coniferous forest. Some of the Palaearctic animals, however, had by then met a worse fate: they had been completely wiped out. Extinct animals of the region include the auroch, a giant oxlike animal, and the tarpan, the wild horse of the Russian plains. Other animals that very nearly suffered extinction but were saved by a handful of early conservationists were the Père David's deer, named after its discoverer, and the European bison, which is now once more thriving well in the Bialowieza Forest of Poland. Both these animals are alive today in satisfactory numbers thanks to the efforts of European zoos. As recently as 1921, however, there were only three wild bison left – and these plus stocks from zoological collections established the future herds.

Odd as it may seem, a number of animals owe their continued existence to hunters. For hundreds of years much of the woodland was the hunting preserve of kings or other privileged people, who jealously guarded the animals living in the forest to make sure that enough deer or wild boar were left to breed and produce game for their future sport.

Some woodland animals have managed to survive

Above right: the red or common fox abounds in the suburbs of London and other cities, though it tries to stay out of sight. Part of its adaptation is to get food out of refuse pails.
Below: the European starling is one of the animals that has managed not only to live in the city, but also to thrive.

in the copses, hedges, and ditches of farmland and in gardens. These include a large number of small birds such as titmice and blackbirds, and small mammals such as voles, hedgehogs, and foxes. In fact, the collared dove has found parks and gardens so much to its taste that during the last four decades it has spread from the Far East across Asia and Europe to Scandinavia and Britain. But such refugees are still threatened because hedges and ditches are being replaced by barbed wire and other fences that destroy their homes. Other animals have adapted themselves to the human presence and made use of it. Swallows, starlings, rats, and mice are among those making their homes in our buildings. The last two, as well as many insects, have found the grain that we grow and store a convenient and plentiful food. The charming little harvest mouse even uses the stalks of cereal crops as a place to build its globular nest.

As people have increased in numbers, so has the waste they produce. Land and air have been polluted to a frightening degree but water, particularly in rivers and lakes, has been even more polluted. Waste from drainage systems and factories are passed irresponsibly into rivers as a convenient way of getting rid of them, and this leads to an enormous increase in the number of bacteria that feed on the waste. These bacteria rob the water of oxygen, making it impossible for fish, other water animals, and plants to survive. The lack of marine life in turn leads to the dying of animals that live on fish such as the otter, kingfisher, heron, and osprey.

Below: the white stork has never been afraid to nest on city rooftops or in chimneys, and has been welcomed in many northern European cities as a symbol of good luck. Its own luck seems to be running out, however. It must go ever farther away from its nest for food among dangerous aerials and wires.

29

Animals of the Arctic

The North Pole, unlike the South, is situated in the middle of an ocean. It is an ocean so bitterly cold that much of it is permanently frozen over with an almost unbroken layer of ice. This ice is so thick – up to 15 feet – that it will not crack under the largest of land animals. The climatic conditions that create the ice, however, are intolerable to all but a very limited number of species. Furthermore, because no plant can grow in pure ice, the animal population is further restricted to those whose diet is strictly carnivorous – that is, eaters of meat including the flesh of fish and fowl. The supply of flesh is severely limited under arctic conditions. Apart from the occasional seabird, it is entirely marine in origin.

This means that, in order for animals to have any chance of survival, they must make their homes relatively close to water: on the edge of the icecap, near the constantly forming and reforming deep cracks in the pack ice or, farther south, on top of one of the ice floes that drift in the frigid sea. Some polar animals, like the various species of seal, live in the sea itself.

To be able to exist for any length of time under conditions so hostile to life calls for special adaptation for conserving heat. With some living creatures this adaptation can be behavioral, such as migration. Certain birds, for instance, will breed in the polar zone and fly south to more temperate regions during the winter. Other animals will escape the worst excesses of the winter by taking shelter, almost like the Eskimos do, in insulated dens made out of snow. Other modes of adaptation are strictly anatomical. Polar bears, for example, grow thick coats of fur in which air, a substance that keeps the heat from escaping, is trapped. Creatures such as seals and whales develop a thick layer of fat, known as blubber, under the skin to keep out the cold. Animals without blubber

Below: the dovekie or little auk is the smallest seabird of the arctic, reaching the size of a starling. It has short wings that are an adaptation for swimming as well as flying. Dovekies migrate as far south as Great Britain and the New England states.

Below: the white fur of this young harp seal is in sharp contrast to the adult's it is watching, but the pup will soon molt the wooly white coat for a shorthaired gray one. Then its pelt will be marked by the harp-shaped band that gives the animal its name. Harp seals are constantly on the move, following the pack ice north in summer and south in winter to eat at its edge.

would die within minutes in arctic waters because water conducts heat 27 times better than air, allowing it out far too quickly.

There is another anatomical method of heat conservation which relies on the fact that a large body loses heat more slowly than a small body. Consequently, arctic animals tend to be big. Polar bears are larger and squatter than their cousins in more temperate climates. The small size of the bear's extremities such as limbs, ears, and tail also help to cut down heat loss. To reduce this rule to absurdity we could say that the best possible shape for a polar animal is a sphere. A seal is about as near to a sphere as any vertebrate can get.

Whales, polar bears, and seals – including their near relation the walrus – are the only mammals that inhabit the most northern reaches of the globe. The polar bear depends on seals for food and hunts them with great skill and patience, flattening its body onto the ice and creeping up on its prey rather like a cat with a mouse. It then makes a final rush and kills the seal with a mighty swipe of its forepaw. Polar bears can weigh up to 1600 pounds, which means that a seal stands little chance against them while on land. Once in the water, however, the seal will probably escape by being a much faster and more agile swimmer. Bears will also attack walruses, but they are more able to defend themselves with their long sharp tusks. Although a good hunter, the polar bear is not above scavenging and will feed on any kind of carrion it may find. This makes the huge creature a hazard to polar communities whose families might have to face a hungry bear that has come to forage in their garbage pail.

The rest of the arctic mammals compete with each other and the arctic birds for the same monotonous diet of fish and small crustaceans or shellfish. These

Above: polar bears often play with each other, even though they generally lead a solitary life. They are great wanderers, sometimes traveling many miles over the frozen wastes in search of seals or fish to eat. They are also good swimmers for sea hunting.

in turn are dependent on the zooplankton, the tiny one-celled plants that abound during the brief summer.

Most species of large whales visit the polar seas in the summer because of the abundance of zooplankton, but the two whales that live in the arctic are smaller species. One is the narwhal with its long single tusk, and the other is the white beluga whale, known also as the sea canary because of the melodic noises it makes.

There are five different species of seal and one species of walrus found on the edge of the icecap and in the surrounding sea. Unlike the whales, these animals must come ashore both to molt and to give birth to their young.

The birds of the far north are all seabirds and include skuas, auks, and gulls. Of these the pure white ivory gull seems best adapted to this grim part of the world, migrating southward during the long dark winter only as far as the edge of the pack ice. It has become partly dependent on the polar bear, feeding not only on the remains of the land animal's kills but also on its dung.

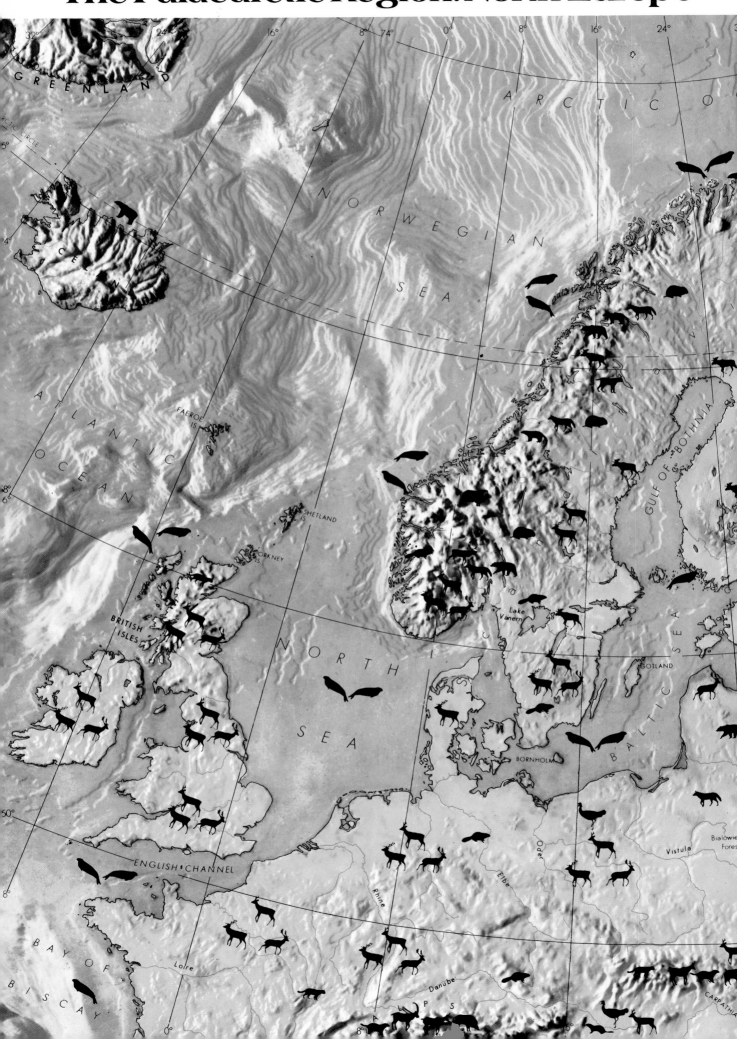

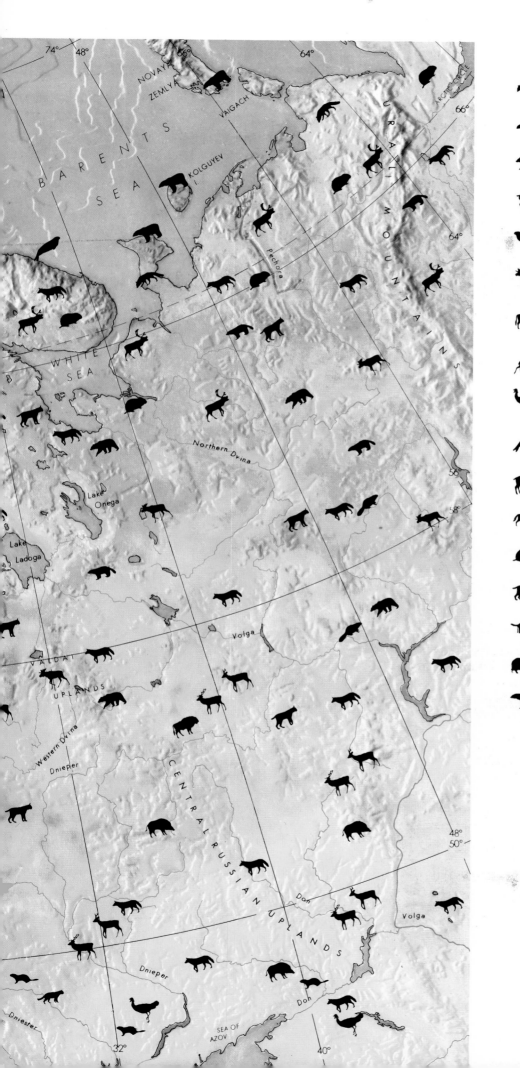

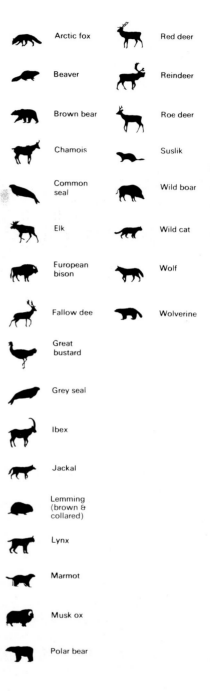

	Arctic fox		Red deer
	Beaver		Reindeer
	Brown bear		Roe deer
	Chamois		Suslik
	Common seal		Wild boar
	Elk		Wild cat
	European bison		Wolf
	Fallow dee		Wolverine
	Great bustard		
	Grey seal		
	Ibex		
	Jackal		
	Lemming (brown & collared)		
	Lynx		
	Marmot		
	Musk ox		
	Polar bear		

Small Animals of the Tundra

Almost all of the Palaearctic Region's northern coastline lies within the Arctic Circle. This 5000-mile stretch of land extending from the Bering Strait in the east to the eastern border of Norway in the west is a forbidding part of the world – flat and featureless, stony and barren, and intensely cold during a long winter. The treeless plains, known as tundra, penetrates inland only a short distance – 300 miles at the widest point. Then it suddenly gives way to the great coniferous forest known as the taiga.

Although the tundra's winter temperature may drop to as low as –70°F, it can reach 60°F during the summer. Despite this comparatively high temperature, the subsoil remains permanently frozen. This permafrost is a very important factor in the ecology of the tundra. It forms a perpetual impassable layer which prevents the melting snow from seeping away so that during the summer it gives rise to vast expanses of shallow lakes and marshland. Unexpectedly these swampy areas provide breeding grounds for many species of gnats and mosquitoes.

Another characteristic of this type of terrain is the spectacular difference between seasons: the deadness

Above: flies, of which there are numerous species on the tundra, are the most common of the insects that pollinate flowers. They are as much a pest to other animals as they are to human beings.

of the long cold winter of drawn out nights, and the very rich flowering of the all too brief summer of 60 days. The length of the day in the summer encourages quick growth and propagation of the varied vegetation that includes lichen and mosses, sedge and bushes. The large number of newly opened flowers invite and sustain such insects as hoverflies, bees, and butterflies. But there are no trees or other deep-rooting plants, which are thwarted by the iron-hard and shallowly sited permafrost.

Sixty days of plenty is followed by 10 months of little when it requires cold grubbing in hard frozen ground for whatever food may be around. At least this is the case for the small herbivores such as the lemmings and voles that do not spend the winter in that state of deep sleep called hibernation. They tunnel themselves in the snow, and feed on what short roots they can find surrounding their dugouts. The temperature in these dens is higher than that outside, but it is unfortunate for the animals if it rises too high because melting snow will soak their pelts and cause them to die of cold.

Much has been made of the lemming's apparent urge to commit mass suicide periodically by rushing headlong into the nearest sea. In fact there is nothing deliberate in their actions, which come about in the following way. At fairly regular intervals of between

Above: the short-tailed weasel, also known as the stoat or ermine, is usually an overall white in winter although the tip of its tail always remains black. This marks it from other weasels.

two and four years, a comparatively long summer is followed by a shorter than usual winter and a large number of lemmings survive to breed. More and more lemmings mean less and less food and living space for each animal, so they go in search of less crowded territory – and they go in mass. Unfortunately, lemmings cannot distinguish between small easily negotiated streams and bigger tracts of water such as lakes, rivers, or the sea. They leap in, and lacking the stamina to get across, they die in droves.

A greater and more constant peril for the lemmings are the vicious predators of the tundra, especially the Arctic fox. It is ever on the prowl for food, always hungry and will eat almost anything. It prefers lemmings, which it will kill and store in the snow when there is a glut, but it will eat voles, birds, and many other small animals. The Arctic fox is not above following the polar bear's example and scavenging, sometimes on the carcass of a whale or portions of dead seal left by the bears themselves. It will even go so far as to consume the polar bear's excrement if times are sufficiently hard. The stoat, which in winter changes its coat to white, its name to ermine, and its commercial value to high, and the snowy owl also benefit from a bumper crop of lemmings. Their populations rise and fall in accordance with that of their victims, though usually in the following year.

Left: the Arctic fox, like many animals in the far north, changes its coat to snowy white in winter. Its thick fur also becomes very long as an added protection against the bitter cold. Most Arctic foxes are gray-yellow in the summer, though some are more gray-blue.

Above: there are several species of lemmings, but all of them are plump and furry with stubby tails and ears almost entirely hidden in their fur. One of the species – the collared or Alaskan lemming – turns white in winter, the only rodent that does.

Right: the snowy owl is one of the lemming's worst enemies, the small rodent being its chief food. Snowy owls have thick dense feathers that extend over their feet to the tips of the toes and almost hide their hooked bill. They are often active in the daylight, operating from the ground as well as from perches on posts or rocks. In recent years they have settled as far south as the Shetland Islands off the northernmost coast of Scotland.

Spring Comes to the Tundra

As the month of May comes to an end the tardy tundra spring begins, and to those brought up in more temperate climates it would seem to do so in quick motion. With the thaw the plants that have waited in bud under the snow burst into blossom, and the ground is spangled with poppy and cranesbill, forget-me-not and saxifrage flowers. Lakes and ponds materialize between the hummocks of lichen and tufts of fescue grass, and with them clouds of gnats, mosquitoes, caddis, and dragonflies. These swarms of insects provide a feast for fish and, above all, for the birds returning from their migration to the south.

The snow bunting is the first to arrive at the beginning of May before the snows have melted, and it is followed by larks, wheatears, and a multitude of wading birds including sandpipers, plovers, and turnstones. Back also are swans, ducks, and geese. They all nest in the tundra and then, at the end of August, fly south again, leaving the permanent inhabitants to their long winter's night. Legend has it that the ancient British, seeing the migrating goose disappear southward over the horizon, believed that they dived into the sea and turned into barnacles. From this they named it the barnacle goose.

As the days lengthen, larger visitors arrive on the tundra. The wild reindeer of Siberia and their semi-domesticated Scandinavian cousins make the migration northward to take advantage of the new vegetation, in particular the reindeer moss which, despite its name, is not a moss but a bluish-tinged lichen. The animals, known as caribou in North America, are goaded on their way by the stinging mosquitoes and flies that attack them mercilessly and hang on relentlessly in the still air of the coniferous forest's edges. Reindeer are able to cope with the snows because of their thick coats and splayed hoofs, which like showshoes, enable them to spread their weight over a wider area to prevent sinking.

As these herbivores arrive from their wintering grounds, so also do their ever-attendant predators the wolverines, also called gluttons, and wolves. The smaller predators among the permanent tundra inhabitants, such as weasels and Arctic foxes, migrate to the more northern part of the region to feed off the voles and lemmings that are coming out of their dens under the snow.

The musk ox, an enormous shaggy beast that winters in the hills of the tundra where the bitter winds keep the vegetation free of snow, moves down to the lusher valleys to feed on the banks of the lakes and rivers. This animal that looks like a cow but is more closely related to sheep and goats, protects

Below: reindeer at rest in the far north of Norway while on their annual migration. The Lapps have domesticated this animal for hundreds of years, but have not been able to breed out the strong migratory instinct. They simply follow the herds on their trek.

Above: the wolverine is extremely powerful for its size and is said to kill more prey than any other animal, which accounts for its other name of glutton. It has been much killed for its fur.
Left: the wolf is a pack hunter but, unlike all the folk tales, it only attacks domestic animals when it has been deprived of its natural prey. Most wolves are tawny with a cream chest and some black markings, but a few are completely white or black.

itself against the cold with a double fur coat of which the dense, soft underlayer is covered by guard hairs that may be long enough to reach the ground. Its method of effective protection against cold is not matched by its way of dealing with its enemies, however. When attacked, the whole herd forms into a tight circle around the calves huddled in the center, and fights with horns and hoofs. Their size, strength, and courage tells against their traditional enemies, but is useless when the predators are humans with guns. In fact, the musk ox was exterminated from the Palaearctic region in the middle of the 19th century, but has recently been brought back into certain selected areas.

There are also two birds which, like the musk ox and the lemming, spend the whole of the year on the tundra. These are the rock ptarmigan and the willow grouse, both members of the grouse family. Because neither of them have great flying speed or maneuverability, they protect themselves against predators by camouflage. Like many other tundra creatures, they change to a snowy white in color in the autumn.

The Taiga: Forest and Swamp

Just as the tundra is an almost continuous strip of land encircling the world, so is the next area to the south a belt going nearly completely around the northern hemisphere. This is the taiga, a Russian word meaning swamp forest. It consists of coniferous forest that starts abruptly at the edge of the tundra, but peters out into mixed woodland on its southern border. The taiga of the Palaearctic covers an area of 4,600,000 square miles – about one-third again as big as the United States.

This woodland is made up mainly of firs, larches, and pines which are able to flourish in the poor soil that is also frozen and snow-covered for a large part of the year. There is little undergrowth, due partly to the bad soil and partly to the small amount of light filtering through the dense canopy of needlelike leaves. These needles carpet the forest floor in a thick layer when they fall, and do not rot down quickly because the lower temperature inhibits bacterial action. During the summer months the snow melts but, because of the relative flatness of the topography, does not drain away into rivers. Instead the water

Above: a closeup of the crossbill (left) shows the unusual shape of its beak, which looks deformed by the way the upper and lower mandibles cross over each other. Crossbills are parrotlike finches that live at the edge of forest clearings. They use their scissorlike bill to cut through twigs for building their nest as well as for extracting seeds from pine cones. Their nest (right) is a loose assemblage of twigs located in a high branch.

forms lakes, puddles, and the swamps that give the region its name.

The animals of the taiga are restricted mainly to two types: those that feed on the conifers together with their predators, and those that take refuge in the forest from the cold in the north or from industrial civilization in the south.

The cones from the taiga trees bear seeds that are the staple diet of a number of birds and small mammals. The bird best adapted to eat them is the crossbill whose scissorlike beak can shear through the tough scales of the cones to get at the seeds underneath.

The pine grosbeak, the spotted nutcracker, and the great spotted woodpecker use their beaks to smash open the cones. At ground level capercaillies and other grouse pick up the fallen seeds, adding to this meager diet with buds and berries. During the winter the birds can even subsist on the actual pine needles, but these make such hard and unnourishing fare that they have to spend most of the daylight hours feeding. By nature the birds are solitary, but in the spring the males congregate for mating displays known as leks in which they exhibit their tail feathers and wattles. Those that put on the most aggressive show win the females.

The taiga mammals that are dependent on cone seeds have, like the birds, reproductive capacities which vary exactly with the amount of seeds available. In a year of abundance, for instance, squirrels may produce litters of as many as eight or nine, whereas in lean years they may have only two offspring. The flying squirrel of the taiga does not actually fly, but glides from higher to lower points in the trees, using as a parachute a fold of fur-covered skin linking its forelimbs with its hind.

Preying on the small herbivorous mammals are the marten and sable, their close relations the weasel and stoat, the fox and the badger, and a number of owls and hawks – and sometimes the larger predators such as wolves, bears, and lynxes. Being extremely agile, the marten is the great enemy of all squirrels but the sable, although a closely related animal of rather similar appearance, prefers to hunt on the ground for voles and ground squirrels. This animal, which was originally found in eastern Russia, was hunted almost to the point of extinction for its beautiful pelt. In 1914, however, a reserve was set up on the eastern shores of Lake Baikal, and the sable began to increase in numbers. The Soviets now farm it commercially.

Lake Baikal is a particularly interesting part of the taiga. Not only is it the deepest freshwater lake in the world, but it is also by far the oldest. Because it has been separated from any other lakes and seas for about 12 million years, it has more than 900 unique species that have evolved differently from other animals. Large numbers of these are invertebrates such as crustaceans and water snails, but there are also several fish and even one mammal, the Baikal seal.

Left: a flying squirrel is only slightly larger than a mouse. The flaps of skin between its fore and hind limbs, which help it glide for distances up to 50 yards, are almost invisible when not in use and do not hinder the animal from scampering up and down trees like other squirrels in search of nuts and fruits.

Above: shafts of sunlight pierce the leafy roof of a coniferous forest, reaching the sparse undergrowth of the floor. Because wide areas of evergreen woods are often made up of a single species of tree, and because ground vegetation is so scanty, such a forest offers a limited variety of environments for animals.

A Refugee Population

Many of the animals that spend at least part of the year in the taiga do so not because of their dependence on the conifers, but because of the shelter it offers. The reindeer and the wolf, for example, winter on the edge of the taiga to escape the bitter high winds of the tundra. The wolf, which once roamed most of Europe and Asia, prefers open ground to dense woodland, but because humans have hunted it more relentlessly than almost any other creature, it has tended to survive only in sparsely peopled areas such as the tundra and taiga. It is only lately that conservationists have begun to question the traditional "big bad wolf" image, and to value the role this animal plays in the weeding out of unhealthy herbivore stock.

The elk, known in North America as the moose, is a fairly common example of an animal that inhabits the coniferous forest but does not feed on conifers It browses instead on whatever undergrowth it can find, and in summer wades far out into the bogs and lakes to feed on the lusher water plants, for which its long legs serve it very well. Like the reindeer, the elk's large splayed hoofs give it surprising mobility in the winter snow and summer mud.

Also feeding in the undergrowth is the varying hare, so called because of its varying numbers, which can be very high one season and very low another. This animal has the misfortune of being the staple food of the lynx, a short-legged cat with tufted ears, a short tail, and a fierce temperament. The lynx lives in both the Palaearctic and Nearctic taigas as well as the mixed woodlands of Asia.

The brown bear is another large predator to be found in the swamp forest. Like most bears it is omnivorous, feeding on both flesh and plants – on birds or small mammals when it can catch them, on birds' eggs, fruit, berries, or roots, according to the season. During the summer they lay up reserve stores of fat in their bodies to see them over the winter, during which they spend a good part sleeping under the arching roots of trees or in other sheltered spots. This cannot be termed true hibernation because neither the body temperature nor the rate of the heartbeat drops significantly.

The wolverine, which belongs to the same family as stoats and weasels, is also found in the taiga as well as the tundra. Its other name, glutton, refers to its

Below: red deer live in herds in more open wooded country over most of Europe. They are reddish or golden brown in summer, turning to a brown-gray in winter. It takes six years for the male's antlers to reach full growth, when he is known as a royal stag.

immense appetite, which makes it gorge itself on carrion or a kill stolen from some other predator. This animal is so fierce that even wolves and bears will give up their kills to it. The glutton sometimes stores the carcasses of its victims in the snow, having first fouled them with its scent glands in order to put off other carnivores.

Some animals more at home in the deciduous woodlands to the south have been compelled to migrate northward to the taiga to escape the hunter. Deer, for instance, are encountered on the edge of the taiga: red, roe, and musk. Other refugees from the game stalkers are the wild boar and the nearly extinct Siberian tiger, which is the largest tiger of all.

The coniferous forest is the home of a number of predatory birds such as the great gray owl and the long-eared owl which hunt rodents and small birds through the night. During the day the smaller animals are harried by the goshawk, the peregrine, and the merlin, while the osprey, a fish-eating bird of prey, is found over the many lakes in the region.

As the taiga changes into deciduous woodland in the south and the lakes become slightly warmer, water birds such as the curiously beaked spoonbill are found. The lakes are also the home of the beaver. Palaearctic beavers, like those of the Nearctic region, were greedily killed off for their fur over the last few hundred years. Although they are now protected, their numbers are sadly depleted. Unlike the American variety, the beaver of Eurasia rarely builds dams or lodges but constructs its home in the banks of a lake.

Above: a young osprey exercises its wings before taking flight. Ospreys live almost entirely on fish, which they catch on the way up from a dive into the water. They eat both freshwater and sea fish, and seldom miss any of the prey under their attack.

Above: the roe deer is fairly common in denser woods and thickets of Europe, Siberia, and China. It is one of the smallest of deer, standing about 2.5 feet at the shoulder, and is not seen about very often because it is active mainly at night.

41

The Temperate Forest

In contrast to the sharply delineated border between the tundra and the taiga, the border between the taiga and the temperate forest to the south is unpronounced. As the climate becomes more temperate, the conifers give way only gradually to the broad-leaved trees that shed their leaves seasonally. There are fairly large tracts of mixed woodland before the conifers die out altogether. Due to the presence of such physical features as the Altai Mountains and the Gobi Desert in central Asia, these temperate woodlands do not form a continuous line across the Palaearctic region. Instead, there is an extensive western section covering a large part of Europe and the western half of the Soviet Union, and a smaller region in the Far East around Manchuria and Korea.

The climate is inviting to a much wider variety of animals than are to be found in the tundra or taiga. Deciduous leaves, being both tenderer and more succulent than pine needles, are a basic source of nourishment for many such larger browsing animals as deer. In Poland the Bialowieza Forest today provides a protected home for the slowly regenerating European bison or wisent, a somewhat larger relative of the American bison that is commonly known as the buffalo.

The habitats of the various species of deer differ. Roe deer, for instance, prefer thickly wooded areas, while red deer tend to inhabit the more open spaces of the forest. In fact, being just as happy to graze as to browse, red deer may even be found on moorland in parts of western Europe. Fallow deer, which prefer moorland, actually originated in the forests that used to exist near the Mediterranean coast.

The leaves are not the only parts of trees that are of interest to herbivores as food. Berries and buds, acorns and nuts all provide nourishment for a great number of small animals: mammals such as squirrels, voles, and dormice, and birds such as finches, woodpeckers, and jays. Most of the rodents carefully store the food they have gathered in the autumn against the winter dearth. Dormice, however, survive the winter by hibernating. In the deep sleep of hibernation, they need only the food they have stored in their bodies during the summer months. Other hibernators include such insectivores as hedgehogs and bats.

In some parts of the forests there may still lurk wild cats and European polecats, both nocturnal in habit, and beech martens. Like so many of the largish carnivores of the woodlands, these three are considered a serious threat by industrial society, and are rigorously controlled. Red foxes, also looked on as a great pest, have by their cunning and adaptability managed to thrive and even extend their natural territories to almost any kind of environment, from

Right: the Eurasian red squirrel is, in fact, usually a rich red-brown in color, although there can be a wide variation in coloration. It has the long bushy tail of all tree squirrels, but the tufted ears are particular to its species. Red squirrels do not hibernate but reduce winter activity by living on stored food.

Below: a red fox crouches in a hunting position, the enemy of mice, rabbits, voles, and other small mammals. This stealthy animal emerges at dusk to search for food, which can also include insects, birds and birds' eggs, and garbage if pushed. Red foxes live all over Europe and in Asia as far south as central India.

tundra to town. Other carnivores that contrive to hold their own against the mechanized world are the stoat and the weasel. The badger which seldom kills chickens and game birds, has been pretty much left alone, and the insect-eating hedgehog has adapted to city life so well that one might be found of an evening rashly crossing a road in a city's suburb.

In addition to predators that proceed on foot are those that go by wing such as the sparrowhawk, kestrel, and tawny owl. They hover on the alert for small mammals, birds, or eggs left exposed. Then there are those that slither underfoot such as the highly poisonous adder and the harmless grass snake. These two snakes have entirely different methods of reproduction, the adder giving birth to live young while the grass snake makes use of the warmth generated by the rotting vegetation on the forest ground to hatch eggs.

The Palaearctic Region: North Asia

Arctic fox	Musk ox
Baikal seal	Polar bear
Beaver	Przewalski's wild horse
Brown bear	Red deer
Common seal	Reindeer
Elk	Roe deer
Fallow deer	Saiga antelope
Giant salamander	Sika deer
Great bustard	Snow leopard
Grey seal	Suslik
	Tiger
Himalayan black bear	Wild ass
Ibex	Wild Bactrian camel
Japanese macaque monkey	Wild boar
Lemming (brown & collared)	Wild cat
Leopard	Wolf
Lynx	Wolverine

Temperate Forest of the East

The smaller eastern sector of the Palaearctic temperate woodland differs slightly in character from the part in Eurasia. Although on the whole it has similar broad-leaved deciduous trees, the warm air flowing in from the nearby seas modifies the climate and, in low-lying areas, such trees are replaced by broad-leaved evergreens or sometimes by bamboo forests.

The animal population likewise has its points of departure from the wildlife found in the larger western sector of the forest. For instance, there are no polecats, wild cats, or hooded crows to be found in the east, but there are Chinese water deer, Japanese dormice, and macaques that do not occur in the west. There are wild boar in both areas, however. The wild boar, which is belligerent by nature, is remarkably fleet-footed for one of the pig family. The male's sharp tusks that sprout from its jaws can easily tear open the body of an adversary, except perhaps the much bigger Siberian tiger. Males also fight each other during the mating season. Although it will eat anything, it is not basically a meat-eater like most other omnivores. All things being equal, it prefers plants and will furrow in the ground for roots, fruit, and berries with its long truncated cone of a snout. Like the Siberian tiger it is much larger than its southern relatives – once more confirming the fact that large bodies lose heat more slowly than small ones.

Tigers are often thought of as being predominantly creatures of the tropical forests, but they actually originated in Siberia. The northern variety is by far the largest, having been known to measure as much as 13 feet in length and weigh more than 700 pounds. In Chinese folklore it towers as the Lord of the Forest, guardian of the ginseng root. This plant, while acknowledged to possess valuable medical properties, is also endowed with magical powers by the Chinese and Tibetans even today.

There is also a monkey native to this coolish region, the Japanese macaque. Inhabiting the higher slopes of the mountain forests of southern Japan, it lives farther north than any other monkey. It is mainly a vegetarian, but it will gladly eat insects when they are available. A neighbor of this intelligent if timid monkey is the Japanese dormouse, the only dormouse species to be found on the island.

Another animal native to the eastern temperate forest is the raccoon dog, a member of the dog family that, unlike most of its relatives, hibernates. It is called the raccoon dog because of its facial similarity to the American raccoon. Oddly enough it resembles the unrelated raccoon in another respect as well – its chosen diet is fish and frogs. The raccoon dog is hunted for its warm furry pelt in the Soviet Union and for its flesh in the Far East, but despite its lack of

speed and agility, it is one of nature's survivors. In fact, its numbers increase yearly. This is due in part to its great fertility, and in part to the steady disappearance of its natural enemies, the wolves and foxes. It has also proved to be extraordinarily adaptable both in its diet and in its habitat.

Another animal that has spread rather than diminished is the sika, one variety of which is the native deer of Japan. The Japanese variety, which has an attractive white-spotted summer coat, has been protected in its native country and has also been successfully introduced into western Europe. The only place that Père David's deer can now be found in

Above: Japanese macaques are one of the few monkeys that can live in a cold climate, even withstanding snow in the mountain forests of southern Japan. They are heavily built monkeys with long shaggy hair and a pinkish face. The parental bond between a young macaque and its mother sometimes lasts for a lifetime.

its native land of China is in the Peking zoo, but this deer named after the 19th-century naturalist-missionary Armand David, thrives today in England. It was taken from the Chinese Emperor's hunting grounds in the 1860s by Père David and brought into England. All the deer were exterminated or died by flood in China by 1900, and they continued to be totally absent from their homeland until 1964. At that time the London Zoo presented four of them to the Chinese Zoological Society in an exchange of animal specimens.

Right: a Siberian tiger at the Los Angeles Zoo gets some relief from the heat by immersing itself in water – a habit that this animal has brought with it from the wilds. Siberian tigers differ from Bengal tigers by having long hair and a paler coat with less striking stripes. They are also the largest of the species. Tigers are very good hunters, stalking their prey at night.

Small Animals of the Steppes

Lying to the south of the western part of the taiga are the steppes, enormous grassy plains stretching 2500 miles from eastern Europe and the plains of Hungary to the Altai Mountains of western China. Large parts of these steppes, which are a yellowish dun color, have neither a break nor a landmark as far as the eye can see. Although they have for centuries been used as grazing land for cattle, sheep, and goats, they are generally speaking unfarmable because of the sandy nature of the soil and the climate of hot dry summers and freezing winters. Whatever cultivation has taken place has been to the detriment of certain species of native animals, especially larger ones, but there is still enough untouched grassland to provide homes for some animals. Among these are herds of saiga antelopes and the occasional wild horse such as the almost extinct Przewalski's horse, named after the Russian explorer Nikolay Przhevalsky (1839–1888) who also discovered a wild camel.

While the grassy nature of the land favors herbivores, its open treelessness and lack of natural cover has given small burrowing rodents a great advantage over other species of animals. The mole rat of this region, in fact, hardly ever surfaces at all. These animals dig extremely complex burrows consisting of separate storerooms, nest, and toilet area, which they seal off when it has been filled. Other burrowers include the common hamster, bigger and fiercer than the golden hamster beloved as pets, and various ground squirrels like susliks, related to the chipmunk of North America, and bobak marmots. These are easier prey for the hawks, eagles, and kites that feed on them because they come above ground more than mole rats. Ground squirrels, which like hamsters are equipped with food pouches in their cheeks, are sociable little creatures that live in huge communities and seldom stray from their burrows. On the occasions that they surface to feed, they post sentinels whose duty it is to warn the others of impending danger, whereupon they all discreetly go to earth. Ground squirrels hibernate in their burrows for half the year. Susliks sometimes go one better than that in times of drought. They spend the summer in a state of suspended animation like hibernation, which is called estivation.

Above: a jerboa at rest. Jerboas look like tiny kangaroos and, like the Australian marsupial, bound away in long jumps when frightened. But, being rodents, they are not related to kangaroos. Their close cousin is the kangaroo rat of the United States, and the two animals are so much alike as to be identical.

Above: the great bustard lives in dry open country across the world except in the Americas. It is as large as a turkey and looks a little like the domesticated bird, but its legs are longer and its beak more pointed. Great bustards are wary and difficult to approach, running swiftly when they feel endangered.

Inhabiting the drier parts of the steppes are a species of small burrowing mammals that have an amazing talent for hopping large distances. These are the tiny jerboas which, though only 2 to 6 inches long themselves, can jump as far as six feet at a time. They do this by means of extremely long hind legs and an equally long tail that they use to balance themselves for the leap. Jerboas have adapted to the high temperatures of their habitat by spending the day in their burrows, the entrance of which some varieties plug tightly to keep out the heat even more. The animal's strange habit of sleeping in a standing position gives it severe cramps on waking, which it relieves by stretching itself and rolling in the sandy soil when it goes above ground. Similar to the jerboas are the gerbils, though not all varieties can leap. These little animals provide a valuable source of nourishment for the local predators – Corsac foxes, marbled polecats, Pallas' cats, and the few wolves that are left – but their habit of hibernating saves them during the cold months.

There is one nonhibernating small mammal that furnishes food for predators during the winter, and that is the Daurian pika. This smaller relative of rabbits and hares has a feeding problem of its own during the winter when vegetation is meager, but it has solved the problem in a way that any farmer would approve of. In the late summer the Daurian pika harvests green plants and spreads them out on rocks to dry in the sun. The animals are constantly on the go, tending their harvest, shifting it so that it is always exposed to the maximum power of the sun, and making a communal effort to collect it swiftly and carry it to some drier spot when it rains. When the vegetation has dried, they stack it within carefully chosen locations in the rocks. These stacks are sometimes hollow in the middle and may reach several feet in height.

The great bustard, which is not normally considered predatory, may sometimes feed on the pika. The great bustard is one of the largest flying birds alive, so large that it will only take to flight when in danger. It is a fast runner, however. Fortunately for the pikas, it is now extremely rare, having been found by hunters to be an easy target and a desirable food.

The Great Desert

The eastern border of the steppes merges gradually from grassland to semidesert, and finally into the harsh, inhospitable Gobi Desert of Mongolia. The Gobi Desert is classified as a cold desert, and although the winters are in fact bitterly cold, the summers are blistering hot. Daytime temperatures can reach as high as 120°F in the shade, while the surface of the earth under the direct rays of the overhead sun may possibly reach 175°F. Despite these severe conditions, there was a time when the region possessed more than a fair share of native animals, especially of the hoofed variety. It was human action more than harsh nature that almost rid the eastern steppes of animal life.

For instance, the saiga once roamed the length and breadth of the steppes. This small antelope of less than 3 feet in height migrated south to warmth in winter and north to better grazing in the dry summer. In the mid-19th century there were still vast numbers of saiga munching their way through the endless plains, but by the early 20th century there were only about 1000 of them left. One of the reasons that they were hunted and killed so callously was the big demand for their horns as a medicine by the Chinese. In 1919 the Soviet government imposed strict controls on hunting saiga in order to save them, and today the animal numbers about 2.5 million.

The rapid regeneration of the saiga herds is due partly to the animal's remarkable reproductive powers. Females are capable of bearing young at the age of 10 months, and generally produce twins. Because males mate with as many as 20 females, and because infant mortality is low, a population increase of between 60 and 80 percent annually is assured. The controls set by the government permit 300,000 head of this fertile little animal to be culled per year. Their hides, fat, and flesh – which is said to taste like mutton – are all put to use.

An animal that has not fared as well as the saiga is Przewalski's horse, a primitive horse somewhat smaller than the domestic varieties and having a large head, upright mane, and long tail. It once existed in great numbers on the eastern steppes. Never much at risk from wolves because it could outrun them easily, Przewalski's horse met a worse enemy in humans, who pushed the wild animal away from its watering places to accommodate their own domestic animals.

At least Przewalski's horse still exists in limited numbers. The same cannot be said of the unfortunate tarpan, another wild horse that was fairly common until the middle of the 19th century. The tarpan partly brought about its own destruction by its habit of enticing mares away from domestic herds. Angry horse breeders hunted it down until the animal was completely exterminated.

Other animals even fleeter of foot than the tarpan and Przewalski's horse find themselves on the danger list as much from competing unsuccessfully against domestic herds for water as from the hunter's shot. These include such mammals as wild asses, goitered and Mongolian gazelles which, like horses and saiga, cannot go without drinking for more than three days.

On the other hand, the wild Bactrian camel of two humps can manage with little water, but this fact has not saved it. Widely hunted for its meat and skin, it is now rare, even though it is protected.

Above: Przewalski's horse is the only wild species of true horse known in the world today. A stocky animal about the size of a pony, this wild horse is rather shaggy with a short stiff mane. It is nearly extinct in the wild but about 150 survive in zoos.

Right: the Bactrian camel is a two-humped species that still survives in the wild, although in its domesticated form it is better as a pack animal than the one-humped species. Untamed Bactrian camels live in small groups of one male and five females. Very shy, they keep away from the other animals of the desert.

The Mountains of Asia

The Palaearctic region possesses many of the world's highest mountains. In fact, in the transitional zone between it and the Oriental region lie the mighty Himalayas, of which Mount Everest is the loftiest peak of all. If, farther west, Europe and North Africa do not have anything as enormous to offer, the Alps, Apennines, Pyrenees, and Atlas Mountains are nonetheless impressive.

Mountains present special problems of survival for animals. Food is scarce, the terrain is irregular, and climatic fluctuations bring troublesome high winds, low humidity, and sometimes exceedingly low temperatures. The atmospheric pressure and oxygen content of the air, both of which decrease steadily as the altitude rises, create discomfort for most creatures. From about 16,000 feet upward there is simply not enough oxygen for lowland animals. Those that live in the mountains have adapted to doing with less oxygen by having proportionately more red blood cells.

Despite all the difficulties, animals of many kinds and all sizes have been compelled to make use of the mountains as a refuge against predators – and have adapted themselves accordingly. The crags and crevices, precipices and pinnacles present no problems to such surefooted creatures as sheep and goats. They are also able to seek for and collect the tiny patches of vegetation that often nestle in hard-to-reach spots. Such inhabitants of the Himalayas as the argali or Marco Polo's sheep, the world's largest wild sheep, can stand the atmosphere at 18,000 feet and will go even higher if threatened by snow leopards or wolves.

The Himalayas also boast the biggest goat in the world, the markhor. Because this goat does not have a heavy coat of hair, it has to descend into the valleys in winter in order to keep warm.

Among the Himalayan animals it is often difficult to tell the sheep from the goats. The tahr, for instance, is a goat, but lacks the beard that most goat species have, and has a thick furry coat similar to a sheep. The bharal is a sheep, but does not have the usual face glands of its species and does have the goat's nimbleness in getting up and down the sheerest of Himalayan rock faces.

There is no mistaking the various species of deer, antelope, and gazelle that inhabit Tibet and northwestern China. These include the shou, a red deer that browses among the dwarf rhododendrons above the Tibetan tree line, and the scarce white-lipped Thorold's deer. The musk deer that lives in the mountains of central Asia resembles the Chinese water deer in not possessing antlers, but the male has long sharp upper canine teeth that make the same kind of useful weapon as antlers. Musk deer derive their name from the musk glands on their bellies, the strong scent of which they deposit on trees and rocks to mark their territory. One species of Tibetan antelope called the chiru has developed an enlarged snout through which it warms up the freezing winter air on the way to its lungs. When the weather is particularly cold it excavates a shallow trench and lies in it – a habit shared by the gazelle called the goa.

Probably the animal that most people think of as typically Tibetan is the yak, a species of cattle. Although domesticated for centuries, yaks still exist in their larger wild state, wandering the coarse pasturages at altitudes exceeding 18,000 feet in herds of up to 100.

Birds of prey and perching birds have their own advantages in adapting to life in the mountains. Birds of prey are usually big enough to withstand the fierce winds; perching birds can often manage to hang onto anything solid. One particularly strong flier is the lammergeier, a large eaglelike vulture. Unlike other vultures, lammergeiers are able to seize large objects and carry them off. They are said to drop bones they have picked clean from great heights in order to shatter them and get at the marrow.

Among the smaller birds that may be found in these regions are choughs, ground jays, and desert chats. The small mammal population includes flying squirrels, pikas, and Père David's voles. Preying upon them are such animals as weasels, foxes, and Pallas' cats.

Left: the snow leopard or ounce likes the cold heights of central Asia and ranges from the Altai mountains south to the Himalayas. Little is known about this nocturnal cat which, with its thick pale gray coat marked by dark rosettes on the upperparts, seems to slip unnoticed over the snow in the dark.
Right: yaks are among the largest of cattle, sometimes reaching over 6.5 feet at the shoulder, and yet they are able to survive on the scantiest of vegetation. This explains why the domestic yak is the chief milk provider as well as the main beast of burden in the harsh mountains of central Asia. In spite of its size and its heavy humped shoulders, it is a skillful, surefooted climber.

The Palaearctic Region:

Southern Europe and the Mediterranean

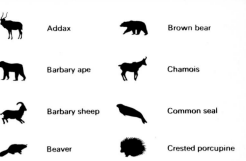

Addax — Brown bear
Barbary ape — Chamois
Barbary sheep — Common seal
Beaver — Crested porcupine

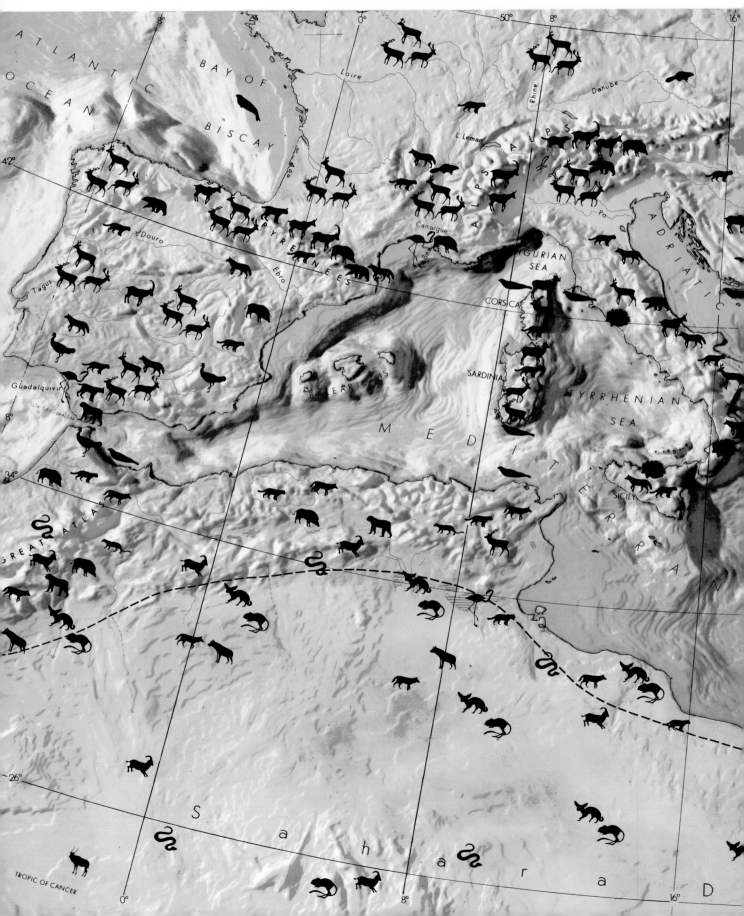

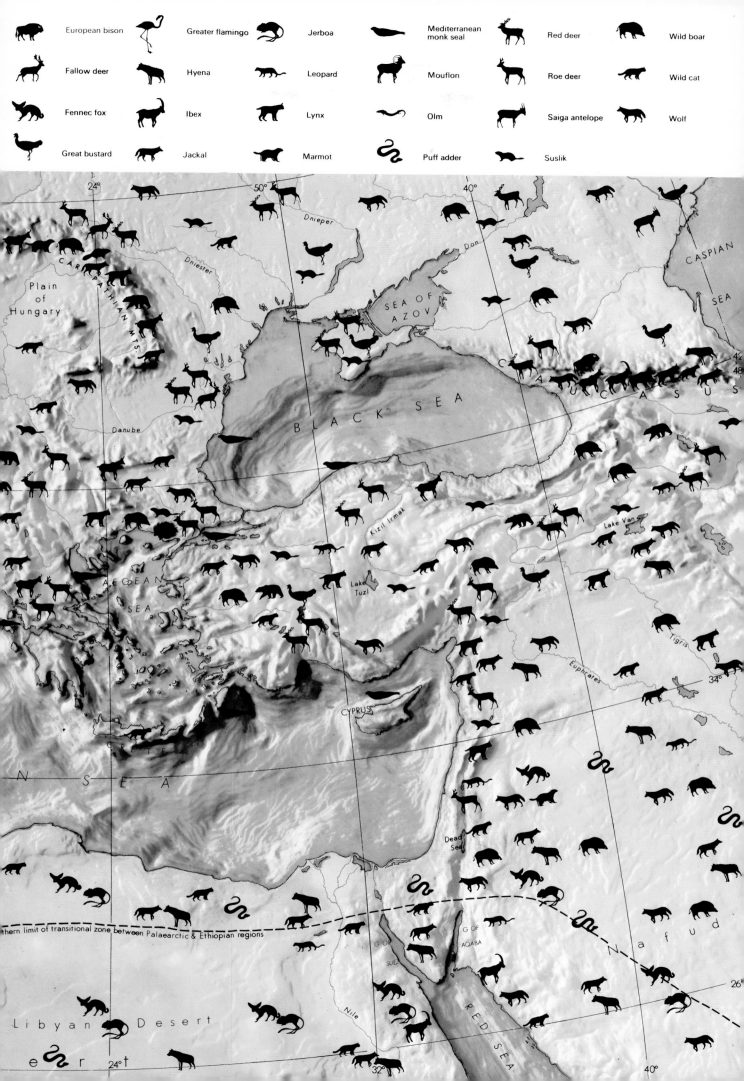

European bison
Greater flamingo
Jerboa
Mediterranean monk seal
Red deer
Wild boar

Fallow deer
Hyena
Leopard
Mouflon
Roe deer
Wild cat

Fennec fox
Ibex
Lynx
Olm
Saiga antelope
Wolf

Great bustard
Jackal
Marmot
Puff adder
Suslik

CARPATHIAN MTS.

Plain
of
Hungary

Dniester

Dnieper

Don

SEA OF AZOV

CASPIAN SEA

CAUCASUS

Danube

BLACK SEA

Kizil Irmak

Lake Van

AEGEAN SEA

Lake Tuzl

Tigris

CRETE

CYPRUS

Euphrates

N S E A

Dead Sea

Libyan Desert

ern limit of transitional zone between Palaearctic & Ethiopian regions

G OF SUEZ

G OF AQABA

N a f u d

Nile

RED SEA

e s e r t

European and North African Mountains

At high altitudes the air becomes sufficiently rarefied to cause discomfort in lowland animals, including humans. In most mountains of Europe and North Africa, however, heights are still just below the threshold beyond which any prolonged activity becomes too difficult. Although the local wildlife has less of a struggle than the animals of the Himalayas as far as physical conditions are concerned, it has had more of a struggle against the intrusion of humans and their domesticated herds. Not only does the wildlife find itself being edged out in its search for food, but it also has industrial pollution to contend with. In fact, hardly any of the mammals of the Alps or the Pyrenees can be said to be thriving, and several species are on the point of extinction. The Pyrenean desman is one example. This aquatic mole burrows in the mountain river banks and subsists on the assorted amphibia, crayfish, and insects it snuffles out with its curiously shaped fleshy nose. It is being exterminated by poisonous factory wastes and the damming of the streams.

The Spanish ibex fell victim to human destruction at a much earlier time. In the Middle Ages it abounded in and around the Pyrenees, but it was highly desired

Below: the Barbary ape is so named because it is found in some areas of North Africa once known as the Barbary Coast, although it was probably brought west by the Arabs as they moved west thousands of years ago. It also lives on Gibraltar, where its colony is under the protection of the British Army. Barbary apes are actually monkeys, and the only ones living wild in Europe.

Below: the alpine ibex, which is one of several varieties of European wild goat, lives high in the mountains. It is extremely rare, partly because its curving ridged horns are much desired as hunting trophies. The ibex roams the rocky slopes above the timber line in small groups that today are widely scattered.

and ruthlessly hunted for several reasons. One was the medieval belief that various parts of the ibex provided cures for innumerable ailments. Another was the prevailing taste for wild goat meat, and another was the challenge it presented to hunters because of the terrain it inhabited. Although the Spanish ibex has been legally protected in recent years, its numbers have increased only slightly. Its cousin, the Alpine ibex, has fared somewhat better and a colony still exists in the mountains of northern Italy.

Closely related to the ibex is the more abundant chamois, a small surefooted animal whose charming appearance is belied by its readiness to use its sharp hooked horns. Even larger in number are the marmots of the Alpine meadows and their predators the eagles and vultures.

Above: because of its black face markings and tufts of feathers on each side of its bill, the lammergeier is also called the bearded vulture. It lives in mountains from Spain to China.

Some animals that were once widespread throughout the whole of the region have been driven back to hard-to-reach mountain retreats. Jackals, for example, today are found only in the most inaccessible parts of the Caucasus Mountains. Lynxes, brown bears, wild cats, wolves, and wild boar exist in small numbers, some in the Pyrenees and some in the bleak coastal mountains of Scandinavia. The Scandinavian ranges provide safe refuge for many endangered species because of the protective policy of the governments. Even the musk ox, one of the nearly extinct species of the Palaearctic region, has been reintroduced into the Dovrefjell mountains of Norway where it leads a sheltered existence.

On the other side of the Strait of Gibraltar are the Atlas mountains, considered part of the Palaearctic region although in Africa. They are home to several unique species, some European and others African in derivation. These animals attract such predators from the Sahara Desert as fennec foxes, genets, and caracal lynxes. Although the Algerian bear and Algerian wild ass are extinct and the last Barbary lion was shot by hunters in the 1920s, Barbary deer, the local variant of the red deer, still browse in the meadows and forests of the coastal side of the Atlas mountains. The dainty dorcas gazelles, having little requirement for water,

Above: like the ibex, the chamois inhabits the highest crags of the mountains from Spain to eastern Asia Minor. It climbs nimbly and fearlessly to seek the twigs and buds, the moss and lichen, and the grass it eats. Chamois groups are led by an old female.

are able to survive well in the dry Atlases on whatever moisture they can obtain from the local succulent plants. Barbary sheep or aoudads, which have horns like a goat's, graze at ease in the crags and high grasslands. There is no shortage of wild pigs which crash about in the rocky forests looking for food, nor of the tailless monkeys misleadingly known as Barbary apes. These monkeys also roam the forests on the search for food – pine cones, leaves, insects, even scorpions. Sometimes they are pushed enough to descend in gangs to forage the farmlands. They have less to fear from predators with the increasing scarcity of the Barbary leopard, the beauty of whose coat has proved to be its misfortune. This big cat has been brought to the verge of extinction by hunters.

The Dying Mediterranean

It would no doubt come as a nasty shock to happy holidaymakers sunning on some Mediterranean beach after a swim if they realized that they had just been bathing in the biggest cesspool in the world. That sadly is the case today. This sea, once renowned for its clear blue waters, has been polluted to an alarming extent just over the past 20 years. This lethal pollution can be attributed entirely to people's thoughtlessness and lack of foresight. The untreated sewage of well over 100 cities is pumped directly into it; factories far inland spew out all kinds of poisonous waste into local rivers which in turn debouch into the Mediterranean Sea; ship's masters have for many years blithely dumped the filthy residue from their crude oil tanks

2000 years since lions were common in the area. All that now remain of any graceful felines are a very few lynxes and wild cats.

Much of the local wildlife is African in origin. Barbary apes, for instance, inhabit Gibraltar's parks and gardens under the British Army's protection. North African crested porcupines can still be found in parts of Italy and the Balkans.

The fallow deer once native to this region has all but disappeared, although it is still common in the northern European forests where it was introduced by the Romans. Another animal that is widespread over much of western Europe but in danger of dying out in its native homelands of Corsica and Sardinia are the wild sheep known as mouflons. The mouflon

Below: the Mediterranean monk seal is a true seal, the largest of the three monk seal species and usually darker in color than the other two. Little is known of its habits except that it spends most of its time in shallow water, venturing on shore to bask from time to time. It is now found in only a few places.

into it. The Mediterranean's only connection with an ocean that could flush it out is by way of the Strait of Gibraltar, which is too narrow to serve this purpose. It has been estimated that it takes the Atlantic waters about 100 years to replace the Mediterranean's. That is why these polluted waters may mean the death of all life within them.

The same kind of devastation has taken place on the Mediterranean shores but it has been going on for much longer. Deforestation, overgrazing, and urbanization have all taken their toll. What was once a land mantled in rich evergreen forest is now a scrubland called by the French word *maquis*. The maquis is relieved at times by such features as the Spanish mountains of Almería, looking for all the world like crumbling stumps of rotten teeth. With the disappearance of the woodland, its natural inhabitants have likewise retreated or been killed off. It is only

prefers the maquis of these islands, where they are found only in small herds today. The leader of mouflon herds is a ewe rather than a ram. Even the common rabbit, which is thought to have originated in Spain, is now more often seen in northern Europe than in its homeland. Brown bears were also once widespread and plentiful, but the few that are left are confined to the Pyrenees and the mountains of Spanish Galicia and the Balkans.

An animal on the danger list today is the Mediterranean monk seal, a fairly large variety of seal whose males sometimes measure over 8 feet in length. These creatures could once be seen basking in many parts of the Mediterranean, especially in the Adriatic and around the Greek islands, but they have found their places on the beaches usurped by human sun seekers. They are also constantly harassed by fishermen, as are the common and gray seals of the Atlantic Ocean.

On the more positive side, bird life in the Mediterranean region continues to flourish, and many reptiles also find conditions to their liking. Among these are the small lizard known as the gecko, a noisy creature with a startling ability to walk on the ceiling by means of claws and flattened toes. There is also a species of chameleon which, like others of its kind, catches insects with its long sticky tongue.

Above: the chameleon is among the slowest crawling reptiles of all, and relies for escape much more on its ability to match its skin color with its surroundings. As for feeding, it has little need of fast movement of the body because of its speed with its long sticky tongue, which it can shoot out for a distance longer than its whole body. The common chameleon ranges from the south of Spain along the North African coast to the Middle East. Unlike other lizards, chameleons have eyes that move independently of each other and in all directions without moving the head. They also have prehensile tails and tonglike toes for extra grip.

Two Thriving Deltas

In the midst of the Mediterranean shores that are so depleted of animal life there are two small pockets of land in which many rare and interesting species are still found. They are the Coto do Donana in Spain and the Camargue in France, both only a few square miles in area. They are similar topographically, both being flat, marshy, highly saline deltas of rivers whose drainage into open waters is sluggish. The Coto do Doñana lies at the mouth of the Guadalquivir near the southern corner of the Spanish-Portuguese border, the Camargue at the point where the two arms of the Rhône meet. Both these areas – which are patchworks of dune, salt flat, grassy marsh, lake, and woodland – are unsuitable for agriculture, though the French have undertaken an intensive program of planting vineyards and rice paddies in the Camargue in recent years. Because of this infertility and consequent lack of intensive cultivation, the deltas offer a relatively safe haven to many animals which have been persecuted to the point of extinction elsewhere in the region. In the last few years, in fact, both the Spanish

Above: the greater flamingo of the Camargue differs from the lesser flamingo of Africa and Asia by the shape of its bill, which is adapted for feeding on the bottom rather than near the surface. However, both feed by filtering tiny marine animals and plants through bristles inside the bill. Flamingos live in flocks of many thousands, seeming to fill the sky with the delicate pink hue of their feathers when they migrate in such number.

Left: the edible frog lives in and near fresh water in countries from France to Russia. Its big eyes help it detect danger, and its long muscular legs help it swim swiftly for cover. Only the edible frog, and only the male of the species, has vocal sacs that it can inflate to amplify its call. These emerge like grayish balloons behind the corners of the mouth below the ears.

wolf may also be found prowling around these areas. The beautifully marked genet and the mongoose, the second of which is an old established refugee from Africa, also find conditions to their liking. Red deer have also settled in this small enclave, although the terrain is far from ideal for them.

The famous white horses and black bulls of the Camargue are basically domesticated, but this delta provides a home for the wild boar and a great variety of smaller mammals including bats, shrews, and voles. There are also foxes, badgers and, somewhat rarer, polecats and otters. Rarer still is a small colony of feral coypus, small South American rodents which were once introduced to various parts of Europe for fur farming. Possibly the rarest mammal in the Camargue is the beaver, once common all over Europe but today existing only in small numbers in a few isolated areas in Norway, Poland, Germany, and the Soviet Union.

The species of reptiles and amphibia to be encountered in these areas are interesting and varied if not large in number. Near the pools and slow-flowing streams are salamanders, frogs, pond tortoises, and viperine water snakes. Drier places attract natterjacks, toads which favor the dunes, skinks (lizard), and snakes such as the ladder snake and the large Montpellier snake. The jeweled lacerta, a reptile whose skin resembles a beautiful beaded handbag, is not often seen in the Camargue itself, but is common in the surrounding neighborhood.

The true glory of these two small deltas lies in their rich and diverse birdlife of both land and marine varieties. Both the Coto do Doñana and the Camargue possess an abundance of edible plants and small animals that mean a plentiful food supply for birds of all shapes and sizes from sparrows to golden eagles. Many species reside on the delta permanently. These include the marsh harrier, water rail, avocet, green woodpecker, kingfisher, and swallow. Others migrate to the region. These include the plover, snipe, golden oriole, cormorant, and black-winged stilt. Still others come for the summer to breed in the marshes or thickets. Among these are the hoopoe, pratincole, little egret, and the very rare Squacco's heron. Many more birds use the areas as a staging post on their seasonal migrations. It must be said that for some of them, such as the gray plover, whimbrel, dunlin, and skua, the short rest is well-earned seeing that their journeys from tundra to tropic and back again are long ones.

Most spectacular of all the delta birds are the greater flamingos with their pink plumage, long legs, and uniquely shaped beaks. These beaks are ingeniously fashioned for dredging their diet of larvae, crustaceans, and seeds from the mud in which they bury their heads for a large part of the time. These two areas are the only places in Europe where flamingos propagate regularly. It has been estimated that in the Camargue alone their population in the spring is usually some 15,000. In climatically favorable years, 5000 pairs of these may be breeding.

and French governments have awakened to their responsibilities and designated sectors in these areas as nature refuges.

By this tardy action the government may have reprieved the otherwise inevitable death sentence on the pardel lynx whose estimated population in the Coto do Doñana is currently not over 200. One of the reasons that the lynx has completely disappeared from the rest of Spain is that, being considered as vermin in the past, there was never any closed season on hunting this feline as there was for game animals. Another feline, the wild cat, and the much victimized

The Transitional Desert

South of the Palaearctic region between the Ethiopian region in the west and the Oriental region in the east is a transitional zone in which the animal life of these regions intermingle. Few species find the terrain inviting with the exception of the densely populated, long cultivated northeastern provinces of China. Apart from these provinces and the remote Himalayas, the transitional zone is virtually all desert, sometimes known as the Great Palaearctic Desert. It stretches almost without break from the Gobi desert in Mongolia, through the Arabian and Iranian deserts of the Middle East, to the Sahara, largest desert in the world. The Sahara desert was not always the vast barren waste it is today, but has reached this state because of several thousand years of overgrazing of their goats by the nomadic tribes of North Africa.

Typical desert conditions – intense, unremitting heat and a dangerous shortage of water – require special adaptations in the sparse wildlife that makes its home in the region. This is especially true in the case of mammals, which depend largely on the evaporation of water to regulate their body temperature. Desert mammals tend to be small, not only because small bodies do not retain heat as much but also because small animals can more easily burrow under the ground to avoid the heat of the sun. They are mostly nocturnal in habit for the same reason. Some go so far in their efforts to elude the day's heat as to suspend their normal bodily functions during the scorching summer months and estivate. Many of the animals have also developed special methods of obtaining the water they must have. Some, like jerboas and gerbils, manage to extract enough from the solids they eat. So do some of the much larger animals, of which one is the very rare Arabian oryx, an antelope whose straight horns and ferocity are both untypical of its species. Another is the oryx's close, almost as rare relative, the much larger yet milder mannered addax. This animal, with large corkscrew-shaped horns, can be found in small herds roaming the Sahara.

Fennec foxes rely on a different source for their fluid intake. They and many other species obtain the necessary moisture from the blood or lymph of the

Above: like most desert reptiles, the horned viper can bury itself rapidly in the soft sand to escape the sun at its hottest. It also hides in the sand to wait for and surprise its prey.

Left: goats climb an argan tree in Morocco to graze on the leaves. Because goats graze so extensively and eat plants right to the ground, they have contributed to the spread of the desert.

Below: the fennec fox, which has a pale buff-colored coat, may be the smallest of any fox but its ears are the largest. This small carnivore is one of the few desert mammals able to live well away from the oases and their limited water supply.

small rodents on which they prey. The fennec is more venturesome in its eating habits than other foxes, feeding not only on rodents and lizards but also on insects. It also has a sweet tooth, eating dates and other fruit.

In common with other species, fennecs have solved the problem of keeping cool in more ways than one. First of all, they stay in their burrows by day and hunt for food by night. Secondly, their enormous ears are well supplied with superficial blood vessels that radiate their body heat very efficiently. They also possess disproportionately large paws that serve the same purpose of heat radiation as well as being useful for rapid burrowing. The large ears provide a second function: they increase the keenness of hearing of this predator, which helps it in its pursuit of the fairly scarce prey.

Small desert mammals like the foxes and rodents have developed special methods of making the most of the water they can get. Many of them do not sweat, and their kidneys are so adapted as to excrete a maximum of waste in a minimum of urine. Sand rats even have cooling mechanisms in their nasal passages which condense the moisture out of the warm air expired from their lungs and retain it in their bodies.

Lions, leopards, and cheetahs were once common on the fringes of the deserts, but all that remains of such big cats are a few leopards and cheetahs. This reduces the number of enemies for the smaller mammals, whose main threat comes from such snakes as puff adders and horned vipers. Desert predators like the Lanner and sooty falcons prefer to eat sand grouse and other small birds or skinks, spiny-tailed lizards, and other lizards which are found in great numbers in the desert.

The wild asses of the Iranian desert also have enlarged ears for keeping cooler. Another means of coping with desert conditions is their swiftness of foot, which makes them capable of traveling long distances in search of water. They can also drink prodigious quantities of fluid in a short time – more than a quarter of their own body weight in a few minutes – and they can stand a water loss of up to 30 percent of their body weight without ill effect.

63

The Wildlife of Szechwan

To the east of Tibet, there is no real barrier hindering the movement of animals between the Palaearctic region and its southern neighbor, the Oriental. Consequently, China gets many immigrants from the steppes and woodlands to the north, from the Himalayas, and from the Oriental region. This is particularly true of Szechwan, the mountainous, permanently cloudy province lying immediately east of the Himalayas and north of the Yangtze river.

From the colder or higher areas come such animals as black bears, wolves, wild boar, deer, tigers, snow leopards, and caracal lynxes. Occupying its own allotted stratum of the Szechwan mountainsides is the takin, a clumsy, slow-witted, Himalayan ox sheep closely related to the musk ox; it lives high in the rhododendron and bamboo thickets. At a lower level there is one of two varieties of goat antelope, the extremely nimble goral or Himalayan chamois. The second variety is the cautious serow, which lurks in the thickly wooded gorges. Its Taiwanese relative owes its inclusion in the list of endangered species to the immense popularity both of its fresh blood as a beverage with the local hunters, and of its flesh.

Probably the best-known native animal of Szechwan is the giant panda, which has been adopted as the symbol for the World Wildlife Fund. Naturalists are not agreed on the panda's classification. While zoologists once believed it was related to the bear, it is accepted today as a member of the raccoon family. Although the giant panda is scarce, it is likely that more exist in the inaccessible bamboo forests they inhabit than was once estimated. Furthermore, it is now being bred successfully in some Chinese zoos. Few animals seem to have stirred the public's imagination to the extent that the huge black and white panda has. The more common red or lesser panda certainly has not achieved the same popularity – though some scientists argue that it is not even related to the giant variety.

Another rare creature brought to light in the 19th century by Pere Armand David along with the giant panda is the golden monkey or snub-nosed langur. It is sometimes known as Roxellane's monkey, so named after the wife of Suleiman the Magnificent because its nose is said to resemble hers. The fur of the golden monkey was once believed to be so effective against

Above left: although the giant panda is probably one of the best known animals in the zoo world today, little is known about it in the wild. This is because the bearlike animal is secretive and solitary by nature and lives in a very inaccessible region.

Left: the caracal is regarded by some zoologists as a true lynx and by others as a serval. One of its distinguishing features is a pointed tuft at the tip of each ear, and another is an ability to leap unusual in a cat. Caracals are mainly nocturnal in habit.

rheumatism that only nobles were allowed to wear it, thus ensuring its survival.

The Szechwan area is rich in pheasants which, although now found throughout the world, originated in the nearby Oriental region. Among the many local varieties are the Reeve's, ring-necked, golden, silver, and blood pheasants. Another is the Lady Amherst's pheasant, which is as resplendent in appearance as it is in name. One of the few pheasants that is in danger is the Chinese monal, an inhabitant of the rhododendron scrubland.

Also scattered throughout the area are deer from both the Palaearctic and Oriental regions. Immigrants from the south include sambars, muntjacs, and water deer. From the north have descended the white-lipped and musk deer. The abdominal secretions of the musk deer are so sought after by perfume manufacturers as a fixative for their scents that the species has become nearly extinct.

There are some animals in this part of the Palaearctic region which are shared only with the Nearctic region. The giant salamander, for instance, is rep-

Above: Lady Amherst's pheasant was named after Lady Amherst, who introduced it into Great Britain. It is a colorful bird with a silvery collaret, green back, white underparts, and black and white wings and tail. The male's crest is red. Lady Amherst's is a ruffed pheasant, which is not considered to be a true pheasant.

resented the world over by only three species. Two are in this area and one, known as the hellbender, is in the eastern United States (Nearctic region). The giant salamander is the largest living amphibian, sometimes reaching 5 feet in length. It inhabits mountain streams, feeding on crabs, fish, and snails.

But the strangest Palaearctic amphibian is the olm, whose natural habitat is the caves of Yugoslavia. This blind, tailed creature looks like a giant tadpole even in adulthood, having undeveloped limbs on a wormlike body, a pale color, and sunken eyes.

Chapter 3

The Nearctic Region

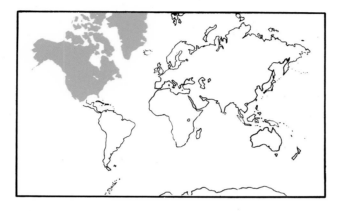

The Nearctic region includes Greenland, Canada, the United States, (except Hawaii), and the northern part of Mexico. It extends from Greenland in the east to the Aleutian Islands in the west, and has the same north-south reach as the Palaearctic region – that is, from the Arctic Circle to the Tropic of Cancer. It closely resembles the bigger Palaearctic in climate, vegetation, and physical features, so it is not surprising that the animals of the two regions are almost identical. Because of these close similarities, some naturalists treat the two regions as subdivisions of a larger one that they call the "Holarctic." Nevertheless, in spite of the basic sameness of the two regions' wildlife, there are several unique animals in the Nearctic, among them the pronghorn antelope, bighorn sheep, and bald eagle. At the same time there are some gaps in the animal population. There are, for example, no wild horses or camels.

The puma is a wide-ranging cat of medium size, noted for its great power of endurance and strength. Also called the mountain lion, cougar, and catamount, the puma has been known to leap 40 feet and to drop from a height of 60 feet. It lives in mountains, grasslands, forests, and swamps, feeding mainly on deer. The slender and graceful puma is like a lioness in appearance, but has a rounder head and ears than most cats.

Man's Impact

It is not unlikely that in the next decade the bald eagle, national emblem of the United States, will be extinct outside Alaska. This sad possibility points up the contradiction of the North American attitude toward its native wildlife. On the one hand the United States has an abundance of nature refuges and national parks including Yellowstone Park, the first of its kind in the world. On the other hand, the United States has severe pollution problems that threaten animal life everywhere, and a seeming indifference to the killing of animals for mere sport.

There was little thought for wildlife in the 19th century. While the State of Idaho was an exception to the rule and tried to protect buffalo in the early 1870s, Buffalo Bill Cody reported: "I killed buffalo for the railroad company for 12 months, and during that time the number I brought into camp was kept account of, and at the end of that period I had killed 4280 buffalo. . . ." That record of slaughter pales beside the record of Billy Tilghman, a hunter who killed 3300 buffalo in only seven months.

At the beginning of the 19th century there had been an estimated 60 million head of bison – known as buffalo in North America – roaming the grasslands, a figure that had remained more or less constant over the centuries. By 1868 there were only eight million left. In only about 68 years, some 52 million animals had been killed off.

Before the advent of European settlers, the Amerinds had maintained a happy balance between themselves and their environment. The newcomers brought with them two novelties that proved instrumental in upsetting this equilibrium. One of the novelties was the horse.

Below: the bald eagle gets its name from the white head and neck that gives it the appearance of baldness. It is a sea eagle living mostly on fish, of which it will sometimes rob other birds.

The horse had totally disappeared from the Americas long before the Spanish conquest in the 16th century, but the conquistadors had brought enough horses with them to breed. After initial terror at the sight of the unfamiliar hoofed animal, the Indians took to horseback as naturally as could be. This increased mobility may not have spelled real danger to the local wildlife on its own. But then the European traders provided another of their miracles of civilization – the gun. Until then, the Amerinds had depended on the bow and arrow for hunting, and had hunted the buffalo to meet only their basic needs for food and clothing. The gun and the horse changed all that. The Amerinds were manipulated to use them in a vicious circle of kill-and-trade. The traders encouraged them

to use buffalo skins as currency to buy the much coveted guns and ammunition. The more guns they possessed, the more animals they could shoot, and the more buffalo they killed, the more guns they got.

Even then, however, the bison's fate was not necessarily sealed, and the population might have stabilized itself at eight million. It took the settlers' insatiable urge to open up the whole of the continent and to extend the recently introduced railroad across the country to finish off the buffalo. Laying transcontinental railroad lines meant cutting straight through the heart of the buffalo's ranges, and the animal was still plentiful enough to cause problems.

A herd of them in tight formation sometimes covered an area of 10 miles by 8 miles, halting work on the lines and later forcing trains to stop while the herd crossed the track. Because of this, slaughter of them became systematic and 4.5 million were destroyed in 1871, 4 million in 1873, and 1 million in 1874.

The disregard of the Europeans for the Amerinds also had something to do with the deliberate killing of the buffalo, which was so important to the local way of life. In the words of General Philip Sheridan, an Indian fighter after his army career in the Civil War: "Every buffalo dead's an Indian gone!" Hunters

Below: this painting depicts a buffalo hunt by American Indians, who used the animal's flesh and hide but did not overkill. The bison's slaughter by European settlers is a well-known story.

buffalo, the fortunate discovery in Canada of a large herd of closely related wood bison helped in sustaining the species. There are 25,000 bison living in comparative security today in the national parks and nature refuges of North America.

Over the years it has rarely been possible to fix the exact moment in time that a whole species dies out. But there is one instance in which the very names of those responsible for finishing off a species is known, as well as the time. The unfortunate animal was the great auk, a large flightless bird of peaceful habits. The entire species met its end at the beginning of June 1844 on a small island in the North Atlantic. It had already been so reduced that there were but two great auks on this island, the last known survivors in the

used other means besides guns to exterminate the buffalo. For instance, it is reported that a herd of 10,000 was destroyed by the torture of denying the animals access to their watering places.

The result of this deliberate carnage was that by 1893 there were about 500 buffalo left in the United States. By 1900 the number had dropped to almost nothing. Apart from a few semidomesticated animals grazing on private parklands, only 20 of them remained in Yellowstone Park.

After about 1913, however, protective legislation was passed and more nature refuges created for all threatened wildlife in the United States. As for the

world. The female had produced one egg. Sigourour Isleffson and Jon Brandsson from Iceland killed one bird apiece, and their companion Ketil Ketilsson smashed the egg. They later received the sum of £9 for the skins.

Another species whose extinction has been recorded to the second is the passenger pigeon, of which it is thought that there were some 5000 million in the 1840s – as many as all the other land birds in the United States put together. The last wild passenger pigeon was shot in March 1900, and the last passenger pigeon of all died of natural causes at 1 pm on September 1, 1914, in the Cincinatti, Ohio, zoo. These birds were slaughtered on an even more monstrous scale than the buffalo, shot at merely as a target much of the time. Such wholesale shooting was still not enough to destroy the fast multiplying species, however. John James Audubon, the famous American animal painter and naturalist, estimated that they reproduced so rapidly that they could quadruple their numbers in a year. But they could not withstand the destruction of their habitat, the vast North American forests that gave way first to the plow and later to factories and housing developments.

The death of the last passenger pigeon in the Cincinatti zoo was followed a few days later by the death of the sole surviving Carolina parakeet. The extinction of this species had been foreseen by Audubon. Farmers justified their destruction of the bird on the grounds of its destructiveness to their apple orchards.

Other Nearctic animals that have become extinct

are the sea mink, Labrador duck, Eskimo curlew, and several varieties of petrel. Grizzly bears, sea otters, jaguars, cougars, bighorn sheep, certain species of seal, the walrus, and the California condor are seriously threatened with extinction today.

The blame for all the damage inflicted on the wildlife in this region cannot be laid solely on hunters. Much of the freshwater life, for example, has been destroyed by misuse of the waterways. Large areas of the chain of Great Lakes between the United States and Canada have been reduced almost to sewers by various forms of industrial pollution. Wildlife has also been disturbed by overfishing and deliberate, though not necessarily malicious, alteration of the natural topography by drainage, irrigation, and damming. Another factor contributing to the disappearance of various freshwater fish like the trout and cisco from some of the Great Lakes has nothing to do with human actions. The parasitic sea lamprey, which invaded these lakes many years ago, adapted to freshwater conditions, and within 12 years had virtually wiped the fish out.

Right: the humpback whale arches its back as it dives below the surface of the water, which is probably where its name comes from. Like most whales, it is now in danger of extinction. Part of the reason is that its course of migration, during which it hugs the coast, is well known and makes it a relatively easy mark.

Left: the now extinct passenger pigeon looked somewhat like the mourning dove, but was larger. Although it did sometimes forage in newly sown grainfields, it did not really damage crops much.

Animal Life in the Far North

The Nearctic and Palaearctic regions were once linked by the Bering land bridge, and still have the same kind of vast layer of permanent ice in their northernmost reaches today. This goes a long way toward explaining why the animal life of the two regions' arctic and tundra terrains are for the most part either identical or very similar. In fact, the distinctions between some of the species are in name only – the caribou of the Nearctic is the same as the Palaearctic reindeer, and the American moose the same as the European elk. New names, however, have not been given to lemmings, wolves, wolverines, and Arctic foxes, which are common to both regions.

Above: baby caribou grazing during the brief summer of the far north. They are born in early June so that they will be strong by the time the severe winter comes. Like the reindeer to which they are related, both male and female caribou have antlers.

Despite almost identical terrain and climate, some shared species have fared worse in one region than the other. The musk ox is a case in point. Although by no means plentiful in the Nearctic, it has been so well protected by the Canadian government that the Canadians had enough to spare to export to the Soviets when they decided to rebuild the Palaearctic population and established some herds in their remote far northern island refuges. Polar bears cannot be said to be plentiful anywhere, their total world population having been estimated variously between 5000 and 18,000, but there are more of them in the arctic islands of the Nearctic than in the Palaearctic. Although polar bears are rigorously protected by law, the law is not easily enforced, especially in international waters. The sport of shooting bears from aircraft is also difficult to control.

The northern or Pribilof fur seal favors the Bering Sea as a habitat. The fortunes of this species have fluctuated somewhat over the years. When their breeding grounds in the Pribilof Islands were discovered in the 1780s, there were 2.5 million of them. When the islands were bought from Russia in 1868, the American purchasers were dismayed to learn that the numbers of seals had been significantly reduced by the Russian sealers. However, the Americans went on their own killing spree and by 1911 there were only 200,000 northern fur seals left. Since then, strict government protection and the high birth rate of the animal has helped it to reestablish itself, and its present population is between 1.5 and 2 million. There is another factor that helps keep the number of Pribilof seals stable. It has to do with unmated males, which leave the breeding colonies when they have been forced out of the running by more aggressive bull seals. About 60,000 of them a year are killed without an adverse affect on the species' breeding pattern, since one male can mate with 50 females. Also found in the Bering Sea are such relatives of the northern fur seal as the common seal, Steller's sea lion, and the walrus.

While not one of the biggest seals, the northern fur seal is fairly large compared with the sea otter which is found floating around in these chilly north Pacific waters, generally about half a mile off shore. These playful animals are, in fact, the smallest of all the sea mammals, and the only such species that lacks a subcutaneous layer of fat. They rely for their protection against the cold on their thick, soft, silky fur. The sea otter might be better off with the serviceable blubber of other arctic marine animals, since its beautiful fur makes it the object of the rapacious hunter. Sea otters hardly ever forsake the sea, mating and breeding there amidst the thick beds of seaweed. At night they moor themselves with strands of kelp to make sure they don't float away in their sleep. This animal has worked out an intelligent way of getting at the meat of shellfish that are too thick to be cracked open with the teeth. Lying on their back, sea otters place a stone on their chest and smash the shellfish on it.

Whales are encountered in all these arctic waters. Some, like the white or beluga whale and the narwhal, are strictly arctic in habitat. Others migrate to the area during the summer months to benefit from the sea's bounty of squid, fish, and krill.

Right: a bull fur seal surrounded by a harem of females. The northern fur seal is larger than the species living in the southern hemisphere, and its coat is softer and denser. Males reach 8 feet in length and 600 pounds in weight, females only 5 feet.

Alaska's Wildlife

About one third of Alaska lies north of the Arctic Circle, and all of it within the forbidding cold region lying 500 miles north of the state of Washington. The forty-ninth state of the United States, Alaska is a vast territory more than twice the size of Texas. The central tundra area of the state is enclosed by two mountains, the Brooks Range in the north and the Alaska Range in the south. Farther north of Brooks Range is more tundra, the desolate Arctic Slope,

Above: the hoary marmot is mostly silvery gray but has black and white markings on the head, and black feet. It has the bushy tail of the squirrel but no cheek pouches. Marmots hibernate for up to six months, after having become very fat in the autumn.

while farther south of the Alaska Range are the evergreen coastal fringes. Scattered among the mountains are clumps of coniferous woodland. The temperatures in the interior range from a bitter –70°F in winter to a sweltering 100°F in summer. A variety of terrains and climates usually means a variety of animal life, and this is true of Alaska. The exception is that snakes are completely absent from the wildlife, and amphibia are few.

Inhabiting the harsh tundra regions are animals that range in size from small hares to large caribou. One of the hare varieties is the varying hare, sometimes called the snowshoe hare.

Barren-ground caribou, one of the larger inhabitants of the Alaskan tundra, are well fitted for the long to and fro treks they make annually, first to their summer home in the high tundra where the cows give birth, and then to their winter retreats several hundred miles away on the outskirts of the forests. *Caribou* is an Amerind word meaning shoveller, and it comes from the fact that the animal uses its splayed

hoofs as shovels to dig out food from beneath the snow. In the 1920s these animals could be counted in their millions, but recently their numbers have declined to the hundred thousands. This fall in population, the repercussions of which have been starvation among Eskimos and Indians and a drop in the number of scavengers and predators, cannot for once be

blamed on human hunters so much as on forest fire.

Among the animals to be found in and around the mountains are rodents such as collared pikas and hoary marmots, and even-toed ungulates like mountain goats with hoofs as sharp-edged as climbers' boots and herds of Dall sheep. Dall sheep are a smaller relative of the bighorns, with wider spread horns.

They are as nimble on the crags and cliff sides as the larger species. The color of their fur is usually white, but this cannot be considered as camouflage because they avoid heavy snow whenever they can. Were it not for the aromatic trails left by the scent glands on their hoofs, Dall sheep would run the risk of being separated from the herd on the misty mountains.

The animals most popularly associated with the mountains of northwest America in general and Alaska in particular are the brown bear and the black bear. There certainly are many of them, though they are not as plentiful as formerly. The most numerous of the two is the relatively small black bear. Although classified as carnivores, black bears eat little meat. Nor are they necessarily black. There are brown and near-white black bears as well and, like cats, they may produce different colored cubs in the same litter. If black bears are not as fierce as their brown cousins, they make up for it in audacity, often begging shamelessly from sightseers in national parks.

The brown bears, of which the grizzly is an inland variety and the gigantic Kodiak – sometimes measuring as much as 12 feet in height – one of the coastal varieties, are solitary creatures. They avoid each other's company as well as other species, except during the summer when they congregate by the fast-running rivers to scoop out the salmon that form part of their diet. Brown bears are often ill-tempered, making dangerous adversaries. On being confronted by a threat, they either flee or attack as a defense. Although grizzlies spend the winter in a deep sleep within their caves, their body temperature does not drop like true hibernators and they awaken during mild spells.

Above: a collared pika makes a tentative move out of the rock crevice that is its hiding place. Pikas, small mammals related to rabbits and hares, can run easily over smooth rocks and can stand snow and cold if their stored food does not get frozen.

Left: the grizzly bear is only one of the brown bears which, with polar bears, are the largest of the carnivorous land animals. Once widespread throughout North America, grizzlies are now only found in any numbers in Alaska. Brown bear cubs, which are born in winter while the mother is hibernating, can climb trees.

75

The Nearctic Region: Canada and Greenland

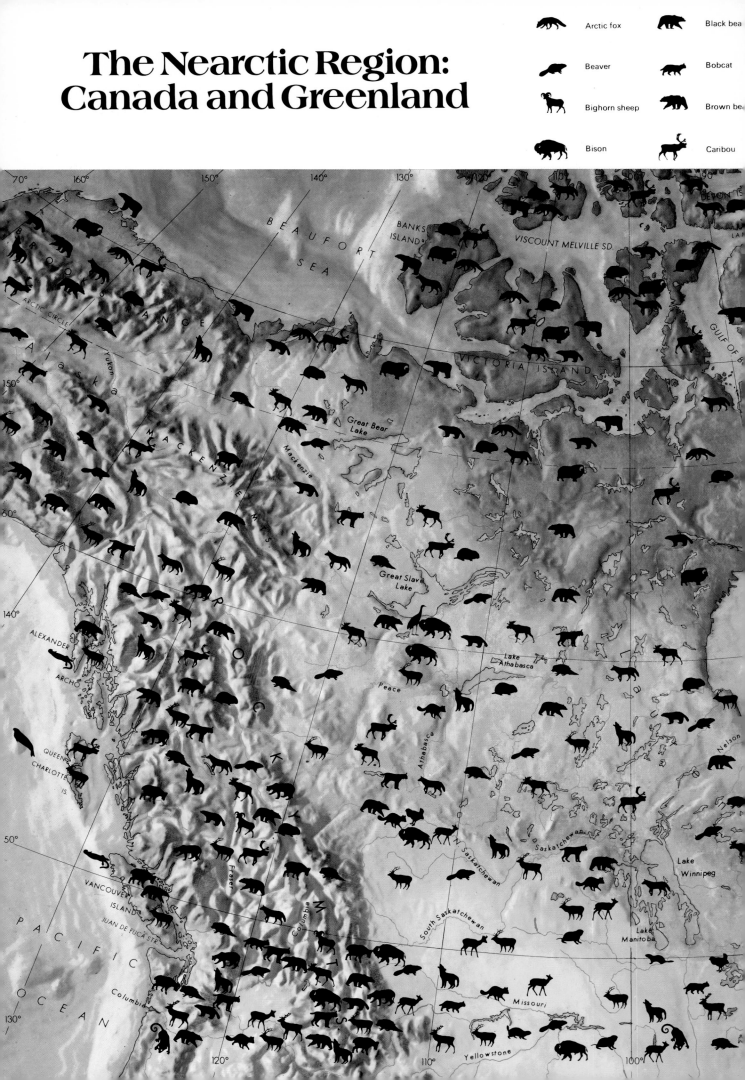

Arctic fox · Black bear · Beaver · Bobcat · Bighorn sheep · Brown bear · Bison · Caribou

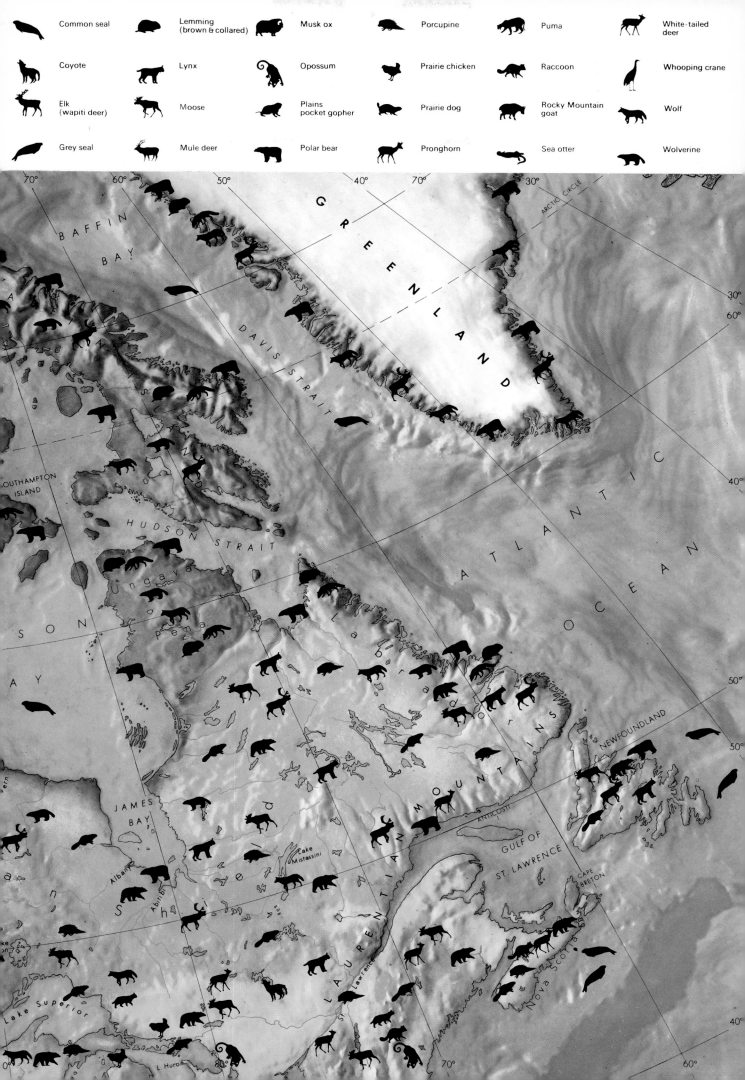

Common seal

Coyote

Elk
(wapiti deer)

Grey seal

Lemming
(brown & collared)

Lynx

Moose

Mule deer

Musk ox

Opossum

Plains
pocket gopher

Polar bear

Porcupine

Prairie chicken

Prairie dog

Pronghorn

Puma

Raccoon

Rocky Mountain
goat

Sea otter

White-tailed
deer

Whooping crane

Wolf

Wolverine

G R E E N L A N D

ARCTIC CIRCLE

BAFFIN

BAY

DAVIS STRAIT

A T L A N T I C

O C E A N

SOUTHAMPTON
ISLAND

HUDSON STRAIT

Ungava
Pen.

HUDSON

SON

AY

JAMES

BAY

Albany

Abitibi

Lake
Mistassini

La
b
r
a
d
o
r

L A U R E N T I A N   M O U N T A I N S

ANTICOSTI

GULF OF
ST. LAWRENCE

NEWFOUNDLAND

CAPE
BRETON

Nova Scotia

St. Lawrence

Lake Superior

L. Huron

Forest Predators

Below: the coyote or prairie wolf is a wild dog of tawny fur and bushy tail, smaller than the wolf to which it is closely related. Because they are clever at avoiding traps, and because they adapt their hunting methods to suit various conditions, they have flourished and spread in the last century. Both male and female help to tend the young, which are born in litters of up to 19.

The Nearctic coniferous forest, which traverses the northern part of the region from Alaska in the west to Labrador and Newfoundland in the east, is not home to many large carnivores. The bear, which eats other foods besides meat, is the largest. Slow, lumbering creatures, bears cannot hope to catch the fleet-footed local hoofed animals. Nevertheless, they will not be backward in making the most of any wounded deer or bison they happen upon, and their great strength enables them to carry off a still struggling body of up to nearly half a ton dead weight. In the absence of such a meat bonanza, bears get by on their mixed diet of edible vegetable matter, small mammals, birds and their eggs, insects, and fish.

Coyotes and wolves, both predators typical of more open country, may also be found prowling around the coniferous forests, but the reasons for their presence are diametrically opposite. Coyotes have had to come north to look for room because they have thrived so well in their natural habitat. Wolves, on the contrary, have been driven north by human enemies. Lynxes, another predator, can by virtue of their speed and stealth live off such speedy creatures as

varying hares, squirrels, grouse, and rats.

Attacking whatever is missed by these mammals are the ever-vigilant birds of prey: the long-eared great gray and saw-whet owls, the eagles, falcons, and hawks. Ospreys live almost solely on fish. Because eagles' wings are too wide for them to get through the close set masses of conifers, they are obliged to hover above the clearings in wait for unsuspecting small deer or rodents. They also wheel and flit around

the topmost branches, grabbing at any bird rising in panic. Goshawks and sparrow hawks, with their smaller wingspan, speed, and maneuverability, are under no such restriction. They operate among the bushes, seizing small birds or sometimes rodents and other small mammals.

Competing with the birds of prey are various members of the weasel family of which the 8-inch-long least weasel is the smallest of all carnivorous mammals. It is one fifth the size of its biggest relative the wolverine, which can reach 40 inches in length. Weasels are extremely adaptable to many different types of habitat and will also eat anything they come across if they have to. They have soft dense pelts as protection against the cold, making many species such as the mink and marten highly desired for the luxury fur coat trade. By the early 19th century, fur companies in North America were exporting 45,000 marten skins annually. Later in the same century, the trumpeter swan fell victim to fashion's demand for long delicate feathers.

Right: a good climber and swimmer, the lynx also has keen eyesight to make it the excellent night hunter that it is. This bobtailed member of the cat family also has large paws that act like showshoes in helping it travel over deep snow. The northern lynx sometimes looks heavier than it is because of its thick fur, which is given a silver cast by silvery white-tipped guard hairs.
Below: brown bears include fish in their diet and can catch salmon right from the stream. The time of plenty is the period in which salmon battle their way upstream to their spawning grounds.

Other Forest Dwellers

American martens and their relatives the fishers have a favorite food animal: the porcupine, a mammal generally considered to be more typical of warmer climates. Apart from these predators, the gluttonous wolverine, and on rare occasions the wolf, coyote, or lynx, animals are not as a rule too anxious to try getting past the porcupine's pointed quills. The porcupine does not commonly loose its quills like arrows leaving a bow, as is often said. It merely thrusts its sharp prickly body with sudden force against its enemy. However, its quills do sometimes detach themselves during the body thrust and stick painfully in an attacker's face.

Today, the chief threat to the Canadian porcupine comes from humans, particularly timber workers who regard the nocturnal tree-dweller as a pest to be eradicated. This attitude arises because the porcupine strips the soft bark of the upper branches of ever-greens for food in winter when its normal diet of leaves and buds is scarce.

The moose is the biggest of all living deer, standing well over 6 feet in height at the shoulders and weighing between 1200 and 1800 pounds when fully grown. They are solitary animals that require a huge territory to supply them with enough food. During the summer months they wade deep into lakes and rivers to feed off the water weeds and lilies to which they are especially partial, or else they browse among the bushes and trees for bark, sometimes in their enthusiasm felling a tree with their 6-foot-wide palmate antlers. To maintain their enormous bulk through

Below: woodchucks never go far from an entrance to their burrow even when feeding. Known also as the groundhog or the common American marmot, the woodchuck is the only woodland dweller of its subfamily. Woodchucks are heavily built for ground squirrels.

the cold and meager winter, they have to find between four and five tons of plants and greenery. No easy undertaking at the best of times, the task of finding food in winter is almost impossible. It is little wonder that they become desperate enough to strip the young trees of their bark.

While porcupines and moose cause deforestation by hurting young trees, chipmunks help to reforest by their habit of forgetting about nuts, berries, and

seeds they have hoarded. Other members of the squirrel family, to which the chipmunk belongs, are not so beneficial. Red squirrels or chickarees, for instance, are alleged to do untold damage to the coniferous forests, particularly when there is a poor harvest of cones and they substitute buds for cone seeds. Red squirrels also have a taste for maple and birch sap and will gouge pieces off the boughs to siphon off such fluid. They are not the confirmed vegetarians that many squirrels are and now and then steal an egg or even a chick from a small bird's nest. Unlike their relations the red squirrels, chipmunks hibernate, although they wake every so often to dip into their store of seeds.

Red squirrels are not the only species to enliven their diet with the occasional egg or nestling. Flying

Like the chipmunk, the woodchuck or groundhog is a true hibernating animal. A member of the marmot family, the woodchuck is distantly related to the squirrel though much larger. It can spend as much as two thirds of the year sound asleep in a burrow or hollow log, breathing only twice a minute in the depth of winter while its heart, which normally beats 200 times a minute, slows down to a mere four or five beats a minute.

squirrels share this taste. These little animals are distinguished from true squirrels by their nocturnal habits. They are also distinguished from such flying mammals as bats by the inability to fly, gliding instead for a maximum of 50 yards. Although incapable of rising into the air, they can maneuver and change direction to escape owls, their chief predator.

Above: in late summer the antlers of a bull moose have grown to their full extent and the velvet or furry skin that has covered them all spring will begin to dry and peel. The velvet will be completely shed in the autumn. Moose wade and swim in shallow lakes a great deal of the time during the summer in order to feed on waterweed, waterlilies, and other aquatic plants. The huge animal will even submerge fully to get at plant roots and stems. Being in the water also helps moose to keep cool in the heat and gives some relief from the swarms of mosquitoes and flies.

81

Beavers and Bobcats

One of the sights in North America which most impressed the original European settlers was the vast expanse of deciduous forest that virtually covered the eastern half of the subcontinent from the Great Lakes in the north to the Gulf of Mexico in the south. Having duly marveled, they then proceeded to destroy it as quickly as possible to make way for farms and villages at first, cities and industrial complexes later. The only forests to escape the ax were those in areas too difficult to cultivate or too uncomfortable to inhabit – areas like parts of the eastern ridge of the Appalachians, which run southward from the Canadian border to Alabama. As the rich forests of oak, elm, hickory, poplar, and others fell before the human advance, so their animal life retreated, adapted, or perished. Some, like the once numerous timber wolves and mountain lions, have almost gone; others such as the wild turkey and white-tailed deer, are exceedingly rare. The white-tailed deer at least has been successfully reestablished in some of the national parks and refuges.

One woodlands species that has suffered in the extreme is the beaver. Before the settlers came along, it was present in the thousands of millions. Perhaps the most hunted animal on the continent for about 200 years, it was rare by the beginning of the 19th century. Beavers depend for their existence on three major factors: the water of lakes and rivers, not only to drink but also to build their dwellings in; tree bark, which is their staple food; and the hard wood of deciduous trees which they use to construct their dams, canals, and lodges. It has been said that their constant dam building and irrigational works may have been as instrumental in changing the vegetational face of North America as subsequent human activities there, but their destruction by humans certainly altered the wildlife population.

The beaver had the misfortune of being discovered in such numbers just at the peak of popularity of the fur hat. Trade in beaver skins was so brisk that European traders hired local Amerinds to help them out with the slaughter, paying them in rifles as they did for buffalo later. It turned out to be a case of killing the goose that lays the golden egg, for beaver skins nearly ran out before the beaver hat fashion ended. Beavers are nothing if not persistent, however, and with the laws passed in the 19th century to protect them, they have made a remarkable comeback.

Almost as much sought after for their skins as the beaver was the raccoon of the forest, whose tails embellished many a trapper's hat. Raccoons are unique to the Americas. They are highly intelligent,

Below: beavers build well-constructed dams of branches, stones, and mud in order to create shallow lakes within the rivers they inhabit. The dams also serve to conceal the underwater entrances to their shelter, which can be either a burrow dug into the river bank if it is steep enough, or a wood-and-mud lodge, sometimes containing several rooms, if the bank is too low. Beavers spend most of their time in the water, being able to stay under for up to 15 minutes at a time. Beaver dams can reach about two thirds of a mile wide and lodges can be as large as 6 feet in diameter.

Above: the bobcat has a bounding gait similar to that of a rabbit, and a short tail from which it probably got its name. The bobcat is smaller than the puma and lynx, the other American cats, and is comparable to the European wildcat. When this predator is in danger itself, it often seeks safety by climbing a tree.

almost exclusively nocturnal animals equally at home in tree or water. Their interesting diet consists of chicken, crayfish, and fruit, but they will eat from the garbage if necessary. In the wild, raccoons dabble their handlike front paws in water instinctively to feel for prey. Because they continue the habit in captivity, it was long erroneously said that they wash their food before eating.

The striped skunk gets a wide berth from other animals who fear the stinging foul-smelling secretions of its anal glands, which it squirts into the eyes of its enemies. Most predators avoid the skunk although mountain lions, which are also known variously as pumas or cougars, but bobcats and bay lynxes have sometimes been known to brave the stench when ravenously hungry.

In the Appalachians

The Appalachians are the oldest range of mountains in North America and, although it is likely that they were once even higher than the Rockies, countless thousands of years of erosion have ground them down until today they are scarcely more than a long chain of rolling hills. The highest point is not much more than 6250 feet above sea level. Although a deep blanket of snow covers these uplands in the winter, they all lie well below the permanent ice line and are consequently heavily tree clad up to their summits. There are both broadleafed deciduous woodlands, which once bedecked most of the eastern half of North America, and coniferous forests of soft wood trees in the colder zones. These wooded slopes and the streams and rivers that intersect them furnish relatively safe havens and well stocked larders for many animals that lead precarious existences elsewhere in the region. Among them are the fox, otter, shrew, and deer mice. The more low-lying areas that merge with metropolitan and populated areas are thick with species that are remarkable mainly for their ability to adapt to human environments. Some of these species were brought to the New World either deliberately or accidentally by European settlers – for instance, sparrows, starlings, pigeons, rats, and house mice. Others, like gray squirrels and orioles, were indigenous to the region.

Most animals prefer more secluded habitats. There are several types of salamanders that find the rivers and watery marshes conducive to breeding and feeding, among them two colorfully named varieties, the mudpuppy and the hellbender. Mudpuppies are closely related to the olms of Yugoslavia but are little like them in appearance and habit. They live in the open, are able to see adequately, and have deep red penniform gills. The hellbender, although much smaller

Above: baby opossums suckling inside their mother's pouch. A female common or Virginia opossum usually has 13 nipples. This means that if her litter is over 13, some of the babies may die.
Below: young opossums ride on their mother's back until they are 14 weeks old, having emerged from her pouch at 10 weeks.

than the enormous Japanese species it is related to, maintains its classification as a giant salamander by reaching a length of over 2 feet. It has the practice, like only two other salamander families, of fertilizing its eggs externally.

Another local species that spends much of its time in the water is the star-nosed mole, although it is a mammal rather than an amphibian. This little creature possesses one singular feature – an extraordinary nasal organ. The fleshy snout is fringed by a starlike halo of no less than 22 sensitive little tentacles with which the animal sniffs out its staple diet of earthworms, beetle larvae, and daddy-longlegs' grubs.

Possibly the most unusual animal to be found in this region is the common opossum – the only marsupial inhabiting North America, to which it spread from its original South American habitat thousands of years ago. This opossum is a survivor, more successful than many marsupials. Among the many reasons put forward for its success are its extreme dietary adaptability, its high breeding rate, and its method of self-defense by which it pretends to be dead – a device that has given rise to the phrase "playing possum."

The upper reaches of the woodlands are attractive to a whole host of birds, both permanent and migratory. There are the ordinary species such as jays, nuthatches, wrens, and chickadees, which are the local equivalent of the European tits. More unusual, there are the ruby-throated humming birds whose native habitat is in the Central American tropical forests, and the rufous hummingbirds which stop over on their yearly journey to southeast Alaska.

The Western Mountains

In the west of the Nearctic region is a complex mountain system over 3700 miles in length from its northwesterly beginning in the Arctic Circle to its termination in Mexico. It varies between 90 and 900 miles in width, and is made up of two roughly parallel ranges, the Californian Coast Range, the Cascades, and the Sierra Nevada counting as one continuous chain along the coast, and the Rocky Mountains a little farther inland. These two branches finally fuse in the north of Mexico to become the Sierre Madre. Being much younger than the Appalachians, these mountains are considerably higher. Vast continuous

Above: crouched in a tree branch, a cacomistle suns itself. This seldom seen nocturnal animal likes a daytime sunbath occasionally, keeping out of sight as is its habit by staying high in the tree. The cacomistle's beautifully marked fur is much sought after, and is sold on the market as "civet cat" and "California mink."

stretches are well in excess of 10,000 feet, while in the extreme northwest several peaks top 18,000 feet. It would be natural to expect a wide range of animals in a region spanning the icy north and the semitropical south, but that would be to forget the tremendous damage humans have inflicted on it during their relatively short occupancy.

The bighorn sheep is a species that, like the buffalo and the beaver, has been mercilessly harried. Audubon, in writing of a journey through the Rockies in 1843, said: "No one who has not seen the Mauvaises

Terres, or Badlands, can form any idea of these resorts of the Rocky Mountain Rams [bighorns] ... or of the difficulty of approaching these animals." He underrated his fellows. By 1905 they had wiped out one species of bighorn – ironically enough, the Badlands variety that Audubon had written about. By 1930 the rimrock variety had followed. Today, many other bighorn varieties are on the verge of extinction, the only one remaining in any appreciable number being that found in British Columbia and the northern United States. This unfortunate creature has suffered in a variety of ways. Not only was it killed for flesh and fleece, but it also died from such diseases as scab that it picked up from domesticated sheep. It was also edged out of the keen race for fodder by reestablished species like the elk and, to add insult to injury, it was hunted down for its magnificent horns, highly prized as trophies.

Rocky Mountain goats are safe from such pursuit because their horns are straight and short. Safe from human predators on that account, they stay safe from animal predators by inhabiting the tallest and least accessible peaks. It is just as well that they are too unapproachable for the puma which, like humans, is known to kill far in excess of its needs. Although these predators have been wiped out in some parts of North America, they are reputed to be making a comeback with the reestablishment of the deer they prey on.

The sewellel is a primitive rodent whose ancestry has never been tied in with any other known rodent. Named after a tribal robe made from its skin by Amerinds, it is also called the boomer or whistler beaver. Stocky, furry, and almost tailless, this burrower grows to about 12–15 inches in length. It is found in the wide valleys of the coastal ranges where it lives by rivers at altitudes of anything between sea level and 9500 feet. Predominantly nocturnal, it feeds mostly on succulent plants and uses its burrow chiefly as a predator-free highway, sleeping quarters, and storage chambers for the food it puts by for winter.

Slightly longer than the sewellel, but boasting a magnificent tail is the strangely named cacomistle, which is a corruption of the Aztec words for half cougar. Like the sewellel it has several other names as well, ring-tailed cat and cunning cat-squirrel being two of them. It is a close relative of the raccoon with similar black and white striations on its long tail. Solitary by nature and hardly ever seen by humans, the cacomistle has managed to adapt to the human environment. It has been known to extend its hunting activities to abandoned buildings in search of the rats and mice it might find there. To their diet of small mammals and birds, cacomistles add whatever fruit and grain they find on the lower slopes of the southernmost parts of the mountains.

Right: the bighorn is one of two wild sheep of North America, so nimble of foot that it can reach the most inaccessible parts of the Rockies above the tree line. Both rams and ewes have massive horns, but only the male's curve into a complete spiral. Both sexes also fight by ramming horns head on after a running start.

The Nearctic Region: The United States

Legend:
- Alligator
- Alligator snapper
- Beaver
- Bighorn sheep
- Bison
- Black bear
- Bobcat
- Brown bear
- Coati
- Common sea[l]
- Coyote

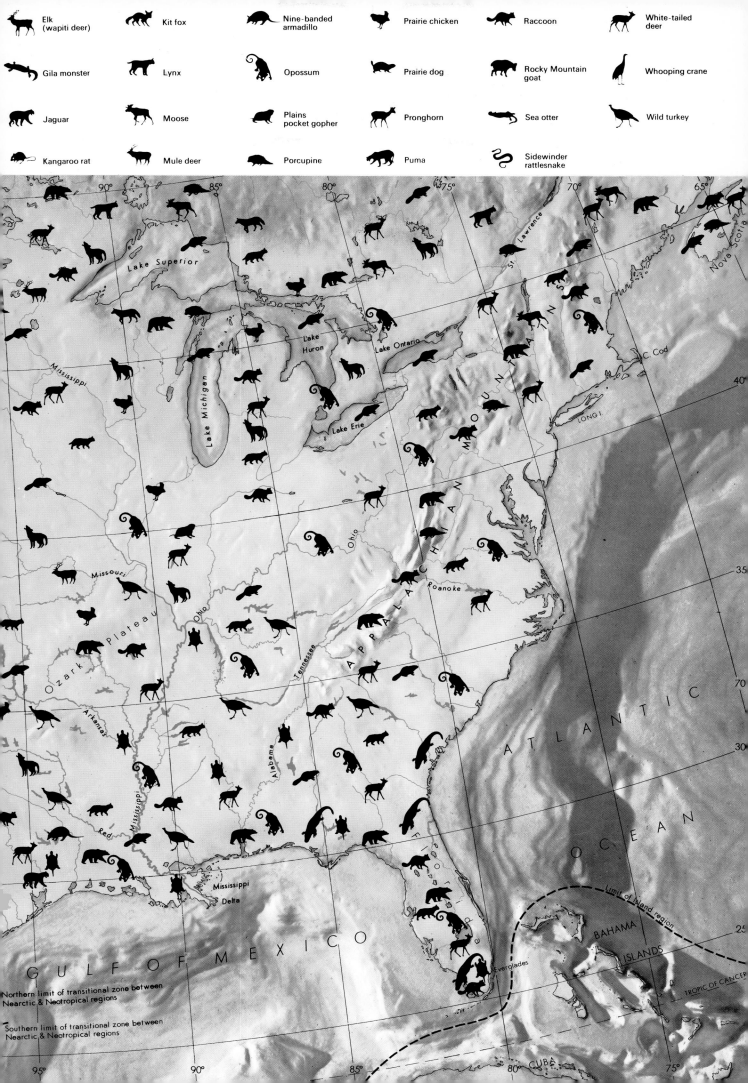

Elk (wapiti deer)

Gila monster

Jaguar

Kangaroo rat

Kit fox

Lynx

Moose

Mule deer

Nine-banded armadillo

Opossum

Plains pocket gopher

Porcupine

Prairie chicken

Prairie dog

Pronghorn

Puma

Raccoon

Rocky Mountain goat

Sea otter

Sidewinder rattlesnake

White-tailed deer

Whooping crane

Wild turkey

Northern limit of transitional zone between Nearctic & Neotropical regions

Southern limit of transitional zone between Nearctic & Neotropical regions

Protected Animals

If in the past the Wild West has been the scene of much slaughter of animals, a great deal has been done during the last 100 years to redress the balance. Not the least has been the provision of protected territories for animals of all kinds. Of the 60 or so major national parks and nature refuges in North America, over two thirds of them are situated in the western mountain regions. These include Yellowstone, Yosemite, Grand Canyon, Glacier, and Mount McKinley National Parks in the United States and the vast Wood Buffalo National Park in Canada. Wood Buffalo Park has an area of 17,300 square miles, just slightly larger than the country of Denmark. This Canadian refuge was established specifically as a haven for the northern bison, but it is the haunt of many other endangered species, including the plains buffalo. It is also the only known breeding ground for the last 50 or so whooping cranes on earth. Because the whooping crane's winter quarters are 2300 perilous miles away in Texas, fewer and fewer birds are surviving the trip. Recently the United States government has been propagating captive whooping cranes in an effort to increase the wild population.

The establishment of Yellowstone National Park as

the first of its kind in 1872 has a long and interesting history. In 1806 a trapper named John Colter stumbled across the source of the Yellowstone River, but his description of the area was greeted with ridicule and disbelief. People put his tales of lakes of hot bubbling mud and great fountains of boiling water down to drink, and dubbed his unbelievable world "Colter's Hell." About 20 years later James Bridger, another hunter, hit upon the same region. His account was even more fantastic than Colter's, and was greeted with the same scorn. Then a businessman, an execu-

Below: black bears roam at will in Yellowstone National Park, where they are among the most popular attractions. Better tempered and smaller than grizzlies, they often stand at the roadside boldly begging for food from passengers in passing cars.

tive of a fur company, published a similar report. Because of his status, he was taken seriously, and in 1851 a small scientific expedition was sent to investigate these miraculous phenomena. The vindicated Bridger was the guide. About 19 years later, a much larger and better equipped expedition went to the region, headed by the Surveyor-General of Montana. One of the members of this team was a judge by the name of Cornelius Hedges. Conscious of what might happen if this "Land of Wonders," as it was then being called, fell into the hands of speculators, he had the revolutionary notion of nationalizing it in the hope of preserving its marvels for the public and posterity. Articles and publicity in *Scribner's Monthly* magazine helped Hedges to kindle the interest of Congress, and in only two years, on March 12, 1872, the federal government passed the bill converting the region into the world's first national park. Today herds of moose, wapiti, mule deer, pronghorn, bighorn, and buffalo as well as bears, white pelicans, and trumpeter swans live there in increasing numbers. Their safety is seldom threatened, but one of the rare occasions

Above: the wapiti is a deer wrongly called an elk by early European settlers in North America. Its name means "white deer" and was given to it by Amerinds, probably because of its light rump patch. Most wapiti today live in national parks.

when protection failed was in 1915. At that time an unexpectedly high number applied for membership in the men's organization called the Benevolent and Protective Order of Elks. Five hundred wapiti or American elks were illegally killed to use their teeth for members' amulets.

Some of the national parks shelter animals unique to them. Grand Canyon National Park, for instance, is the one and only habitat of the kaibab squirrel, which over the ages has virtually been marooned on a small plateau by the impassable canyon itself. Opinions vary on whether the present population of about 1000 is enough to insure the future of the kaibab.

Life on the Prairie

Once the prairies were an ocean of grass stretching virtually from the Rockies to the Appalachians, from Canada to Mexico. That they were full of buffalo is common knowledge. It is not so well known that the pronghorn antelope also inhabited the wide plains in great numbers. The pronghorn is not an antelope at all, there being no members of the antelope family in the Nearctic. It resembles the true antelopes in having a bony core to its horns but, unlike them, it sheds the horny exterior annually.

Possessing far greater speed and staying power than the horse, the pronghorn had an assured future until the coming of the crackshot with the long-range rifle. Animal predators could hardly ever catch it except at certain times in the winter when the snow slowed its progress enough for coyotes and bobcats to match its speed. Before they got guns, Amerinds sometimes caught pronghorns by having several small groups of horsemen chase the creatures back and forth between them until the animals were too exhausted to go on – but even this ploy was frequently unsuccessful. With efficient guns in sure hands taking the place of the slow cumbersome bow and arrow, however, it was not long before the pronghorn was on the way out. By 1910 only a few, small, widely dispersed herds remained. Since then stringent protection combined with good management has saved this unique species from what looked like certain extinction, and today they exist in sufficient numbers in parts of Wyoming and Montana to be hunted once more, under legal restrictions this time.

Another story of being saved from extinction concerns the mule deer, but it has a twist ending. Less restricted than most deer to a purely woodland habitat, the mule deer moved into the prairies as the buffalo and pronghorns were killed off. They in turn were picked off and then rescued by strict protective measures. The irony is that they have increased by so

many that they face starvation in winter when there is not enough food to go around.

The once luckless bison's future became more secure from the time that statutory measures of protection were taken. Montana passed legislation in 1897 making buffalo shooting a felony punishable by two years' imprisonment, for example. More recently, it has been suggested that there is potential economic value in the bison based on the facts that it is stronger and more able to withstand the cold than domestic cattle; it will eat grasses the tamed variety will not, which reduces the likelihood of overgrazing the pastures; and its meat is by no means unpalatable.

Tied to the bison's fate is that of the brown-headed cowbird. This relative of the cuckoo earns a free ride on the buffalo's back by feeding off the parasitic ticks that the big animal cannot get rid of by scratching against a tree or rolling in the mud. The brown-headed cowbird is something of a parasite itself. It does not build its own nests, but dumps its eggs into another bird's. When hatched, cowbird chicks manage to get a share of the food brought to the nest.

Below left: a pronghorn herd of any size is rare today, even though this animal is now protected. A large mammal of great speed, the pronghorn is sometimes called the American antelope. However, it is not a true antelope and has no close relatives.

Below: mule deer are so called because of their long mulelike ears. Related to the Virginia deer, the mule deer ranges throughout western North America from Alaska to northern Mexico. This photograph clearly shows the velvet of the antlers. This soft covering remains for the four years antlers take to grow fully.

Small Animals of the Prairie

Some inkling of the immense size of the prairies as they once were might be gleaned by considering that their grasses provided ample sustenance for 60 million bison, 40 million pronghorn, countless wapiti and mule deer, and a teeming population of smaller herbivorous animals all of which have prodigious appetites. It is also well to remember that an exclusive diet of plants does not satisfy the hunger as much as the same amount of meat.

Of the big predators only the coyote exists in any number – the gray wolf and puma are very scarce today. Smaller predators such as prairie falcons, spotted skunks, the nearly extinct black-footed ferrets, and various species of snake ranging from the poisonous rattlesnake to the nonvenomous hog-nosed snake, are still able to find enough food.

Burrowing rodents such as prairie dogs and pocket gophers are perhaps the most characteristic animals of the prairie. These animals' ceaseless burrowing has undermined the surface of the land with an extensive labyrinth of small tunnels, and has had a fundamental effect on the actual nature of the prairie. Its dearth of shrubs and trees is due in no small measure to these tireless little creatures' fondness for the tops and long roots of thistles, shrubs, and saplings, and to the speed with which they devour any small seeds blowing in from the surrounding woodlands. Farmers have found that where these animals have been exterminated, the prairies have quickly become a wilderness of sagebrush, cactus, and mesquite.

The more threadbare patches of the prairie are pitted by bison's wallows and pockmarked by burrowing animals' homes. Pocket gophers, so-called because they have food pouches or pockets in their cheeks, do not hibernate but hoard their winter forage in the storage chambers of their burrows. The gopher's name is a corruption of the French word *gaufre* mean-

ing honeycomb – an allusion to the effect the entrance to their burrows has on the appearance of the terrain. This solitary little creature has a short, extremely sensitive tail that enables it to run backward.

Unlike pocket gophers, prairie dogs lead a sociable existence, living in highly organized underground

Opposite: larger than its European cousin, the American badger is just as skilled as a burrower. It has exceptionally strong front claws, which help it in digging a large deep den. Leaving its den only at night, it hunts for small rodents and usually goes along the same familiar paths in its search. The badger puts up a hard fight when in danger, but is otherwise mild and peaceful.

Left: a prairie falcon feeding a small mammal to its nestlings. This bird of prey, which is one of the fastest winged animals in North America, often attacks smaller birds in midair while in full flight. It is becoming increasingly rare these days.

communities called towns. These towns, which can have as many as 1000 inhabitants, are subdivided into closer knit communities known as wards, made up of several family groups called coteries. The community as a whole is connected by burrows that extend for miles and that are served by hundreds of entrances and communicating corridors. Another feature of these burrows is the mound surrounding the entrances as a protection against flooding. Prairie dogs are constantly forced to extend their colonies because rattlesnakes take over their burrows as hibernating quarters every year, occasionally eating the outgoing tenants into the bargain. Prairie dogs, which are not dogs but members of the marmot tribe of the squirrel family, are beset by enemies from all quarters: birds of prey from above, human and animal predators at ground level, and rattlesnakes, American badgers, and black-footed ferrets underground.

Even the ability to fly away from danger has not saved the prairie chicken from possible extinction. Basically ground birds, their relative, the sage grouse, prefers the drier sagebrush plains to the west. Like other members of the grouse family, the males at mating time strut about in front of the nonchalant females, proudly displaying their bright yellow plumage, puffing out their orange throat sacs, and fighting among themselves in order to win a mate.

Opposite: a prairie dog sentinel, standing guard at its burrow entrance. Prairie dogs are not related to dogs at all, but are ground squirrels. They get their name from the barking sound they make. This large plump rodent has an interesting kissing ritual by which it identifies members of its own large community.

A Desert Habitat

Between the Rocky Mountains and the west coastal mountains lies a large, arid, scrubby plateau known as the Great Basin. It is the most northerly of a whole chain of arid areas extending into Mexico. These include the scorching, below sea level Death Valley in eastern California, the yucca-studded Mojave Desert in southern California, the state of Sonora in northwest Mexico and the neighboring state of

Like many reptiles, it immerses a large part of itself in the loose sand which serves the double function of shading the animal from the glare of the sun and acting as a heat-conductor for its cold-blooded body. In addition to the horrifying appearance of its spiked body, the horned toad possesses another highly efficient if rather gruesome way of keeping its enemies at bay. When excited, its blood pressure rises so sharply that the small blood vessels in the conjunctiva of its eye burst and it shoots a squirt of blood at its enemy.

The chuckwalla is a much larger lizard that inhabits the North American deserts. Its methods of escaping danger are less startling than the horned

Left: a kangaroo rat is surprised by a rattlesnake, against which it can defend itself by kicking sand into the predator's eyes. Kangaroo rats, which are not of the kangaroo family, are able to live wholly without water.

Below: horned toads mainly eat plants, although most other members of their species live on insects. It is the spines on their head that give them their name.

Chichuahua.

The climates range from temperate in the Great Basin and the salt flats abutting it to the east, to tropical in the Mexican wastelands. In such varied environments there is a wide variety of animals to be found. In the northern zones, for instance, the wildlife is basically similar to that of the surrounding mountains and includes coyotes, bobcats, pumas, and buzzards, while the Mojave Desert is the domain of sidewinder rattlesnakes, kangaroo rats, and desert tortoises. Woodpeckers, diminutive elf owls, and several species of snakes find convenient lodgings in the gigantic seguaro cacti of the Sonoran desert area. The mesquite-dotted Chichuahuan desert region supports antelope jackrabbits, tarantula spiders, scorpions, and a wide range of lizards. Some of the lizards are unique, many are rare or bizarre or both.

The horned toad, which is an inguanid lizard rather than a toad, is widespread throughout the more torrid deserts of the southern United States and Mexico.

Above: elf owls like to live in a saguaro cactus, often moving into a home vacated by a desert woodpecker. This bird, which is a little bigger than a sparrow, lives only where saguaros grow.

toad's. Like the chameleon, it tries to escape the notice of less keen-eyed predators by changing its color to that of its background. If this stratagem fails, it can resort to another: it scuttles into a crack in the rocks and inflates its body until it is wedged in so tightly that it cannot be dislodged.

Some Nearctic desert animals have adaptive patterns markedly similar to those in the Palaearctic desert regions. The American kit fox, for instance, has developed enormous ears like the Saharan fennec with the dual purpose of radiating heat and hearing its prey better. Like a large number of desert animals, it is able to extract its water requirements from the body fluids of the rodents it preys on. Grasshopper mice derive all their water from their diet.

Jackrabbits, which are really hares, have developed very large ears in proportion to their bodies in order to avoid danger through keen hearing. Other species, such as the kangaroo rat, rely for survival on their ability to spring great distances.

Florida's Fauna

Both on its Pacific and Atlantic sides, the Nearctic region terminates in a peninsula. The western peninsula is called Baja California and is a long thin promontory of mostly arid desert land. In contrast, Florida on the east is one of the lushest parts of North America. Farther inland from Florida, the banks of the lower Mississippi are lined by an evergreen forest of magnolias, bay trees, palms, and evergreen oaks under whose canopy springs a thick mantle of rank vegetation – orchids, creepers, and ferns. The river winds its leisurely way downstream, through the bayous south of New Orleans, eventually emptying out of the ever-growing head of the delta into the Gulf

glades end in mangrove swamps and salt water marshes.

The lush vegetation encourages an abundance both of the brightly colored flowering plants from which Florida derives its name – *florida* is the Spanish word for flowery – and a wide variety of animal life especially in the vicinity of the hammocks. There are some of the same species encountered elsewhere in the Nearctic – raccoons and opossums, muskrats and otters, bobcats, white-tailed deer, and black bears, for instance. Several aquatic and avian species could not exist in conditions other than those of a swamp.

As with the Camargue and Coto do Doñana in the Palaearctic region, the presence of both fresh and sea water in these coastal marshes insures a generous supply of aquatic plants, insects, crustaceans, small reptiles, and little fish. These go to feed wading birds like the egret, heron, flamingo, and roseate spoonbill. Less well known are the jacana, whose elongated toes

Above: the American alligator is one of only two species of this reptile in the world, the other being found in China. Alligators bask in the sun during the day and hunt at night. They have been killed off for their hides, used for shoes and other accessories.

of Mexico.

In Florida's northeast lie the remains of what at one time was a dense deciduous forest of hickory, holly, and oak, which is replaced in the less well drained lower areas toward the coast by subtropical pine woods, peatland swamps, and salt marshes. In the southern part of the Florida peninsula are the Everglades, a vast tract of swampland covering more than 5000 square miles. The Everglades start at Lake Okeechobee, after the Great Lakes the biggest lake in North America. Dotted in the marshy expanse are small islets known locally as hummocks, upon which grow such tropical trees as palms, mahogany, strangler figs, and others with fascinating regional names – gumbo-limbo, joewood, and pond apple. The Ever-

and flattened claws allow it to walk on the saucerlike leaves of water lilies, and the anhinga or darter, whose pointed bills act as harpoons to spear fish.

The Everglade kite, although not belonging to an aquatic family, has adapted itself to preying on freshwater snails. It uses its curved and sharply pointed upper mandible to paralyze its victim and, with the steadying help of a foot, extracts the flesh from the shell with its beak. Never very common despite the glut of freshwater snails, this bird has become very rare, forced back from its natural habitat by drainage of the Florida marshes. It numbered only 10 in 1965 and, although it breeds in a sanctuary in a tiny corner of Lake Okeechobee, its future is much in doubt because of attacks by its natural predator the grackle.

Among the aquatic animals to be found in this area; none is stranger than the manatee, a mammal weighing from 600 to 2000 pounds. It is almost as strictly confined to the water as the whale, but considerably less intelligent. Of a placid and trusting disposition, these animals inhabit the warm muddy coastal shallows and turbid estuaries. They eat up to a hundredweight a day of seagrasses, water hyacinths, and lilies.

Among the reptiles of the Everglades are many varieties of turtles, including the alligator snapper turtles whose hooked jaws can inflict serious injury. Unique to this area is the American alligator, one of the largest of the reptile family. It divides its time between sunbathing on the river banks and floating in the streams, totally submerged but for the top of its head. Although it will feed on any kind of water animal, it will also attack land animals that come within range on the river bank. Larger still than the alligator is the American crocodile of southern Florida. It is also found in the West Indies and Central and South America.

Below: the brilliantly colored American gallinule lives among plants in semistagnant water, and has the special skill of being able to run fast over floating vegetation. It is a close relative of the moorhen, called the common gallinule in North America.

Mexican Variety

Mexico is a very varied country geographically with deserts, semideserts, high mountains, and tropical forests. It is even more varied zoologically. Its position athwart the Tropic of Cancer neatly symbolizes its zoogeographical role as a transition area between the Nearctic and the Neotropical regions. Although these two regions have a number of animals in common, each possesses several peculiar to itself. This transitional zone, which runs through the center of Mexico, contains a mixture of the two wildlife species. The pronghorn and white-tailed deer have infiltrated from the north as have the puma, coyote, and peccary. Of the same family as the pig, the peccary has also spread from the Nearctic region into Central and South America. Among the animals that have strayed

Above: the gila monster is one of the largest lizards in North America and one of only two poisonous lizards. It is nearly 2 feet in length and looks somewhat like a prehistoric reptile.

in from South America are armadillos, sloths, and anteaters, all members of the edentate order that is unique to the Neotropical region. Edentate means toothless and is somewhat misleading because only the anteaters are actually without teeth. In fact, some species of armadillo possess as many as 100 teeth – more than any other land animal – although they are of a primitive kind. They lack both roots and enamel and are all simple molars, but they are adequate for the armadillo's insect diet. Edentates also have small brains but they have held their own against the competition of many more highly developed mammals. For example, the nine-banded armadillo has spread not merely throughout Central America but into the southern states of the United States.

The tapir, another mammal almost exclusive to South America, is represented in Mexico by a variety

Right: turkey vultures, also called turkey buzzards, use the tall cardon cactus as a perch from which to keep an eye out for carrion. This scavenger has a wingspan of 6 feet in width, and will spread its wings to the full in order to catch a cool breeze.

known as Baird's tapir. This shy, velvety, nocturnal herbivore's chosen habitats are the rivers and marshes which are made perilous for it by the occasional lurking alligator. Its only other enemy is the jaguar which, with its smaller cousin the ocelot, is the most feared predator of this area.

Small predators include the crab-eating raccoon and

Above: the collared peccary is so called because of the semi-circle of lighter hair on its shoulders. Peccaries look similar to wild pigs of the Old World, but are not of the same family. Two differences are fewer teeth and upper tusks that grow upward.

the tayra, which is the South American equivalent of the marten. Two carnivores of the raccoon family that eat fruit as well as meat are the olingo and the kinkajou, often nick-named the honey bear. It is said to visit Mexican bars and drop from the ceiling and steal a customer's rum and coke to satisfy its sweet tooth. Both olingos and kinkajous are tree dwellers and a little like monkeys in appearance, especially the kinkajou with its prehensile tail.

There is no shortage of genuine monkeys in Mexico, among which are tamarins, marmosets, capuchins, howlers, and douroucoulis. Nor does it lack birds, including toucans and brightly colored parrots, pelicans and flamingos. Mexico and adjacent Guatemala

boast a particularly beautiful bird all their own: the quetzal. When it flies through the upper branches of the tropical forests, its scarlet belly and long green tail feathers can be seen.

Another unique animal is the Mexican burrowing or digger toad. While this curious pink and brown amphibian can tolerate the extremely dry conditions of the coastal plains where it feeds on termites, it can spawn only after the heavy rainstorms which now and then occur. The axolotl is also an amphibian, but it is not at all like the digger toad even though it is just as vitally affected by the humidity. As long as its surroundings are wet, it retains its larval characteristics – a phenomenon known as neoteny – remaining in its tadpole stage indefinitely. If the water in which it lives happens to dry up, however, it is possible for the axolotl to lose its external gills and become an adult salamander.

101

Chapter 4

The Neotropical Region

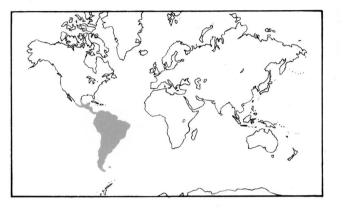

The Neotropical region, which extends nearly 5500 miles from north to south, embraces most of Mexico and the rest of the Central American isthmus, the whole of South America, Trinidad and Tobago of the West Indian islands, and the Falkland Islands. It is generously endowed both geographically and zoologically. It has in the Andes the longest continuous and second highest mountain range in the world. It also has the world's largest tropical rain forest in the basin of the Amazon River, which itself is the world's longest river. Of the many large tributaries feeding the Amazon, 17 are themselves over 1000 miles in length. There is a great diversity of climate and terrain from desert to jungle, from mountain to pampa and bleak foggy moorland, from the tropical waters of the Caribbean Sea in the northeast to the Pacific Ocean's cold Humboldt Current on the west. In these various environments is found a great wealth of animals, many of which are unique and many remarkable.

Few marsupials live outside Australia, the opossum being one of them. This tiny murine opossum – only the size of a large mouse – is found in Central and South America. It seems to be fearless, opening its mouth in a menacing gesture whenever anything at all threatens it.

103

The Terrain

Of the world's zoogeographical regions, the Neo-tropical is the one that has been least disrupted by the human presence. In fact, the conquering Spaniards of the 16th century actually redressed a balance by reintroducing the horse. This animal, which had originated in North America and migrated to South American, had long since disappeared from both continents.

The reasons for the region's comparatively pure state are many and may be ascribed partly to economics, partly to politics, partly to historical accident. The chief reason, however, lies in the geography of the region. Much of it is tropical, and some of it is even equatorial. South of the Central American isthmus lie steamy savannas relieved in parts by highlands. South of this is the vast Amazon basin, below which is the enormous tract of thick scrub called the Mato Grosso. This gives way to the arid plains of the Gran Chaco, which merges into the more temperate pampas or Argentine prairie. Then comes the Patagonian desert and, to the far south, the foggy cold tip of the continent and the inhospitable chain of islands called Tierra

del Fuego. In the west of South America from the northernmost to the southernmost shores, the mighty Andes mountains stand sentinel. To the west of this range lies a very narrow coastal strip, a large section of which is desert.

The Amazon basin covers the enormous area of 2.5 million square miles – more than five times as big as the Mato Grosso and nearly 10 times the size of the state of Texas. The river system itself is so vast that 18 percent of all the fresh water running into the world's oceans flow through its complex network at an average rate of 7.5 million cubic feet a second.

The constant strong sunlight, the huge amount of rain, the minerals carried down from the Andes and deposited by the slow-moving rivers – all combine to provide ideal conditions for unbridled forest growth. Some trees reach gigantic heights of up to 160 feet; others grow beneath them so abundantly that hardly an inch of ground is left uncovered. Even so, enough light filters through the leafy canopy for shrubs, creepers, and epiphytes to fill the rest of the ground space. This jungle, which contains more than 400 species of trees compared with a dozen or so in the average mixed temperate forest, has proved so impenetrable that it was not until 1958 that the geographical center of Brazil was reached. Furthermore, few of the explorers who ventured into the interior of the Mato Grosso ever returned to civilization,

Right: llamas inhabit the windswept grasslands of the high Peruvian Andes. This humpless camel, which is nearly half the size of its cousins in Asia, is often domesticated but never becomes fully tamed. It gives birth to only one baby a year.

Left: Chilean pines or monkey puzzle trees grow on a mountain in southern Chile. The harsh terrain of this region of South America requires great hardiness in an animal to survive, but at the same time it has kept humans from interfering so much with animal life.

whether the victims of disease, hunger, or hostile Amerinds is not known. Even today some of the remote Indian tribes are unaware of what is going on in the rest of Brazil, but this state of affairs is not likely to last much longer. The Brazilian authorities have finally realized the enormous potential of their natural resources, and have made a start in opening up the interior of their huge country which is some 313,000 square miles larger than the United States. They have shifted the capital from Rio de Janeiro on the coast to Brasilia, an entirely new city 600 miles inland to the northwest. They have also started to build a road some 3300 miles in length, which on completion will cut through both the Mato Grosso and the heart of the tropical forest. It is only to be hoped that the Transamazônica highway will not significantly affect the self-perpetuating forest nor the incredibly rich and varied wildlife it shelters.

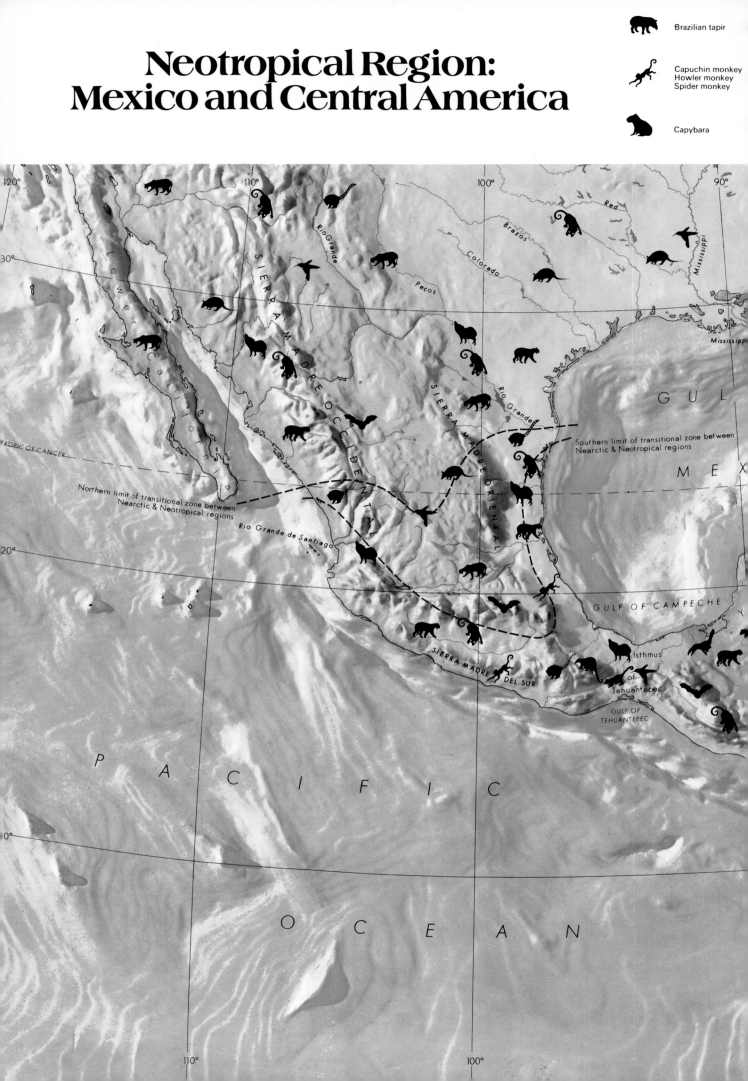

Neotropical Region: Mexico and Central America

Brazilian tapir

Capuchin monkey
Howler monkey
Spider monkey

Capybara

TROPIC OF CANCER

Northern limit of transitional zone between
Nearctic & Neotropical regions

Southern limit of transitional zone between
Nearctic & Neotropical regions

Rio Grande

Pecos

Colorado

Brazos

Red

Mississippi

Mississippi

SIERRA MADRE OCCIDENTAL

SIERRA MADRE ORIENTAL

Rio Grande

Rio Grande de Santiago

SIERRA MADRE DEL SUR

Isthmus
of
Tehuantepec

GULF OF
TEHUANTEPEC

GULF OF CAMPECHE

G U L

M E X

P A C I F I C   O C E A N

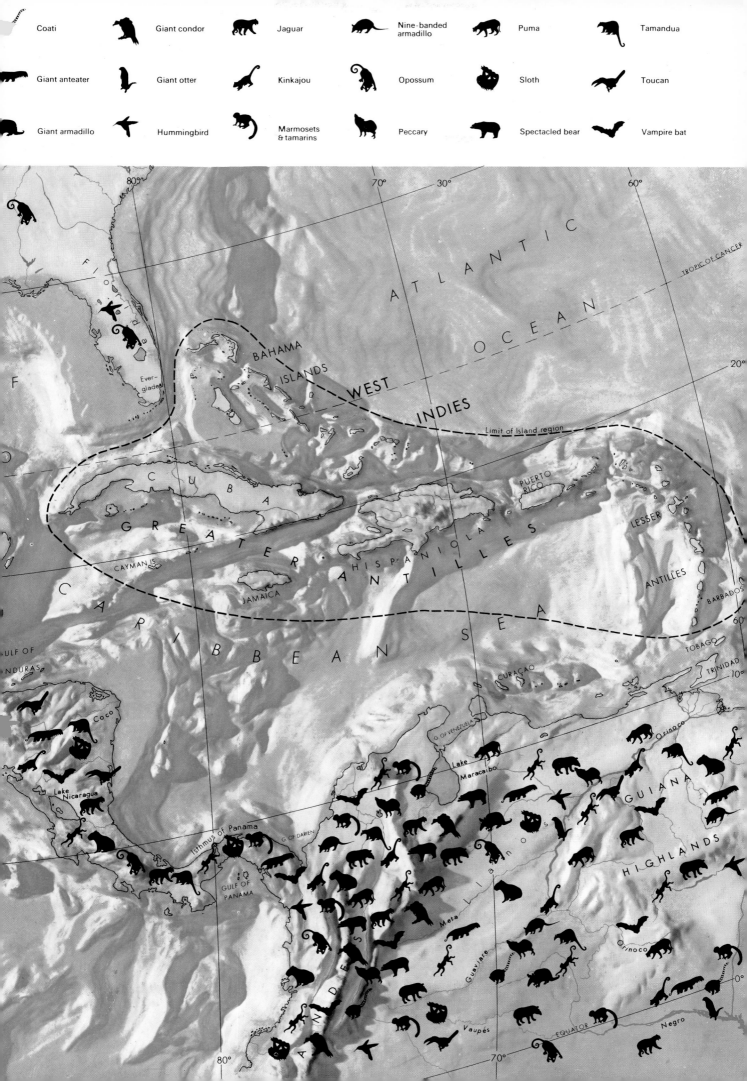

Coati

Giant condor

Jaguar

Nine-banded
armadillo

Puma

Tamandua

Giant anteater

Giant otter

Kinkajou

Opossum

Sloth

Toucan

Giant armadillo

Hummingbird

Marmosets
& tamarins

Peccary

Spectacled bear

Vampire bat

An Exotic Wildlife

If the Neotropical region's physical features are spectacular, much of its wildlife is even more so. For example, it boasts the largest living rodent, the capybara, the world's largest freshwater fish, the arapaima, and the enormous Andean condor which, with its 9-foot wingspan, can sustain a glide longer than other birds. It is also the home of two huge and extremely dangerous snakes, the bushmaster and the anaconda. The bushmaster is the biggest of all the pit vipers and, after the king cobra, the largest venomous snake in the world. The mighty anaconda, which can

and a variety of manatee. Still to be encountered in the surrounding seas and oceans are many species of whale, even though it has been hunted as ruthlessly as any animal on earth. Happily, not all of the local species of seal have been wiped out. Both the South American fur seal and the southern sea lion are relatively abundant and widespread, and the southern elephant seal, which not so long ago was brought to the verge of extinction on account of its oil, is growing in number today.

Several species of animals are unique to the Neotropical region while others are shared with only one or two other zoogeographical regions. Originally the whole of the *edentate* (toothless) order was found solely in South and Central America, but some have wandered north to the Nearctic. Occasionally the process has been reversed; the peccary, for example, has

Above: the anaconda is one of the world's biggest snakes. It seldom strays far from water and becomes increasingly aquatic as it grows older. The liking for water is also tied in with size, the largest ones spending almost all their time submerged.

attain a length of 25 feet, is the biggest of the boa family. From the water where it lies, the anaconda coils itself around its victims, pulls them from the bank into the water, and squeezes them to death.

The rivers are the home for other vicious animals as well. One is the piranha, a voracious fish with needle-sharp teeth. It is said that a school of piranha can pick a bulky 3-foot-long capybara clean of all its flesh in a matter of seconds. Another predator fish is the electric eel, which can be about 8 feet in length. The electric eel employs its powerful equipment for hunting as well as attacking. It navigates and locates its prey radar-like by means of a moderate electrical charge, and then turns up its current to as much as 600 volts to stun it.

Besides the giant otter that has been hunted to the point of extinction for its fur, there are many other aquatic mammals inhabiting the region's lakes, rivers, estuaries, and coastal waters. There are sea dolphins and porpoises as well as three species of river dolphin

migrated south into the Neotropical region. Species of the primitive lungfish and side-necked turtle are to be found in Africa and Australia as well as in this region, and species of the tapir in the Oriental region and here.

Among the unique animals are the New World monkeys – 70 species including capuchins, marmosets, and uakaris; the chinchilla, much hunted for its beautiful pearl-gray fur; the rhea, which resembles the ostrich; and the guinea pig, popular as a pet.

Not for nothing has South America been called the Bird Continent. Birds outnumber all other animals and also outdo them in raucousness and colorfulness. To name but a few there are the toucans, macaws, ovenbirds, jacamars, oropendolas, and manakins. The enormous harpy eagle swooping through the upper branches in search of sloths or monkeys contrasts with the tiny hovering hummingbird.

South America also has an exceptional number of bats, there being 140 species, and rats, of which there are no less than 340 species.

Below: the Andean condor, being slightly bigger than the California condor, is both the largest bird of prey and the largest flying bird there is. Although unrelated to the true vultures of the Old World, the condor has the bare head and neck of true vultures. The Andean condor's is red or blackish red in color. It also has loose folds of wrinkled skin hanging from its face.

Birds
of the Jungle

One of the characteristics of the teeming life in tropical forests such as the Amazon basin is that the various species inhabit one particular level and, on the whole, seldom depart from it – a fact probably accounted for by the overcrowding. With certain exceptions, this stratification applies even to birds and bats which, more than any other animal, are just as mobile upward as they are horizontally.

Hovering above the forest, often called jungle when tropical as in this region, is the yellow-headed vulture. Like the nocturnal, cave-dwelling oilbird, this bird is one of the few to possess a sense of smell. But unlike the fruit-eating oilbird, it lives on carrion.

The animals that live at the top of the trees are

Above: the long migration of the tiny ruby-throated humming-bird is one of the most remarkable examples of the great endurance and skillful navigation of birds. It covers well over 2000 miles from eastern North America across the Gulf of Mexico to South America, flapping its wings over 50 times a second.

generally free from predators, the main danger being the harpy eagle. The harpy in turn is in danger from the forest Indians who capture and cage it to use its feathers for decoration. Although this bird is the world's largest eagle, its wings are disproportionately short, and this adaptation enables it to swoop through the upper branches of the trees to snatch a bird, monkey, or somnolent sloth. Other tenants of the upper reaches are the brilliant toucans with bright blue eyes, whose raucous cries blend with the raspings of parrots and macaws and the stentorian yells of howler monkeys to give the jungle its distinctive pattern of sound. The toucan's huge and gaudy bill is ideally suited for probing about in the thick foliage of the slender branches high up in search of fruit. The strong pincerlike beaks of the equally showy parrots and macaws are just as well suited to their diet of nuts.

Also inhabiting the canopy are the cotingas or chatterers such as the cock of the rock, the male of which has a helmet shaped crest completely obscuring its beak. Cocks of the rock are like a crow in size, but of a bright red or orange color. They are not per-

petually confined to the upper strata of the forest. During the mating season they come to earth to perform their highly formalized courtship rituals. A group of cocks clear a kind of arena, preferably surrounding a rock, and one male after the other displays for minutes on end in slow succession before the hens.

Above: the orange cock-of-the-rock, like the rarer and paler Peruvian species, has a noticeable crest in the shape of a double fan going from the crown of the head to the base of the bill. The habitat of the two species is separated by the Andes.

Manakins are not as fussy as many species about which layer they inhabit and, like the cock of the rock, descend to the ground for their courting ceremony. This takes the form of an acrobatic competition of often frenzied dancing, swooping, and whirling – after which the female selects her mate.

The quiet and solitary trogon, which belongs to the same order as the quetzal of Mexico, is an insect eater. So are its close relations the puffbirds and jacamars. Although they spend their days in the topmost branches making swift sorties to catch their prey, they return at night to their homes in termites' nests or ground burrows.

The many gorgeously feathered species of hummingbird have a somewhat varied diet. They eat insects or the nectar of flowers, which they extract with their slender bills. Their ability to hover is based on an incredibly high rate of wing beat, detectable more by sound than by sight. The energy these tiny birds expend requires constant stoking up by incessant feeding; in order to survive through the night they go into a torpid state.

The tinamou, one of the larger jungle birds, is

Below: an emerald hummingbird, named after a gem to reflect its jewel-like brilliance. Unrivaled for colorful plumage, the hummingbird family includes other species with names like ruby, topaz, and garnet. There are over 300 species of this bird.

unique among them. It lives on the ground, grubbing for seeds and insects and occasionally emitting an eerie whistle. In times of danger it runs for cover, although it can take short flights if pressed.

The strangest bird of the tropical forest is the hoatzin, which resembles the archaeopterix of prehistoric times. The hoatzin, whose call is more reptilian than avian, is born already possessed of claws. These claws, which are situated on the front of its wings, enable it to climb around the nest during the first few weeks of its life or to scuttle to safety along the branches of the trees if in danger. The adult lacks such claws and avoids its foes by diving into the water and swimming out of harm's way.

New World Monkeys

Sharing the tropical forest's rich offering of fruit and insects with the birds are a host of mammals and a good many reptiles and amphibians.

Although they have many features in common, the South American monkeys are not closely related to those of the Old World. They are dissimilar facially, having different teeth and shorter snouts with widely separated, flattened nostrils. Unlike the Old World monkeys, it is notable that their thumbs are not opposable, but like several other Neotropical animals, their tails are usually prehensile.

Higher up, toward the tops of the emergent trees, dwell the woolly monkeys. Their gluttonous appetites often result in potbellies, which has earned them the Brazilian nickname of *barrigudos* (big bellies). Their close cousins, the spider monkeys, are unusual among monkeys because of the lack of a thumb.

Possibly the commonest of the South American monkeys is the squirrel monkey. Found mainly in the riverside forests, they live in large groups sometimes of several hundred. The squirrel monkey has a beautiful coat of yellowish-green, and is said to be of a charming disposition.

The cebids also include the world's only nocturnal

Below: a family of golden lion marmosets or tamarins, whose long silky hair and mane of red-gold make it one of the brightest of all mammals. It is the father that usually carries the young around, handing them over to the mother only when they are fed.

The New World monkeys consist of two distinct families, the Cebidae and the Callitrichidae. The cebids include the capuchin, the spider, woolly, squirrel, and howler monkeys, among others. Equipped with enlarged larynxes, the howler is capable of producing sound carrying a distance of one or two miles. Howlers use this shout to defend their territory. Big as dogs, these monkeys roam the upper branches in bands of about 20.

Inhabiting the middle level of the jungle trees in larger groups are the capuchins, probably the most intelligent of all the monkeys. They are, for example, able to use simple tools such as stones to crack open nuts. Like the more developed apes, they have been known to produce drawings and paintings in captivity.

monkey, the douroucouli, whose eyes are sensitive to daylight and adapted to night. It is sometimes known as the owl monkey because of the saucerlike shape of the eyes. They sleep in hollow tree trunks and, being light sleepers, are often roused. They are extremely inquisitive, which sometimes leads to their capture for sale as pets, illegal though that is.

In the fine twigs of the topmost branches live three unusual and shy types of cebid monkey: the slow-moving titi, the swifter saki, and the very rare uakari. Titis, which are said to smell like orange juice, sleep with their tails intertwined with their mate's. The red uakari has a bare face and head of bright scarlet, which flushes even redder if the animal is disturbed. The bald uakari may have a harsh looking face, but it is as gentle and timid as any of the cebid monkeys.

The other family of New World monkeys, the Callitrichidae, consists of 21 species of marmosets and tamarins. One of these, Goeldie's marmoset, may occupy an intermediate position between them and the Cebidae, possessing as it does some features of each family. For example, it has cebid teeth and, like Cebidae, bears a single offspring. However, it has the claws typical of the Callitrichidae. The golden lion tamarin, so called because it has a mane, is of a

Above: Geoffroy's spider monkey, which lives in the densest forests of Central America, swings beneath the branches like an ape. In common with several other Neotropical monkeys, it has touch pads on the underside of its prehensile tail for better grip.

particularly beautiful glowing gold color. It has been so hunted for the pet trade that only about 500 are left.

Seven other species of New World monkeys, including the red uakari, Goeldie's marmoset, and the woolly spider monkey, are also endangered.

113

Tree Dwellers

If the number of species of monkey in the South American tropical forests is substantial, it still falls far short of the varieties of bat. It has been estimated that the five families of bat are made up of no less than 140 different species. Nocturnal creatures, they hang upside down from the branches while asleep during the day. Although the bat is ungainly and perhaps even ugly in appearance, it is relatively harmless to humans and the larger animals even if it can sometimes inflict a vicious bite.

Even the dreaded vampire bat, which sticks unswervingly to a diet of blood alone, takes an amount that is not enough to do the victim any harm. The real danger from a bat is that it can carry such diseases as rabies and horse fever. It is just possible that they were the cause of the strange disappearance of native horses from this region. Less than 3 inches long, with a wingspan of some 6 inches, vampires feed so carefully and lightly that they will not wake a sleeping victim. Alighting like a feather on their prey, they slice off a thin layer of skin with their sharp incisor teeth and lap tiny quantities of blood from the wound, aided by a chemical in their saliva that prevents clotting. They consume about an ounce during the night. The great false vampires, which have a 28-inch wingspan, are not vampires at all but eat only fruit and insects. The tent-making bats fashion themselves shelters by chewing half through the ribs of palm leaves until the leaves droop like tents over the branches on which they roost.

Living even more of an upside down existence than bats are sloths, which go so far as to mate and give birth hanging upside down from the branches while attached by their powerful claws. Even when shot dead, sloths remain obstinately suspended in the foliage until they rot. When forced to move, they can climb trees easily enough, if only at a maximum speed of about one mile an hour. Should they find themselves in the water, sloths are strong swimmers but they are lost on the ground, able only to crawl painfully. Predatory harpy eagles do not always spot them easily because of the camouflage of green algae that cover their fur. The fur itself grows downward from the belly toward the back in order to shed water.

Two other toothless nocturnal animals may be found dangling head down from the branches, but by their tails rather than their claws. These are the tamandua, and the pigmy anteater. The tamandua measures a little over 3 feet long from the tip of its long tubular snout to the end of its 16-inch tail. It splits its time between the ground and a tree branch, while the pigmy anteater is completely arboreal. Both rely for food mainly on the contents of the termites' nests in the trees or on the ground. These they rip open with their efficient claws and then probe repeatedly with their amazingly long sticky tongues. At each insertion of the tongue, hundreds of insects adhere to it. When unable to escape from an enemy, both these animals rear back on their hind legs, holding their viciously clawed forepaws up in a belligerent attitude.

Another Neotropical animal with a prehensile tail,

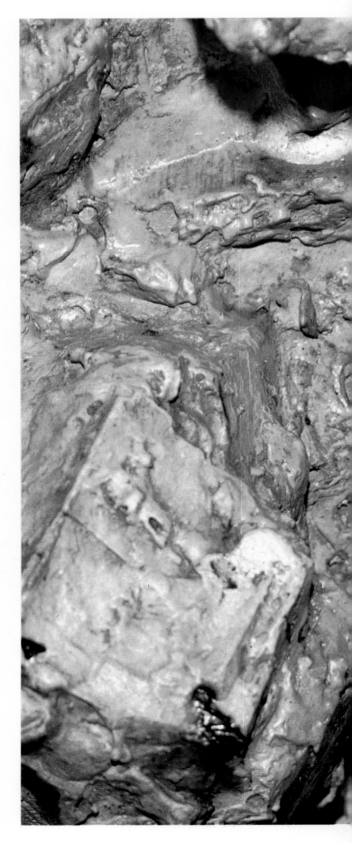

the tree porcupine or coendou, has no need to resort to a trick like camouflage to confound its foes. In addition to the usual sharp quills possessed by all porcupines, they have tiny barbs that work themselves deeply and painfully into the adversary's flesh.

Below: the tiny vampire bat has special adaptations for its diet of blood. One is a grooved tongue that fits over a notch in the lower lip for sucking, the other is a long tube in the stomach.

There are also two prehensile marsupials making their homes in the jungle treetops – the woolly and the mouse opossums, both nocturnal in habit. Although even more primitive mammals than the sloths, they are much livelier – lively enough to catch the insects that make up the bulk of their diet. Whereas the woolly opossum possesses a vestigial pouch in the shape of a flap of skin, the mouse opossum has none.

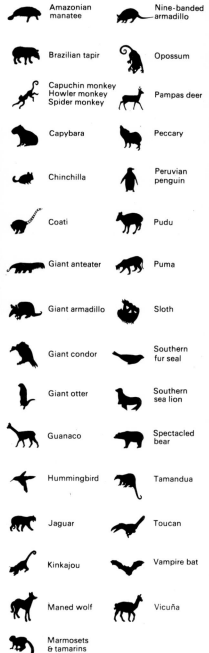

	Amazonian manatee		Nine-banded armadillo
	Brazilian tapir		Opossum
	Capuchin monkey Howler monkey Spider monkey		Pampas deer
	Capybara		Peccary
	Chinchilla		Peruvian penguin
	Coati		Pudu
	Giant anteater		Puma
	Giant armadillo		Sloth
	Giant condor		Southern fur seal
	Giant otter		Southern sea lion
	Guanaco		Spectacled bear
	Hummingbird		Tamandua
	Jaguar		Toucan
	Kinkajou		Vampire bat
	Maned wolf		Vicuña
	Marmosets & tamarins		

The Forest Floor

Below: capybaras, although they are rodents, are also known as water pigs or water cavies. Some conservationists believe that this mammal, whose flesh is already used for food by humans, could be successfully farmed as a new source of meat protein.

The floor of the Neotropical forest is packed with trees and shrubs, matted with creepers, and alive with insects – an ideal environment for insectivores and herbivores and the carnivores that in turn feed on them. Reptiles and amphibians also find the perpetual high temperature much to their liking. Some of these animals are remarkably large considering how difficult it is to move in the dense growth. As a rule, however, the larger species center their activities on the more open riverside, most of them being well adapted for a partly aquatic life.

Of the world's rodents the capybara is the biggest, sometimes reaching over 3 feet in length. A member of the cavy family which, together with the agouti and the porcupine makes up the relatively small suborder of Hystricomorphs, the capybara looks like a jumbo guinea pig with just a suggestion of the hippopotamus in it. It has partially webbed feet to facilitate its activity in the water where it feeds, mates, and seeks refuge from its few enemies. Unfortunately these few include jaguars which, unlike many cats, are good

swimmers. Capybaras are more vocal than most rodents, having a whole range of clicks, grunts, and squeaks. They are also easily tamed and give every indication of liking human company. Despite their friendliness, however, they have been much hunted for their fish-flavored meat, which is often falsely sold as salmon. The smaller paca or spotted cavy is related to the capybara although it is a burrowing animal. It comes out at night to hunt for fruit, leaves, and roots, heading for water if pursued by an enemy.

The agouti and acouchi are closely related to the paca, but have developed somewhat differently and in some respects have come to look like small ungulates. The agouti and acouchi are similar to each other in their pattern of life, differing mainly in their size and their tails. The agouti is about the same size as a hare and almost tailless, having hardly more than a black stump. The acouchi is smaller and has a short but obvious white-tipped tail. Although the fruit that makes up their diet is available all year round, these creatures nonetheless follow the practice of many other rodents and hoard their food away – often promptly forgetting where they buried it. Described as "the basic diet of the South American carnivores," which include not only bush dogs, big and small cats, raccoons, and weasels but also the human fur hunter, they manage to keep their population stable by their fast breeding.

The South American jungle possesses three kinds of true ungulates: the odd-toed tapir and the even-toed peccary and deer. Among the deer are the white-tailed variety also found in the Nearctic and, in the depths of the forests, the brocket.

Tapirs, like capybaras, are confined to the wooded areas by the lakes and rivers. They are shy nocturnal animals whose great bulk not only deters all predators apart from jaguars and alligators but also is useful for bulldozing their way through the dense vegetation. The velvety dark brown of the Brazilian tapir's coat is always encrusted by a thick coat of mud with which the animal daubs itself as a protection against insect bites. If grotesque and unpleasing to human eyes, the tapir's long, pliable, trunklike upper lip and snout are very useful to its owner, enabling it to browse among the leaves and twigs or pull up water plants and transfer them, like an elephant using its trunk, directly into its mouth.

Although resembling a large pig, the tapir is more closely related to the rhinoceros of the Old World. The peccary, however, not only looks like a small wild boar but is actually a member of the pig family. The white-lipped peccary roams the forests in leaderless bands of up to 100 as a way of defense against predators.

Left: baby capybaras, which weigh about 2.5 pounds at birth, are born in litters numbering between two and eight. There is only one litter a year, so allowing the young to stay with their parents until well into the next breeding season. Like their relative the guinea pig, the babies of this water-loving rodent are well developed when born. Their life span reaches 12 years.

Above: this young Brazilian tapir will lose its stripes and spots as it matures, finally becoming a uniform dark brown in adulthood. Such markings provide camouflage among the forest shadows for the defenseless young. The fully grown tapir, which weighs between 500 and 700 pounds, may reach 8 feet in length though 6 feet is more usual. It is from 29 to 40 inches at the shoulders.

Cats and Other Predators

Despite the profusion of small animals, the tropical forests of South America are not as filled with the kind of large carnivorous mammals that make the African jungles such a peril for smaller species. Of the predatory dogs, cats, weasels, and raccoons, the largest is the jaguar.

Owing to its popularity as a fur animal, the jaguar has virtually disappeared from some of the less inaccessible parts of the forests. This animal is much the same size as the leopard of the Old World and, apart from the black variety, is similarly spotted although its spots are larger than the leopard's as a rule, and each rosette usually has a black dot inside. Furthermore, it is shorter in the tail, squatter, and less graceful in general than the leopard. The black

jaguar confines its activities to the densest and dankest depths of the jungle, but the spotted jaguar ranges more widely. It might go as far south as the Argentine pampas in its search for deer and agouti, although its favorite haunts are near rivers where the peccary, capybara, and tapir abound. Before jaguars attain their maximum weight, which may be as much as 250 pounds, they are great climbers and will often hunt for food in the sturdier branches of trees. This cat also swims, unlike most of its species, and catches fish as well as meat animals.

Although similar in name, the 4-foot-long jaguarundi is more like an otter or weasel than a jaguar. Their coats are dark in color, either of a red-brown or gray. Extremely short in the leg, shorter by far than any other New World cat, they are nevertheless swift enough to catch the large rodents that constitute the

Below: the ocelot's spotted coat provides good camouflage in the dappled sunlight of the forest. Its beautiful fur varies from pale gray or grayish yellow to warm brown, and has large brown spots bordered in black. This cat sees and hears especially well.

Above: although a coati usually digs for its food, it will also climb for it. There are three species of this ring-tailed relative of the raccoon, and they are extending their range into the southwestern United States from Central and South America.

main part of their diet, and agile enough to scale the trees in order to pounce on birds, small mammals, reptiles, and amphibians. They also like fruit and occasionally have a feast of green figs.

Even more popular for its fur than the jaguar is the spotted ocelot which hunts its food in the open spaces but spends a great deal of time shyly hidden in the branches of trees. Just as beautifully marked as the ocelot and even more retiring are the tiger cat and the big-eyed, nocturnal margay. These two species are so rarely seen that little is known of their ways of life.

Shyness is not a quality that can be attributed to the 2-foot-long bush dog, another short-legged animal and the most terrierlike of all wild dogs. Wild though it may be, the bush dog is intelligent and easily tamed, often kept as a pet in Brazil. Like many of the forest carnivores, the bush dog becomes active in the evening when it emerges from its burrow to go hunting with a dozen or so other bush dogs. They prey on pacas and small deer. Although little is known about the bush dog's life, as with so many jungle animals, it has been discovered that the female has a singular way of leaving her scent. This is done by urinating on a tree trunk.

The coati, a brindled member of the raccoon family with a typical ringed tail, has a long flexible snout which it uses somewhat like a snorkel when it swims, which it does well. An omnivore, the coati eats fruit, insects, birds, and lizards. Although the females and young are gregarious, living in groups of between five and a dozen, the male adults are kept at bay. They lead solitary lives except during the short breeding season when they are allowed to join the group, though in a subordinate capacity.

121

Cold-blooded Creatures

The hot humid conditions of the tropical forests are very favorable for animals incapable of keeping their body temperatures constant, so it is not surprising that the Amazon basin is the habitat of many cold-blooded species of reptiles, amphibians, and fish.

In addition to the enormous anaconda and bushmaster snakes, there are also the brilliantly colored coral snakes. There are about 40 species of these front-fanged reptiles, most of which prey on other snakes. Like the cobras to which they are related, coral snakes are venomous although the strength of the poison varies from one species to another. Several species of false coral snakes also live in the leaf mold on the forest floor. They are uncannily similar in appearance to the true coral snake, but differ by being either totally harmless or only mildly venomous, and by having either no fangs or rear fangs.

There are also members of the pit viper family to be found. Being fonder than coral snakes of warm-blooded prey, they are consequently much more dangerous to humans. The fer-de-lance, despite being considerably shorter than its cousin the bushmaster, is highly lethal and has been responsible for many human deaths.

The snakes are not the only poisonous creatures of the jungle. The arrow poison frogs, so named because of the use the Amerinds make of their toxic skin secretions, live both in the trees and on the forest floor. In common with many other venomous species, they give fair warning of their deadly presence by their vivid coloration.

Many of the frogs and toads of South America do not spawn in still waters. Some lay their eggs in nests hanging over ponds and streams, some in water-filled holes in trees, some on damp earth where the young leave the eggs as fully formed frogs. Others make nests of foam that float like a raft in the water, while the females of some species carry the eggs in pouches on their backs. These untypical breeding habits are made possible only by the extreme humidity of the tropical forests.

More restricted to water are crocodiles, caimans,

Below left: raised eyes and nostrils enable a spectacled caiman to breathe and see while most of its body is hidden under water. This helps it ambush animals that come to drink at the river.
Below: a male anole lizard displays its brilliantly colored dewlap during courtship or in territorial fights with other males.

and a great variety of turtles. Caimans, although similar in habit to crocodiles, differ in having shorter, broader, and blunter heads. The black caiman is the biggest and most dangerous member of its family, growing to a length of about 15 feet, or around the same size as the American crocodile.

The most bizarre of the turtles is the matamata, a member of the side-necked family. Like all side-necked turtles, it bends its neck sideways rather than backward to withdraw its head. The matamata has a rough bumpy shell with three ridges running front to back, and a flat head that extends to form a flexible snout. So ungainly is this animal that to liken a human to it is the highest insult among the Amerinds. Fortunately for this turtle, fish find the many fringes of flesh on its head, jaws, and long neck irresistibly attractive, and all the matamata has to do when it is hungry is wait, open its mouth suddenly, and make a feast of the fish that is sucked in by the inrush of water.

Above: hungry arrau turtles go in a swarm to look for food. This freshwater species, which grows to 2 feet in length, is eaten as a delicacy by South American Indians. Freshwater turtles have partly or fully webbed toes and are quicker than land species.

The caiman lizard, which lives in the lower Amazon, is one of the most aquatic of the lizards. It subsists on a diet of snails and mussels which it cracks open with its large flat teeth, spitting out the shards of shell before eating the flesh. It gets its name from the fact that its flattened tail has a double crest like that of a caiman.

Living in the trees of the forests are other lizards such as the small anole, which can change color like the chameleon and has friction-padded toes for climbing like the gecko, and the big tree iguana, which can measure up to 7 feet in length, although most of that is tail. Tree iguanas are unusual among lizards in that they are almost exclusively vegetarian when fully grown.

Life in the Water

The streams and lakes of the South American tropical forests are the habitat of a few unexpected aquatic mammals and many strange forms of fish, some of them remarkably ferocious. The piranha, moving in shoals, is one of the fish that prefers the flesh of mammals for food, and is said to make deadly attacks on even very large animals with incredible speed.

The large arapaima, measuring up to 15 feet in length and weighing some 400 to 500 pounds, is the largest living freshwater fish, and also one of the biggest eaters. It will eat almost anything, though preferring other fish and especially its smaller cousin the arawana. Being fleshy itself, the arapaima is one of the chief food fishes of the Amazon.

Above: armored catfish are so called because of two rows of plates along the sides of their body. There are more than 50 species of this water animal in the rivers of South America.

Electric eels and knifefish are nocturnal creatures that rely on their "radar" system to find their way about. Catfish are also nocturnal. The Amazonian waterways are the home for many species of catfish, several of which are blind and lack skin pigmentation because they live on the river floors or in caves. Some of the armored catfish that probe in the mud for food with their mouth barbels are able to take to the land for several hours when their pools dry out in order to search for new territory, keeping their gills moist by closing the gill chamber. The male of another species, the Brazilian catfish, expands its lower lip to form a hatching chamber during the incubation period.

Helping to make the Amazonian waters generally dangerous is the stingray, one of the world's few *cartilaginous* (having a skeleton mostly of cartilage) freshwater fish. It is armed for protection with poisonous spines on the upper surface of its tail. Living on the river floor like the stingray is the

candiru, one of the several parasitic catfish of the Amazon. It is almost transparent with a yellowish tinge, big eyes, and spines on the sides of its head. Only about an inch in length, the candiru burrows into bodily orifices. When it gets into the human urinogenital tract, an operation is needed to remove it.

Two odd fish of the region are the four-eyed fish and the Amazon molly, both members of the same sub-order. The four-eyed fish has only one pair of eyes, but the top half of each is used to see in air and the bottom half for seeing in water, as though there were four eyes. Like many other bony fish of the Anablepidae family, four-eyed fish give birth to live young. The Amazon molly is an oddity. Its eggs are not fertilized, but merely stimulated toward growth by any sperm that enters the female's body – not always that of a male molly. Only females are born, but some of them later undergo a sex change that enables them to produce sperm.

Besides the amazing variety of curious and colorful fish, the rivers also contain some aquatic mammals including one species of river dolphin, one marine dolphin, and the South American manatee. The bouto or Amazon dolphin should not be confused with the marine Amazon White dolphin, which is found only in the part of the river that meets the sea tides. The bouto lives in the river's muddy upper reaches. It uses the short sensory bristles on its snout rather than its tiny eyes to guide it to the piranhas on which it preys. It is such a scourge to the vicious piranha that local fishermen know they are safe if a bouto is near.

Below: although it is a small fish, the piranha has a massive jaw and large razor-edged teeth. The jaw is strong enough and the teeth sharp enough to chop large chunks of flesh easily.
Right: rushing waterfalls of mighty power are one of the hazards facing marine animal life in the nearly 4000-mile-long Amazon river, yet there are more than 750 species of fish living in it.

Some Toothless Animals

The Amazon Basin jungles and the Mato Grosso are flanked by grasslands. To the north lie the Ilanos of Venezuela and eastern Colombia, to the southeast the Brazilian campos, and to the south the great pampas of Argentina. Separating the pampas and the eastern foothills of the Andes from the tropical forests is a transitional zone of deciduous woodland, scrub, and marsh called the Gran Chaco.

Of the rare animals indigenous to the Gran Chaco, the strangest is the loalach or South American lungfish, whose only relatives are found in Africa and Australia. As its name implies, this fish possesses lungs which, primitive though they may be, account for more than 95 percent of its oxygen consumption. In abnormally dry conditions, these 3-foot-long fish may become dormant and, covered in mud with a breathing hole provided, can survive for about three months. They live on the large amounts of food they ate and converted into fat during the wet season.

Although the giant anteater is widespread throughout the northern half of the Neotropical region east of the Andes, it is a natural visitor to the swampy Gran Chaco. A close relation of the forest-dwelling tamandua and dwarf anteater, the giant anteater is the largest of the edentates. Gray-brown in color, it is marked with a long, narrow, black triangle outlined in white and running backward across the shoulders. It often attains a length of more than 6 feet – to which an extra 8 inches is added when it extrudes its sticky tongue in order to help itself to termites from the nests it has ripped asunder with its powerful claws. Giant anteaters have a strange gait because of the way they move on their knuckles with their claws folded inward. They lead a wandering life on the pampas, alone and constantly on the move in search of food. They sleep unsheltered in the grass, using

Right: the giant anteater has a body that measures from 3 to 4 feet long and a tail of from 2 to 3 feet. A female anteater carries her young on her back until she is ready to give birth again, even though the offspring gets to be almost half her size during that period.

Below: the plains viscacha has a disproportionately large head on a heavily built body, and black and white lines on each cheek accent the head even more. Its fur is coarse in contrast to that of its relative the chinchilla.

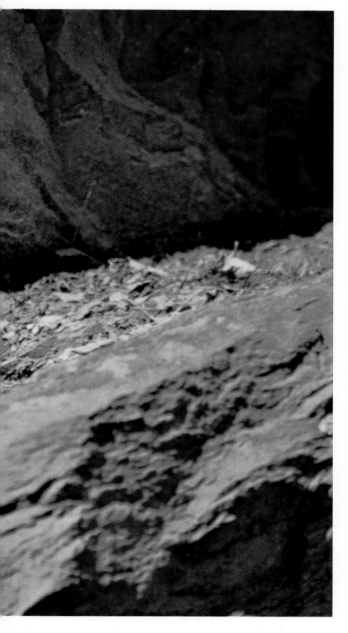

their enormous bushy tails as covers.

The grasslands are a popular habitat with another branch of the edentate order, the armadillo, which lives in burrows of its own construction or those abandoned by other species. Armadillos range in size from the 4-foot-long giant armadillo to the 5-inch fairy armadillo. All armadillos rely up to a point on their armor of small plates of bone covered by bony scales as a primary defense against would-be attackers, but some of them are so supple that they roll themselves up into a tight ball when danger looms. One of the three-banded variety's many nicknames is *tatu naranja* (orange armadillo), not because of its color but because of its spherical shape when rolled up. Most armadillos can dig a burrow very fast if necessary to their safety. Their ability to hold their breath for extended periods while burrowing is supposed to allow them to cross narrow rivers by walking across the bottom, although they can also swim a little. Generally resting by day, armadillos emerge at night to root for insects and berries.

A burrowing rodent of the pampas is the plains viscacha, a close if much larger relation of the chinchilla. Plains viscachas live somewhat like prairie dogs of the Nearctic do. They belong to colonies of some 20 to 30 animals and occupy warrens of a dozen or more burrows called viscacheras. Although self-contained and sometimes as big as 200 square feet, one community will associate with inhabitants of other nearby viscacheras. It is said that plains viscacha burrows are passed on from one generation to the next – sometimes for centuries. The animals constantly extend, improve, and keep their burrows in good repair. These burrows are characterized by large mounds around the tunnels' wide entrances, mounds constructed from earth, vegetation, and a collection of rubbish and refuse from bones and boots to whips and wallets.

Pampas Predators and Prey

Although the plains viscacha is by no means the only grassland inhabitant that constructs burrows, its excavations seem in particular to attract squatters. Perhaps the piles of earth bedecked with grass and trash around the entrances make them conspicuous and attractive landmarks to other species in the vast flatness of the pampas. Frightened but guileless animals like the Patagonian cavy will occupy them, often in preference to digging their own, while more wily and opportunistic creatures such as the burrowing owl and pampas fox find them a source of food as well as of shelter.

The Patagonian cavy, or mara, is the most harelike of all the rodents, and as such is also known as the Patagonian hare. Like the hares, for example, one of its courtship rituals is to drench its prospective mate with a jet of urine. As with many of the pampas animals, the mara is endowed with exceedingly long legs, even longer proportionally than a hare's, which give it the speed it needs to escape from predators. A timid animal of about 3 feet in length, the mara is much hunted by bigger predators. The adult's principal enemies are foxes, pumas, and pampas cats, but the young are more in danger from weasels, buzzard eagles, and red-backed hawks. One of the borrowers of viscacha burrows, maras use them only for sleeping and not as a daytime refuge from enemies.

Other uninvited guests that move in on abandoned viscacha burrows are birds such as miners, swallows, and burrowing owls. Because of the absence of trees, miners and swallows nest in the entrance mounds and wax fat on the plentiful insects in the grass; burrowing owls use the mounds as vantage points from which to survey the passing parade of small rodents, reptiles, and insects that make up their diet.

The pampas or Azara's fox often will occupy viscacha burrows while viscachas still remain, seeming to live in harmony with them and feeding on other rodents such as wild guinea pigs. Young viscachas are a different story, however. Once the newborn have been weaned and left the burrows, they are subject to attack by foxes.

Closely related to the pampas fox is the maned wolf which, after the true wolf, is the largest member of the dog family. The maned wolf is much like a fox in appearance, although it has especially long legs which give it an elevation so useful in these flat treeless grasslands, and also enable it to run after its prey extremely fast. This animal's neck is covered by a long, thick, furry mane that stands on end in times of stress or excitement. Unlike true wolves, maned wolves are not pack animals. They hunt on their own, preferably under the cover of night. Although their prey includes insects, birds, reptiles, most small mammals and, when their luck is in, sheep, they are not averse to feeding on vegetable matter, including fruit and sugar cane.

Above: the local name for the maned wolf is "fox on stilts," which describes both its face and its long legs. In spite of the fact that maned wolves have no natural enemies, they are becoming rare because they are hunted as suspected sheep killers.

The pampas is the home of a primitive burrowing rodent called the tuco-tuco. a short stocky animal which is sometimes also called the South American mole rate. Like the viscachas, the tuco-tucos are gregarious and live in large colonies, although each animal digs its own tunnel often extending several yards in length. Because their tunnels are only about a foot below the surface, their activity in the soft sandy soil often causes subsidence of the land. The tuco-tuco derives its name from its call of "tuc-tuc-tuc-tuc" which it makes loudly, starting slowly and repeating it faster and faster, over and over.

Left: a small bird with long legs and a short tail, the burrowing owl usually lives in holes abandoned by other animals, sometimes enlarging them if necessary. This predator of rodents and squirrels stays on the ground so much that it has become almost flightless. It is more active in the daytime than many owls.

129

Birds of the Pampas

Living in surroundings as flat, treeless, and devoid of shelter as the pampas is bound to present grave problems to many animals. This is especially true of birds, many of which depend on the cover and accommodation of trees for the nesting and raising of their young. Therefore, although some 200 different species of bird may be seen on the pampas during the course of a year, the great majority of these are migratory. Some are only passing through; others are avoiding the harshness of their own winters, like the burrowing parrot from the Patagonian desert to the south, or Wilson's phalarope from the North American prairies. However, the very difficulty of existence for birds has given rise to a few unique and extremely interesting species that have managed to adapt.

The relatively primitive, almost flightless tinamou, for instance, has markings that make it blend into the background, and often it simply waits out any danger from attack. Unlike most birds, it is the female that takes the lead in courtship and the male that builds the nest and hatches the eggs.

Another nearly flightless species, the widespread tapaculos, have nesting habits as varied as the terrains they inhabit. Some burrow, some utilize naturally occurring holes, some build nests from grasses. One of the family, the barrancolino of Argentina, can take a stride of 6 inches although it is only 7 inches in length itself.

One of the most remarkable nest builders is the rufous ovenbird, which has been adopted as the national bird of Argentina. This small stocky bird, known locally as *el hornero* (the baker), is one of a family of over 200 species and is found all over Central and South America. It has spread from the more wooded grasslands to the north into the pampas, and has brought some of its tree-dwelling habits with it. Nest construction is an operation carried out jointly by the mating pair, and may take several months to complete. The building material, which is a mixture of sand and cow dung reinforced by root fibers and bits of twig, is attached to any suitable base – the roof of a house, the occasional tree, crossbars of telephone poles, or even the ground if nothing else is available. When finished, the nest is a neat edifice looking exactly like an old-fashioned bread oven with a door on one side. It also has an outer lobby separated from an inner nesting chamber by a steeply sloping sill.

The Neotropical region has the distinction of sharing with Africa, Australia, and New Zealand the only living *ratites* (completely flightless birds). All of them – the rheas of South America, the ostrich of Africa, and emus and cassowaries of Australasia, and to a lesser extent the kiwis of New Zealand, have certain physical features in common. For instance, they all have long legs, well-developed thigh muscles, very small or totally absent tails, almost no toes, and little plumage.

Rheas are the largest birds in the New World, sometimes reaching a height of 5 feet. Until the coming of the horse, this three-toed bird was the fastest animal of the pampas. Rheas, like ostriches, will sometimes join herds of cattle and graze alongside them. Although particularly vicious to their male rivals at the start of the breeding season, the dominant cocks become highly domesticated later on, digging out the nests and sitting on the eggs, of which there may be more than 30 from the various females he mates with. The rhea defends its nest vigorously, though it sometimes resorts to a ruse such as running off and trailing limp wings as if wounded. It is said that if the cock becomes broody before its mates have finished laying, it will drive them away in order to sit on what eggs there are, leaving the females to deposit the other eggs in the open. The male guards the chicks in his charge throughout their five-month growing period.

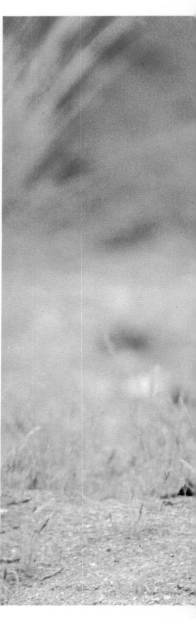

Above right: the eggs of the tinamou are smooth and so shiny that they look like porcelain. Chicks hatch in just under three weeks, which is not very long for such a big bird.

Right: the crested tinamou or martineta spreads its crest when it is agitated. Although widely hunted as a food bird, the tinamou has good protective camouflage in its dull coloring.

Animals of the Andes

The Andes is the world's longest and second highest chain of mountains, running virtually unbroken from almost 10° N of the equator to 55° S, not much more than 10° from the Antarctic Circle. Although only a few miles south of the equator, the tip of Mount Cotopaxi, just under 20,000 feet in height, is perpetually snowclad and bitter cold. There are several peaks in the Andes that even top Cotopaxi including Chimborazo, Huscarán, Sajama, and Aconcagua, the highest peak in the western hemisphere at 23,000 feet. Conditions on either side of this enormously long, towering, yet comparatively narrow mountain range differ markedly. The thin coastal strip to the west is, if not actual desert throughout most of its length, at least largely barren. The eastern foothills, apart from the south where they descend into the pampas and Patagonian steppes, are excessively humid. In places they are endlessly dripping, wet cloud forest, and as such merge into the northern savannah, the tropical forests, and the Gran Chaco.

Lack of oxygen presents a problem to animal life, requiring adaptations in breathing apparatus and the circulatory system. For example, the hearts of many of the high-dwelling mammals of the Andes, including human beings, are considerably larger than normal. The nimble vicuña, which inhabits the high plateaus from 14,000 to 18,000 feet, manages to extract sufficient oxygen from the rarefied air by possessing blood nearly three times as rich in red corpuscles as a human's.

Left: alpacas are smaller than their cousins the llamas, and have a soft silky fur that is light and warm. They are usually of a uniform black or reddish brown, but can also be of mixed colors.

them in the wild, although they are known to be good climbers able to ascend trees over 100 feet high, and are thought to prefer plants to meat. The spectacled bears are now in danger of extinction in their natural habitat, though many zoos have them.

If only one species of bear has established itself in the Neotropical region, not even one member of the bovid family has. Instead of sheep and goats, those natural mountain dwellers, there are representatives of the camel family. These consist of the wild vicuna and guanaco, and the domesticated llama and alpaca. So ungainly is the guanaco that it was once described as "a careless mixture of parts intended for other beasts and turned down as below standard."

The vicuna is the smallest member of the camel family. Living near the snow line in herds of up to 100, they feed on the grasses and broad-leaved succulent plants. In turn, they provide nourishment for pampas cats and colpeo foxes. Although unexpectedly timid

Right: although the blue-crowned motmot is brightly colored like the other seven of its species, it is difficult to find because it lives in dark mountain forests.

Low temperatures demand not only a sound circulation, but also efficient insulation and a larger than average body volume. Such an adaptation is seen in the mountain tapir, sometimes known as Roulin's tapir, which lives at levels of between 10,000 to 13,000 feet in the northern half of the Andes. It is more thickly coated than its cousins of the tropical forests, and attains the height of a small pony.

Frequenting the same regions but at much lower altitudes is the spectacled bear, the only member of the bear family in the Neotropical region. As bears go it is not very large, reaching a height of a little over 2 feet. Its coat is black or dark brown and shaggy, but much less dense than that of bears from more temperate regions. The overall darkness of the hair is relieved around the muzzle by a lighter yellow coloration that extends to form circles around the eyes, giving the animal its name. Little is known about

133

for members of such a bad-tempered family, vicuñas nonetheless fiercely defend their territory against intruders, biting them viciously or spitting regurgitated food at them. Vicuñas have been much sought after both for their meat and for their wool, which is the finest and lightest in the world. During the time of the Incas, the use of vicuña wool was reserved for royalty.

Herdsmen farm any vicuñas they can catch in an orthodox way – rounding them up, shearing the wool, and then liberating them again. Recently vicuñas have been crossed with alpacas, their close relation which has been domesticated for hundreds of years. Alpacas are also valued for their soft warm wool, which is the staple cloth for the South American Indians. The successful hybrid is known as the paco-

vicuña and is as easily farmed as the alpaca, with the additional advantage that its wool retains to some extent the fine quality of the vicuña's.

Best known and largest of the four humpless South American camelids is the llama. Like the alpaca, the llama has not existed in its wild state since the days of the Incas. The llama is very important to the South American Indians. They use it as a pack animal and its coarse wool for rugs and rope. They convert its hide into sandals and its fat into candles. They eat its flesh and use its droppings as fuel. Llamas are temperamental creatures that have to be fed and rested regularly and treated with special care to avoid a kick from them. They refuse to be overloaded, and will not accept a load of more than 100 pounds.

Inhabiting all levels of the Andes up to 20,000 feet

Above: the Andean condor's vast wings enable it to soar effortlessly at heights up to 20,000 feet. This condor is one of the longest lived of all birds.

Left: llamas measure about 4 feet at the shoulder and weigh up to 300 pounds. They can be white, various shades of brown, black, or piebald in coloration.

is the chinchilla, a little animal with a particularly beautiful coat of long gray silky fur. The higher the chinchilla's habitat, the longer its fur and the shorter its ears – both adaptations to retain heat. Said to be of a nervous temperament to start with, the chinchilla does not thrive well in captivity, often beset by duodenal ulcers and alopecia, a disorder that causes heavy loss of hair. This animal has been killed nearly to the point of extinction for its fur, which is one of the most expensive on the market.

The Andean forests provide a home for many species of wildlife including the tree porcupine, mara, deer, and pacarana, which are heavily built relations of the pampas paca with flesh just as edible. Andean deer are found up to nearly 15,000 feet in the central sector of the mountains. A variety of the diminutive pudu confines its activities to the more elevated forests of the northern part while the small red brocket with the single-spiked antlers browses on the lower slopes. Inhabitants of the tropical forests such as coatis and kinkajous have spilled over into the Andes, living up to fairly high altitudes in the northeastern mountain forests. In the woodlands of the foothills howler and spider monkeys and other primates find an abundant diet of fruits, shoots, and leaves.

Stealthily roaming the mountains up to considerably high altitudes in search of prey are pumas, also known as cougars. Much bigger than the more nocturnal lowland variety of puma, these beasts stalk their victims until such time that they can leap out and knock them down. They are just as likely to attack domestic herds as wild animals, which makes them public enemy number one in these parts. Despite the view of conservationists, every effort is made to wipe them out. Other South American cats – jaguars, ocelots, margays, and jaguarundis, for example – also sometimes make forays to altitudes of up to about 10,000 feet.

Other predators making their way into the mountains from time to time are the maned wolf and crab-eating fox. Sometimes hovering over all, ready to swoop on anything left over – provided it is dead – is the now rare Andean condor.

West of the Andes

Separating the Andes from the Pacific Ocean is an extremely narrow coastal belt that is as opposite in character as possible from the tropical forests lying only about 200 miles on the other side of the mountains. Apart from a small area of tropical forest at the extreme north and a somewhat longer but thinner strip of mixed forest in the far south, the whole length is grim and barren. In fact much of this coastline, from the north of Peru well into Chile, is absolute desert. It is characterized in many places by vast tracts of drifting sand unrelieved throughout its length of 2000 miles except for an occasional river.

This desert owes its existence to the Humboldt

northern forests and river valleys were well stocked with animal life, the intensive cultivation that has taken place over the last few decades has reduced their numbers drastically. The best survivors have been cottontail rabbits, nine-banded armadillos, reptiles, and tayras, that fierce South American version of the marten, all of which are in the north. In the southern mixed forest lives the very rare, very shy Chilean pudu, smallest of all deer.

Few mammals live in the drier parts of the region, though lizards, geckos, and toads are relatively common. The odd guanaco in search of fodder may be seen at any level up to 13,000 feet, while on the shore coastal foxes scramble through the sand after their favorite diet of sea birds. Another shore-dweller, the coast otter, often ventures along the river valleys to

Right: the guanay or Peruvian cormorant has the white underparts found exclusively in species of the southern hemisphere. There are 30 cormorant species, of which 11 are white breasted.

Above: the male great frigate bird has a sac that it inflates only during courtship, when the throat turns a brilliant red. The bird seeks a mate after it has selected the site for a nest.

Current, which washes the Peruvian coast with icy waters from the Antarctic. The prevailing winds blowing off this cold current turn the normal pattern of coastal climates topsy-turvy, for far from bringing rain as usual, they actually absorb what little moisture there is present in the ground. This has created one of the world's few coastal deserts. Although the desert continues up the slopes of the Andes all the way to their summits, higher altitudes bring a blanket of mist, fog, and clouds that provide enough moisture to stimulate the growth of some vegetation.

Because of its aridity, this area's wildlife is limited. Although at one time the more fertile areas like the

feed on freshwater prawns that are being farmed.

Along this extended coastline are many birds of different kinds – land birds such as cactus wrens, flycatchers, and ovenbirds; forest birds such as parrots and hummingbirds; water birds such as egrets and herons, attracted by the infrequent lagoon or mangrove swamp.

It is offshore that life really thrives. The Humboldt Current on its journey from the Antarctic brings with it innumerable shoals of anchovy which have gorged themselves on the plankton the sea is so rich in. These anchovies are an irresistible temptation to sea birds, especially the brown pelican, the Inca tern, and the guanay or Peruvian cormorant. The guanay's excrement, known as guano, is one of the best fertilizers available anywhere, and is exported worldwide.

Neotropical Region: Southern South America

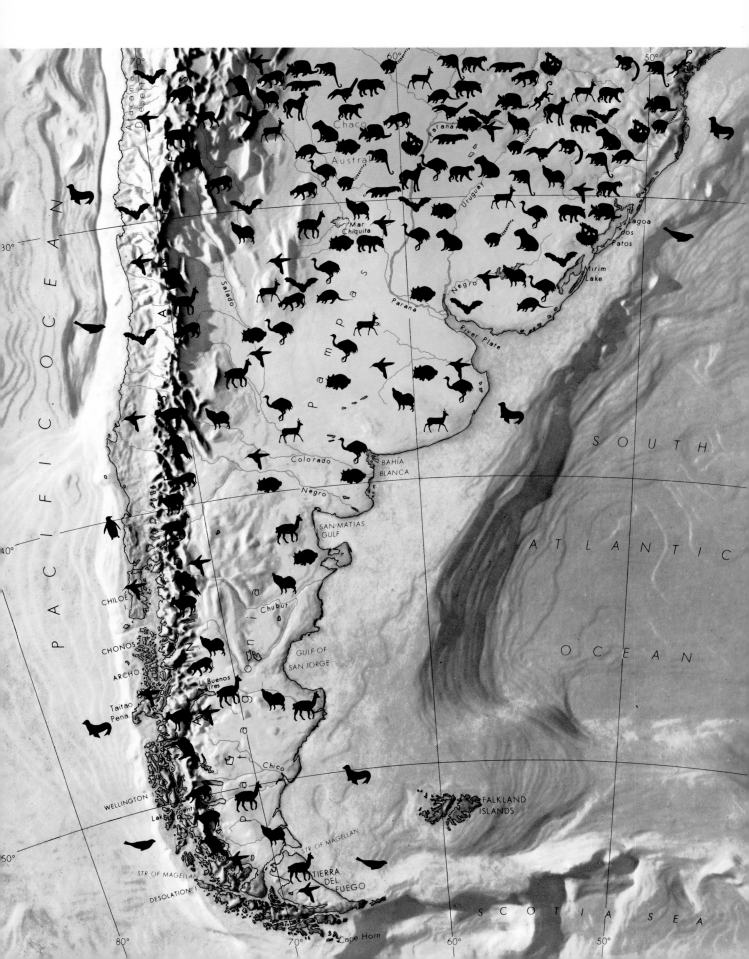

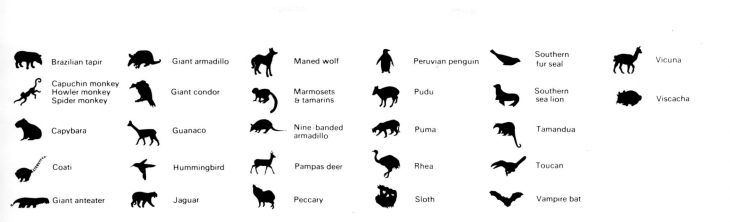

Brazilian tapir	Giant armadillo	Maned wolf	Peruvian penguin	Southern fur seal	Vicuna
Capuchin monkey Howler monkey Spider monkey	Giant condor	Marmosets & tamarins	Pudu	Southern sea lion	Viscacha
Capybara	Guanaco	Nine-banded armadillo	Puma	Tamandua	
Coati	Hummingbird	Pampas deer	Rhea	Toucan	
Giant anteater	Jaguar	Peccary	Sloth	Vampire bat	

Above: tremendous clashes take place between southern elephant seal bulls, who fight for their territories and their harems. They use their canine teeth in battle, and seem to inflict terrible wounds on each other. This seal is the largest of all seals, although between the sexes the female is a good deal smaller than the male. Its name comes not only from its large size but also from the male's elongated and somewhat flexible nose. Elephant seals breed on many of the subantarctic islands.

A Harsh Homeland

The southern part of the Neotropical region east of the Andes stretches nearly from the pampas to Tierra del Fuego. Separated from the mainland by the Strait of Magellan, Tierra del Fuego is gloomy, foggy, and cold. It's name – Land of Fire in English – comes from the natives' fires Magellan saw as he sailed past.

Rising sharply from the Atlantic seaboard to a height of about 1000 feet, the land on the main island climbs step by step to an altitude of some 5000 feet. Then it drops again to form the 2000-foot-high trough that abuts the Andes. Dry cold winds whistle and howl down from the mountains to rip across the plateau, creating a semidesert naked of vegetation save tufts of coarse parched grass and thin clumps of viciously thorned bushes and shrubs. The higher slopes of Tierra del Fuego boast beech, laurel, and myrtle forests, and its lowlands are well enough grassed to provide good pasturage, but they do nothing to lessen the general dreariness caused by incessant winds and almost total lack of sunshine. Harsh as it is, the region abounds in a unique mix of wildlife accustomed to eking out an existence the hard way, from peccaries to penguins, from cavies to cormorants, from hummingbirds to whales. Even the arctic tern considers it worth the 24,000 mile journey from its north polar habitat to spend its time in Tierra del Fuego during the Antarctic summer.

Some birds, such as the canastero or basketmaker, make the most of the protection afforded by the thorn bushes. The tawny-throated dotterel, on the other hand, relies on its coloring for camouflage. This is effective not only for the bird itself, but also for its nest and eggs which lie completely exposed but undetectable among the pebbles.

Among the larger mammals to be found in these inhospitable parts is the guanaco, too big to be threatened by other animals except the occasional puma. Patagonian gray foxes may be seen lurking slyly among the bushes, feeding on the bright red berries until the next small rodent, reptile, or bird appears. Two species of opossum are also common in the area. One is the tiny, pouchless, murine opossum which is widespread throughout the continent. The other is a larger thick-tailed opossum which has habits similar to the weasel.

Magellanic penguins are to be encountered in their thousands, living in burrows on the shores, particularly of Tierra del Fuego and the many small islands in the strait.

There are also several species of seal inhabiting these bleak regions, including the South American fur seal, the South American sea lion, and the southern elephant seal or sea elephant with its curious inflatable nose.

140

Left: Magellanic
penguins were named
in honor of Ferdinand
Magellan, who sighted
them when he rounded
the southern tip of
South America in 1520.
These penguins are
closely related to the
jackass penguin that
lives at the southern-
most point of Africa.

Chapter 5
The Ethiopian Region

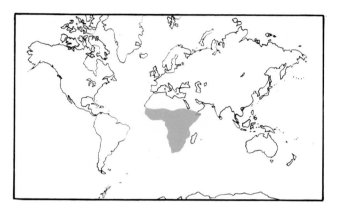

The Ethiopian region consists of all of Africa south of the Sahara desert and the southwestern tip of Arabia. The Sahara desert, which separates the Ethiopian from the Palaearctic region, today forms an effective barrier between the two regions. But because the Sahara has not always been as dry as it now is, the Ethiopian region shares some animals with the Palaearctic and Oriental regions.

Africa has an enormous wealth of animal life, possessing almost as many unique families as does the Neotropical region. There is also a great diversity of species within the families, especially antelopes.

Because Africa was part of the great Gondwana land mass that split up some 180 million years ago to form the continents of the southern hemisphere, the Ethiopian region has some fish, amphibia, reptiles, and birds in common with South America and Australia.

African elephants have been caught up in a strange web of circumstance in regard to their preservation. Although they live in protected park areas, such parks do not provide enough trees to meet the heavy food needs of this largest land animal. Because the elephants have nowhere else to go after they destroy the forests within their preserves, they are dying off rapidly. One authority has estimated that African elephants will be virtually extinct by the end of the 20th century.

Man's Impact

Since the days of the Roman Empire, Africa has been plundered for its animals, and Roman circuses were well stocked with many African animals that looked exotic to European eyes. Even before that time, however, the ancient Greeks had been hunting elephants for their easily carved ivory, a substance that was ideally suited for covering the Greeks' immense statues. Through the years ivory has been used continually for making such varied items as furniture, musical instruments, jewelry, scientific equipment, and artificial teeth. The east coast of Africa became known as the Ivory Coast because it was from there that the merchants shipped cargoes of tusks that countless elephants had died to provide. Arab traders found a way of killing two birds with one stone by making newly enslaved Africans from the interior carry elephant tusks to the coast, and exporting both of them.

Elephants, however, weathered this early exploitation. Being so large, they were difficult to kill in great numbers with unsophisticated weapons and, being intelligent animals, they quickly learned ways to avoid their hunters. The elephant and all other African animals were not threatened with extinction until the 17th century brought European settlement.

The rhinoceros was and is still much hunted for its horn, used as a fake sexual tonic. Although today the hunting is done only by poachers, the white rhino is seriously threatened.

The early European settlers were tireless hunters, and in southern Africa they found a hunter's paradise of unimaginably large herds of animals living on the vast grassy plains. By 1800 the bluebuck antelope had been wiped out and in 1883 the last quagga, a brownish partially striped zebra, died in Amsterdam Zoo. If zoos in the 19th century had been as conscious of their conservationist role as they are today, they might have saved this animal in the same way that they later rescued the European bison, Père David's deer, and Przewalski's horse.

However, although some settlers slaughtered anything that moved, there were others who saw the need to protect these animals. In 1898 Kruger Park, the first African game reserve, was established and since then many reserves and game parks have been set up throughout the African continent. Many of these have become a source of revenue as tourist attractions. Careful management of such parks has proved necessary, both in the control of the number of tourists and in the prevention of poaching. Strangely enough, the animals themselves have sometimes posed a threat to

Below: these waterholes in Tsavo National Park, Kenya, would once have been thronged with animals drinking at sundown. They are a grim comment on the depleted state of Africa's wildlife.

Above: Ethiopians had to ration water for their livestock during the drought of 1975. Some conservationists suggest that elands be farmed because they can go for up to 18 months without water.

the ecology of the parks and, consequently, to themselves. In the national parks of East Africa, for example, elephants which have congregated there in large numbers from the more dangerous surrounding country have destroyed so much vegetation that the country is turning into a huge barren waste. The animals are starving as a result.

Preservation of animals has been aided by two major factors keeping the human enemy at bay. The first has been the difficulty of penetrating the interior of Africa, where the rivers have so many rough rapids and waterfalls that the settlers were unable to navigate them for many years – years that would undoubtedly have led to the slaughter of millions more animals. The other is the existence of the tsetse fly, carrier of the dreaded sleeping sickness that is fatal to humans and domesticated cattle. This insect has stood in the way of colonizing Africa between the Zambesi and the Sahara.

Because indigenous mammals are immune to sleeping sickness, it has been suggested that some of them be farmed instead of domestic herds. The eland, for example, has flesh which tastes like veal, and milk that, while it contains more fat and protein than cow's milk, keeps longer than cow's milk. Experiments in such farming are now being carried out.

145

Ethiopian Region: Northern Africa

Aardvark		Cheetah	
Abyssinian ibex		Chimpanzee	
Addax		Crocodile	
African buffalo		Dugong	
Black rhinoceros		Elephant	

Northern limit of transitional zone between Palaearctic & Ethiopian regions

Southern limit of transitional zone between Palaearctic & Ethiopian regions

Limit of Island region

S a h a r a   D e

AHAGGAR MTS.

TROPIC OF CANCER

ATLANTIC OCEAN

GREAT ATLAS

MADEIRA

CANARY ISLANDS

STR OF GIBRALTAR

MED

Senegal

Gambia

FOUTA DJALLON

Niger

Black Volta

White Volta

Volta

Niger

Lake Chad

Chari

Logone

Benue

Sanaga

Mouths of the Niger

FERNANDO PÓO

GULF OF GUINEA

SÃO TOMÉ

EQUATOR

Congo

Forest-living monkeys (e.g. colobus)

Gaboon viper

Giant eland

Giraffe

Gnu

Gorilla

Grant's gazelle

Grassland monkeys (e.g. baboon)

Hippopotamus

Hornbill

Hyena & jackal

Impala

Leopard

Lion

Mediterranean monk seal

Okapi

Oryx

Ostrich

Pangolin

Potto

Puff adder

Red duiker

Secretary bird

Shoebill

Springhaas

Warthog

White rhinoceros

Wild ass

Zebra

The Many Antelopes

The most common animal of Africa is the many species of antelope. Although the Palaearctic and Oriental regions have a few species such as the dorcas, the saiga, and the blackbuck, the vast majority of the world's antelopes are to be encountered on Africa's grassy plains, and to a lesser extent in its forests, swamps, and deserts. The Union of South Africa has even adopted one – the small springbok – as its national emblem.

Antelopes are first and foremost grassland animals, their bodies being beautifully adapted to their habitat. Grass is a difficult food to digest, and antelopes, like cattle and most other even-toed ungulates, have found an efficient way of digestion. They ruminate or chew the cud, passing food through their complicated four-chambered stomachs twice, and regurgitating and rechewing it each time. This means that they can browse or graze a great deal of grass in a short time while keeping a wary eye out for predators and, having filled their stomachs with unchewed grass, can retire under safe cover to go through the lengthy process of chewing and digesting it. Odd-toed ungulates such as zebras, horses, and asses, have to chew their food as they eat it, and have not been able to survive as well.

Having fewer toes – two or four in the even-toed ungulates and one or three in the odd-toed – together with the elongation of the foot and ankle bones gives the typical thin long-legged look of most of the hoofed animals, and is also an adaptation for speed for most. Such an adaptation is vitally necessary for creatures that inhabit vast open spaces and have few defensive weapons. Usually both the female and the male bear horns, which are hollow and which vary widely in size and shape among the different species.

Within the antelope group the species are legion, varying in size from the giant eland that is almost 6 feet high at the shoulder to the tiny royal antelope of somewhat less than 1 foot.

Those most closely related to wild cattle and to domestic cows are the spiral-horned antelopes such as the kudu, eland, and nyala. They are large animals usually inhabiting wooded areas or forests or, in the case of the sitatunga, marshy land of central Africa. They have unringed spiralling horns – in most cases only the males – a crest of hair down the neck and back, and a coat decorated with a few thin white stripes. The closest relatives of this group of antelopes are the nilgai and the four-horned antelope, both of South Asia, and the various species of the cattle tribe.

Another group of African forest or bush-dwelling antelopes consists of the duikers. These tiny animals are plentiful but rarely seen because of their shy and retiring habits. Measuring between 1 and 3 feet tall, both sexes have a pair of diminutive spiked horns often hidden in a crest of long hair, and a scent gland under each eye with which they mark twigs and branches.

There are also some large antelope that are all closely related and are counted in the same subfamily. All possess spectacular horns, in most cases ringed and pointing backward. This direction of the horns is a necessary adaptation for the continuation of any species in which the males battle with each other for

Below: two male gemboks locked in combat. One of the myriad types of antelopes of Africa, the gembok has long straight horns that can reach 4 feet in length. Both male and female have them.

Above: the lead animal of a group of Thompson's gazelles makes a leap known as "stotting." These gazelles, which are fawn colored with white and dark brown markings, were once plentiful in East Africa, but are rarer now. Only the male has horns.

the females. One group of these large animals, containing waterbucks, lechwes, reedbucks, and the kob, lives mainly in or near water. Others live in much drier habitats, either in open grassy country or in desert or semidesert; these are the oryxes, the roan and sable antelopes, and the addax which, unlike the others, has horns twisted into a loose spiral. Still others – the gnu or wildebeest, the hartebeest, the blesbok, and the topi – are familiar savanna animals. All the members of this group have shoulders higher than their rumps, giving them a curiously clumsy look and a peculiar rocking gait.

The most typical antelopes are a subfamily of animals all medium-sized to small. The first tribe of this group contains various species, but the common factor is the smallness of its members. It includes the tiny dik-dik and royal or pygmy antelope as well as the steinbok, oribis, grysboks, and klipspringer that live on the grassy plains and stony mountainsides. The slender, graceful, and fleet animals often known as gazelles are of the antelope group. They inhabit not only Africa but have spread across Arabia into Asia. Among these are Thomson's and Grant's gazelles, the springbok, the impala, and the gerenuk, which stands on its slender elongated back legs to browse from the acacia trees.

At the Sahara's Edge

South of the Sahara lies the northernmost limit of the Ethiopian region, a strip of semidesert stretching all across Africa from west to east into the southwestern corner of Arabia and downward into the Horn of Africa, interrupted only by the Ethiopian Highlands. As expected, the animals found in this arid region are those that can exist with a minimum of water or that can travel a long distance between one source of water and the next.

Although the camel is found here, it is not an indigenous African animal. It originated in North America from which it spread south into South America and northwest into Asia at a time when there was a land bridge between the continents. There are a few two-humped Bactrian camels living in the wild Gobi Desert, but it is the one-humped Arabian variety that is used for riding and as a pack animal in Africa. This camel exists only in its domesticated form. Even though it has been described as "a horse put together by a committee," this animal is beautifully designed for hot parched conditions.

Animals too large to shelter by burrowing have two interlinked problems if they live in a desert – the heat and the lack of moisture. Mammals must maintain a constant temperature, for which they have such mechanisms as sweating to keep them cool in hot places. In the desert the problem becomes severe because the amount of sweating required to keep cool is so great, and the water needed to replace the moisture lost in sweating is so rare. People lost in the desert will lose some 12% of their body weight through perspiration, by which time their blood will have become too concentrated to carry the heat efficiently from inside the body to the skin, where it could be dissipated. Their temperature will soar, causing what is known as "explosive heat death." Even if they were lucky enough to reach water, they would not be able to replace their lost body weight immediately because the human system cannot cope with so much. The unfortunate person would die of "water intoxication" instead of heat explosion.

Compare human inadequacy with the way the camel can cope with its torrid habitat. To begin with, this mammal does not absorb as much heat as most mammals because its fat is concentrated in its hump rather than being a continuous insulating layer beneath the skin, and its fur prevents heat from entering as well as from escaping. It voids a minimum of water in its urine and feces, and it loses little if any water through sweating because its skin has almost no sweat glands. Camels also have a fluctuating body temperature which stays about 105°F in the heat of day and drops to about 93°F in the cool of night. They also sweat only if their temperature rises above 105°F.

The camel's trump card in resisting drying out is that it loses water from its tissues instead of its blood so that it can withstand a loss of 30% of its body weight without showing signs of stress. Moreover, when it does reach water it can replace most of its lost weight in one long draft of drinking water – perhaps as much as 27 gallons – without doing itself any harm.

The indigenous animals of this harsh area employ the same methods of survival as the camel, but less efficiently. Therefore they depend on being able to travel long distances between water sources for the water they need. Only a few animals are able to live this specialized life, mostly some species of antelope, two races of wild ass, and the carnivores that prey on them. Three species of large antelope are found on the stony edges of the desert – the common oryx including the biesa and gemsbok races of south and east Africa, the scimitar-horned oryx of north Africa, and the addax of north Africa. All of these except the common

Left: the wild ass of northeast Africa likes the arid regions, being able to live without much water. It is believed that most wild asses have interbred with domestic ones for some time past.

Below: some of the few Arabian oryxes left in the world. The only survivors live in captivity after a rescue operation in 1961.

oryx are now on the endangered list. Before the advent of the car, these animals were fairly safe because their speed and the desert's heat made hunting them very difficult. Hunting from jeeps, however, has made the lives of the Somali and Nubian wild asses less secure. The African wild ass is probably the ancestor of the domestic donkey. Certainly the wild and domestic species can breed together, and wild herds are probably contaminated by mating with tame donkeys that have reverted to the wild state.

Three small antelopes, the mountain, the dorcas, and the slender-horned gazelle or rhim, are also to be found in this semidesert strip. The rhim is also on the endangered list.

The main mammal predator of this region is the cheetah, but caracal lynxes, wild dogs, jackals, and sand foxes also menace the herbivorous animals.

Wildlife of the Savanna

While the Ethiopian region's heart, like the Neotropical's, is a huge tropical rain forest situated in and around a river basin, it is distinguished from the Neotropical by an enormous savanna – a grassland that takes up more than one third of the total land. The quality of this is not consistent, however. On the edges of the semidesert it is no more than a treeless expanse sparsely dotted with stunted perennial plants and thorn scrub that burst briefly into luxuriance after the infrequent but heavy showers. This area, known as the Sudan savanna, merges into grasslands that are still relatively dry but scattered with broadleaved and acacia trees. The large center of the continent surrounding the Congo Basin to the north, east, and south, is Guinea savanna. This has a lush growth of tall grass studded with numerous trees that become increasingly evergreen as the jungles come nearer until it is difficult to say whether the terrain is grassland or tropical forest. In the southeast there is a relatively small area of subtropical and temperate grassland.

Because there are no physical barriers such as long mountains to inhibit the movement of wildlife, many species are as much at home in the treeless savanna as they are in the similar bushveldt on the edges of the Kalahari Desert. These include ostriches, aardvarks, hyenas, jackals, and Cape hunting dogs. Giraffes can be found wherever there are trees of the right species and the right height for them to browse on, though they prefer acacias.

Other animals – some of the many varieties of monkey for instance, seem to be conservative and unadventurous in their choice of home, remaining much in one area. The patas monkey limits its habitat to the dry grasslands stretching from the Atlantic to the Nile from west to east, with the Sahara to the north and the tropical rain forest of the Congo to the south. The chacma baboons favor the rockstrewn savannas in the southeast, while the yellow baboons choose the broad band of wooded savanna running all the way across the breadth of Central Africa.

One of the most remarkable aspects of the wildlife on the African savanna is that many species coexist in close-knit harmony without any suggestion of competition, behaving almost like partners. This arrangement does not, of course, apply to predators like the big cats. In fact, one reason it happens is that it is a method of mutual protection against them. It is no uncommon thing for mixed herds of gnu, hartebeest, and zebra to be joined by ostriches and giraffes

Left: herd of zebra and gnu in the Ngorongoro Crater Conservation Area, Tanzania. It is not uncommon for herds to contain mixed animals as a way of mutual protection against natural predators. The government protects the animals from human hunters.

Above: a copse of acacia trees in the Serengeti National Park, Tanzania. The African grasslands are interspersed with isolated clumps of trees, which tend to have wide-spreading root systems.
Right: not an aggressive gesture, but a big yawn from a ratel or honey badger. This animal is found in most of Africa from Senegal and the Sudan to the Cape Province. It is getting very rare.
Below: a young male chacma baboon uses a termite heap as a lookout post to guard the rest of the troop against predators.

which, with their keen eyes on a long neck can spy an enemy from afar and raise the alarm.

This community spirit is not confined to self-protection only. The feeding habits of the cooperating species often fit together like the pieces in a jigsaw puzzle. For instance, the red oat grass that constitutes much of the grassy fabric of the savanna and provides staple fare for many of the herbivores is fed on by the zebras, gnus, and topis in rotation, each preferring the grass at a different stage in its development. Tree and bush browsers do not compete for food either, because they eat at different levels. For example, dik-diks, not much more than a foot in height, eat the lowest leaves of shrubs; elands munch among the middle branches of trees or bushes; and giraffes make the most of their enormous reach to feed on young foliage up to 18 feet above the ground.

Left: ostriches are unique to Africa's dry grasslands. The myth that they bury their heads in the sand probably arose from their habit of stretching the neck flat on the ground if threatened.
Below: honeyguides locate bees' nests for themselves and others.

A much more intimate partnership is that of the ratel or honey badger and the small indicator bird often called the honeyguide. An inhabitant of the wooded savannas, the ratel is a black-and-white member of the weasel family, although it does not have any close relatives. It is a solitary creature traveling alone or in pairs to find the ants, beetles, lizards, and snakes it mainly feeds on. It is the ratel's fondness for honey that accounts for its common name of honey badger. The honeyguide also looks for bees' nests and, if by chance the bird meets the ratel, it will attract its attention by an urgent chatter. Responding with curious chuckling noises, the ratel jog trots over to the bird which, calling continually to the following ratel, flies around until it finds a bees' nest. The ratel then does its part by tearing the nest open with its strong claws. After the honey badger eats its fill, the honeyguide feeds on the bee larvae and then the wax. Honeyguides seem to have a strong taste for wax. The bird was first recorded in the 16th century when a priest in Mozambique noticed that it was eating his candles.

Grassland Grazers

The northernmost area of savanna in the Ethiopian region is the habitat of such typical grassland dwellers as the hartebeest, the enormous Cape or African buffalo, and the eland, and also of some animals, like the ostrich, that divide their time between the grassland and the desert with which this area merges.

Some 8 feet in height and weighing up to 350 pounds, the ostrich is the largest living bird. There is only one species left today, although formerly there were nine. Its survival in hot conditions is facilitated both by its thick body feathers that insulate it against the heat of the day, and the almost total featherlessness of its head, neck, and legs, which is useful in helping to radiate excess heat. The ostrich has also adapted to arid conditions. While it prefers to live in places that have a convenient water supply, the ostrich does not care if that water is brackish or even very salty because it has a gland in its nose that excretes excess salt. Furthermore, it extracts a certain amount of moisture from its diet of succulent vegetation and berries and the occasional reptile and insect. Like its

foot is an added threat to any would-be attacker. As a final protection, the ostrich often grazes in the company of four-footed herbivores like antelopes and zebras, all of which share the task of watching for enemies. The ostrich has a penchant for gobbling up bright metallic objects, and the contents of its stomach often include such indigestible items as keys, nails, and penknives.

As with so many birds, it is the ostrich cock that is the more strikingly feathered. Gregarious and polygamous, they do not waste much time on nest building – they just scrape a hollow about a yard across and a foot deep in the sandy soil. All the laying females deposit their clutches of eggs, usually between 10 and 12 each, in the hollow and both hens and cocks sit on them – the hens during the day when their drab plumage makes them less easy to spot and the cocks at night when their black plumage makes good camouflage. Although the laying of so many eggs at a time might seem to be overproduction, it is vital for survival because ostrich eggs are plundered by Egyptian hyenas, jackals, cheetahs, leopards, and snakes among several others. The hatched chicks are

Below: the Cape buffaloes of southeastern Africa are very hardy, like most of the water buffalo family. Buffaloes do not need a great variety of food and do not notice extremes of temperature. They are also seemingly immune to diseases carried by insects.

South American relatives the common and Darwin's rheas, the ostrich can also live on the plains through adaptations for escape from plains predators. Its long neck and huge eyes – nearly as big as tennis balls – enable it to spy trouble from afar, and its long legs with strong thigh muscles and two toes per foot allow it to run at speeds of 28 to 30 miles an hour. The ostrich can keep up this speed for about 20 minutes without showing undue fatigue. This huge bird also has a powerful kick, which has been known to bend thick iron bars, and the vicious nail on one toe of each

also in danger from these same predators, although they can run with the parents when they are 48 hours old. They can reach a speed of 35 mph in a month.

Another inhabitant of this area is the warthog, an almost hairless mammal whose face is said by some to be the most grotesque among animals. The excrescences on the cheeks below the eyes look like huge warts, which lend the animal its name, and the long head with small eyes set back nearly to the ears does not add to its appearance. Its curling upper tusks scare off many predators, leaving the leopard as its

main enemy. Jackals will sometimes attack the young, however. At night warthogs retire into burrows vacated by other animals, entering backward in order to threaten any followers with their formidable tusks.

Although the name aardvark means earth pig in Afrikaans, this animal is not of the pig family. In fact, it is the sole member of the Tubulidentata (tubular toothed) order. These tubular teeth lack enamel and grow continually. Aardvarks are solid animals nearly 5 feet in length, and have strong claws on their front

Above: a giraffe reaches down to have a taste of a salt lick. Salt licks are important to large herbivores like giraffes because there is little or no sodium in their usual vegetarian diet. The ostrich looking on indicates that this is a mixed herd.

feet which they use to tear down termites' nests in a single night, though humans using picks have trouble doing so. They are covered with a tough bristly skin to withstand the bites of the soldier termites on which they feed along with other soft-bodied insects. They do not eat hard-bodied insects such as true ants, but will add some fruit to their diet.

157

Savanna Scavengers

Like the aardvark, the aardwolf feeds mostly on termites, though the two animals are not at all related. The aardwolf is a near relative of the scavenging hyenas. In fact, it is similar to the striped hyena in outline and coloration and pattern of its crested coat, although much shorter and slighter in build – less than half the length and not even a third of the weight. Unlike its genuinely carnivorous cousins, the aardwolf's jaws are feeble and its teeth small, but these are adequate for its diet. Not being very fast on its legs, the aardwolf is easy game for predators, but it manages to defend itself fairly well by secreting a substance reported to be even more foul than that of the zorille, the African equivalent of the American skunk. The aardwolf shuns the forests at all costs, restricting itself mostly to the open dry plains and thorn scrub of Somalia, Ethiopia, and Kenya, although it also inhabits pockets of savanna in Rhodesia, South Africa, and Namibia. During the day the aardwolf often borrows an aardvark's burrow in which to rest rather than construct an earth of its own.

Above: the aardwolf is a solitary animal whose name means "earth wolf" in Afrikaans. It is not a wolf, however, and it differs from the hyenas it is related to by feeding mainly on termites.

The aardwolf's cousins, the spotted, striped, and brown hyenas, have long been known as scavengers and undoubtedly rely on the leavings of other predators to a large extent. However, it is now known that they do their own hunting in certain areas at night, giving chase to their prey in packs of up to 30. In one area, for instance, spotted hyenas have been found to procure 82% of the meat they eat from killing such animals as wildebeest, zebras, and Thomson's gazelles. In fact, lions will as often be found finishing off a hyena's kill as a hyena scavenging a lion's. The hyena laughs a wild laugh when it is alarmed or when it has found food. This habit, along with the fact that hyenas are extremely difficult to sex because the external organs of male and female resemble each other closely, has given rise to a myth. Local legend has it that every hyena can act as a male or female as its fancy takes it – hence the laughter.

There are also three species of jackal in Africa, two of them inhabitants of the savannas. Popularly linked with the hyena as a scavenger, the jackal and the hyena have little in common. Hyenas, although doglike in appearance, are more closely related to cats, while the jackals are true members of the dog family – so closely related to the domestic dog as to be able to interbreed with it. The black-backed jackal occurs mainly in the grasslands of eastern and southern Africa and the side-striped jackal more widely in the northern and central savannas. The black-backed jackal is less nocturnal in habit than the larger, more timid, rarely seen side-striped species. Happy enough to lead a solitary existence, black-backed jackals prefer to live in small groups, occasionally congregating in a bigger group of as many as 30 when there is a large carcass to scavenge. Like the hyenas, this species is not restricted to eating carrion and will hunt living reptiles, birds, and mammals as big as young antelopes. Black-backed jackals have even been known to attack large pythons when the snake is not in too active a state – perhaps at rest after

Above: jackals are wild dogs that live mostly by eating carrion but they will also hunt prey for fresh meat. They are nocturnal.
Left: spotted hyenas devour the remains of a kill while vultures wait their turn. The largest and strongest of Africa's scavengers, spotted hyenas are one of three species. They have a somewhat scanty coat of gray or yellow-brown with many brown spots.

eating. The Simenian jackal, which lives in northeast Africa, is rare and little known.

The necessary task of scavenging is not entrusted solely to terrestrial animals. Many avian scavengers wheel around in the sky over the savannas, ever watchful for carrion. Some, like the marabou stork, also hunt small mammals and reptiles as well as scavenge. Not so the vultures, whose keen sight and high flying range allow them to see for miles around. Various vulture species are well adapted physically to avoid competition with each other. Ruppell's griffon and the white-backed vulture are usually first on the scene. They have a long hooked bill and a rough tongue especially designed for feeding on the softer tissues of the internal organs. Then it is the turn of tougher beaked species like the lappet-faced and white-headed vultures that use their great strength to rip off skin and eat tougher muscles and tendons. All these four species have the bare neck and head so hygienically necessary to scavengers that spend a large part of their time with their faces immersed in bloody and putrefying flesh. Finally come the Egyptian vultures to feed on the scraps torn off and tossed aside by the others. Egyptian vultures also have a marked liking for ostrich eggs and are enough of a tool user to break the eggs open with a stone.

Small Mammals

Although monkeys evolved in and are thought of as forest animals, there are eight species that have adapted to living in other areas of Africa. Three species – the patas and guenon monkeys and the olive or anubis baboon – may be found in the northern savanna belt, the patas monkeys being restricted to the northernmost and driest areas and even venturing into the desert. The guenons, which are much wider spread throughout Africa, leave the forest only for the edges, but the olive baboons prefer rockier regions. Although all savanna monkeys live in groups, various species form their groups differently. Those inhabiting the arid regions where food is scarcer will have but one male, for example, and those in the somewhat lusher areas will include several males.

Unlike the majority of South American monkeys, the Old World species do not have prehensile tails. Patas monkeys use their tails as props when they stand up to peer over the long grass, while the olive baboon has a tail that droops in apparent disuse.

Above: the patas monkey is a large red primate that has a deep chest, long legs built for speed, and a supple back. The male has much brighter coloring and is twice as big as the female.

Inhabiting the more arid and less fertile areas, patas monkeys live in groups of up to 30, consisting of about a dozen females, their offspring, one dominant male, and a couple of immature males. The leader does the mating, the young bachelors living apart, and also serves as sentinel. The decisions about when to move on or stay in the day-to-day comings and goings are left to the females – unless the leader disagrees outright, when they bow to his wishes.

Olive baboons live in much larger communities than patas monkeys, and there are always several males battling for ascendancy within each group. When not fighting each other or an external enemy, male olive baboons spend an enviably pleasant life,

Right: olive baboons, which live in the grasslands from Senegal to Ethiopia, are one of several savanna species. They are among the largest of the baboons, none of which are highly colored.

Below: the serval is unusual looking among cats because of its large ears. These are both erect and particularly wide at the base, and give this cat keener hearing than most of its family.

feeding in the mornings and lazing in the shade in the heat of the day. They do not have family ties or responsibilities to a harem, mating with any female during her fertility cycle of one week per month. Like other animals in the savannas, baboons will form mixed herds with antelopes to benefit from their more acute hearing and sense of smell in return for fighting their main enemy, the leopard.

Never going too far away from trees, the vervets, one of the guenon monkeys, include leaves and bark in their mainly vegetarian diet, which they sometimes supplement with insects, eggs, nestlings, and even rodents and hares at times. Vervets, also called green or grass monkeys, are like the patas monkeys in that they seldom need to drink. Among the commonest of the African primates, vervets have been described as having the least organized community of the savanna monkeys. They live in groups of 20 or more in which males are slightly outnumbered by females. Males are dominant over females, although there is no strong sense of hierarchy among the various males. Because of their varied vegetarian diet, vervets are considered to be a nuisance by fruit growers as well as crop farmers and are hunted accordingly. The animal is also in danger from predatory birds and cats.

The serval is possibly the most beautiful of all the cats with its slender frame, its long elegant legs, and its heart-shaped face. It is also one of the swiftest cats, able to catch birds on the wing and at times leaping some 6 feet to do so. A vigorous hunter, the serval often kills domestic dogs and, being a good climber, can capture fleeing hyraxes in a tree. Otherwise, it saves its arboreal activities for making a speedy escape from its own pursuers. The serval spends its nights hunting for grass monkeys, lizards, duikers, rats, birds, and hares, while it spends its days resting in thick bush or in an aardvark's abandoned burrow.

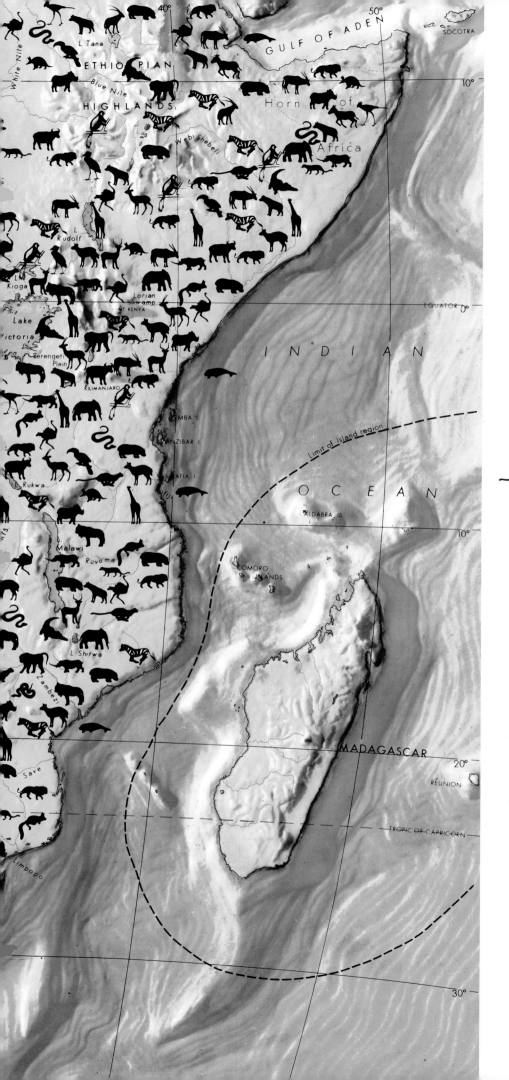

Ethiopian Region: Southern Africa

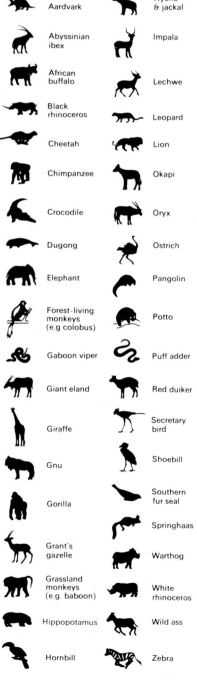

Aardvark	Hyena & jackal
Abyssinian ibex	Impala
African buffalo	Lechwe
Black rhinoceros	Leopard
Cheetah	Lion
Chimpanzee	Okapi
Crocodile	Oryx
Dugong	Ostrich
Elephant	Pangolin
Forest-living monkeys (e.g colobus)	Potto
Gaboon viper	Puff adder
Giant eland	Red duiker
Giraffe	Secretary bird
Gnu	Shoebill
Gorilla	Southern fur seal
Grant's gazelle	Springhaas
Grassland monkeys (e.g. baboon)	Warthog
Hippopotamus	White rhinoceros
Hornbill	Wild ass
	Zebra

163

The Largest Land Mammals

African elephants are a separate species from Asian or Indian elephants, and bush and rain forest elephants are merely variants within the African species.

As if flatly to contradict the general observation that body bulk is a characteristic of animals inhabiting the colder areas of the world, the African bush elephant is the largest of all living land mammals. However, it has developed several adaptations for ridding its huge volume of excess heat. Like the fennec fox and many other animals of hot climates, it has

Above: the elephant's trunk is almost like a combination of the human hand and nose – it is used for touching and grasping as well as for breathing and smelling. With this long flexible proboscis, an elephant can reach to and break off leaved twigs and branches of trees, and then stuff them into its mouth to eat.
Opposite: an elephant also uses its trunk for drinking water.

huge ears that are sometimes 6 feet from top to bottom and which house a huge network of blood vessels. Besides contributing to the elephant's acute sense of hearing, acting as fly swatters at times, and serving to terrify all standing in the animal's path

when they are flapping wildly, these gigantic ears are also used as enormous fans and radiation panels

themselves with cool soothing mud, and sucking up the water with their trunks to spray over their bodies. This regular irrigation has a second purpose of maintaining the suppleness of their skin which otherwise cracks severely.

Adult bulls can measure up to 11 feet in height at the shoulder and weigh as much as 6.5 tons. Due to their strictly vegetarian diet, elephants have daily to consume up to 600 pounds of food and 40 gallons of water, which they squirt into their mouth by means of the trunk in two gallon gulps. It is hardly surprising, therefore, that the animal often comes within danger of eating itself out of house and home. To procure such vast amounts of food elephants have have become both browsers and grazers. Before the days of national parks and reserves to which they are now largely restricted, they preferred to find their food in the forests. Rough, wasteful, and messy feeders, they tore down branches and uprooted trees with their tusks to get at the foliage and, when that had gone, to eat the bark. Having turned forest into open woodland, they then turned their attention to the savanna. Now some are starving because, as extensive as the national parks may be, they are nonetheless limited, and once the elephants have laid waste to this food supply, there is no more.

Elephants' trunks are muscular marvels of pliable versatility. They are strong enough to pull down tree branches, yet delicate enough to pick up a cube of sugar. They are sensitive organs of smell and touch. They are used as siphons, bugles, and semaphores.

Elephants have problems with their teeth. During their lifetime they have a total complement of 26 teeth of which two are the tusks. These enormous tusks – of which the largest ever measured was 13.75 feet long – are irreplaceable upper incisors. The other 24 teeth are molars, equally distributed between right and left upper and lower jaws. Of these only four are in use at any one time. As these four teeth in use wear out, they are pushed forward and out by their erupting replacements. When the elephant's full ration of 24 teeth has gone, the animal must live where it can find food that needs no chewing, usually near a river. Its only alternative to this is starvation and death.

Contrary to expectations, the largest land mammal ever to have existed was not the elephant's predecessor but that of the rhinoceros, another herbivore. The prehistoric monster, the Mongolian *Baluchitherium*, was 18 feet high and 28 feet long, making even the original African elephant look puny let alone its descendants. Present-day rhinos are not exactly small. The black rhino, more common than its white cousin but by no means abundant, stands as much as 5.5 feet high and weighs as much as 1.5 tons. The very

rare white rhino is actually the same gray color as its black cousin, and probably got its name from the Afrikaans word *weit* (wide) in reference to its mouth. It is about a foot higher than the black one and tips the scales at 5 tons, making it the largest land mammal extant after the elephant. These two rhinoceros species have developed differently to adapt to their different eating habits. The white rhino inhabits two small pockets of grassland and open scrub-dotted savanna, one in north central, the other in southeastern Africa. Being a grazer, it has a longer neck and head to allow it to feed comfortably at ground level, and a square-ended muzzle which enables it to remove a full mouthful of grass with each bite. The black rhino, which is much more widely spread throughout the dry bush and thorn scrub of mideastern Africa, is a browser. It is shorter in the neck because it feeds at eye level, and it has a long, pointed, mobile lip which is essential for plucking foliage, buds, and leaves.

Above: a pair of black rhinos feeding in the Masai Amboseli Game Reserve, Kenya. The two species of African rhinoceroses have two horns while their Asian cousins have only one. These horns are built up continuously by fibers that cover a hump on the nasal bone. They are the rhinos' self-defense weapon.

Left: a white rhinoceros cow nurses a calf. The infant white rhinos can stand up about an hour after birth and often begin to graze after a week. However, they suckle for not much less than a year and usually stick close to their mother even after.

Below: oxpeckers, which are related to starlings, have a close feeding-warning relationship with rhinos and other large plant-eating animals. They perch on the back of their host, and from their higher vantage point and with their better vision, warn of approaching danger. In turn they feed off the ticks and tsetse flies on the rhino's back, from which they also get warmth.

Animals of the Serengeti

Of Africa's many national parks and nature reserves, nearly all the biggest and most important are situated in the savannas. Of these, the best known if not the largest of all is Serengeti, which without doubt possesses the most impressive collection of plains animals in the world. These include herbivores with all kinds of feeding methods and predators. It was not until after World War I that this 5700 square mile tract of mixed savanna became popular, a popularity that initially lay in its big game. Hunters found the big cats and large ungulates easy targets. Worried by the rapid depletion of their local wildlife, the authorities of what is now Tanzania managed after years of striving to impose protective measures. First they converted the area into a reserve and later, in 1940, into a fully fledged national park. But the battle was not won. After World War II one of the country's governors derestricted part of Serengeti – namely the richly stocked and spectacular sunken cap of the inactive volcano Ngorongoro and the surrounding highlands – for the use of hunters like himself.

Right: wildebeestes have a migration cycle that brings them to the southeast of the Serengeti in time for the birth of their young. This gives them the best conditions for that purpose.

Below: giraffes once had a range extending into Asia and Europe but today are confined to the savannas and semideserts of Africa.

Below: zebras move in small groups across the grassy plains in which they live, although they sometimes join a mixed herd of other grassland animals. Even though they are a stark black and white, the stripes actually helps to hide them in the tall grass. Most zebras today are found in the Serengeti area of east Africa.

Although the subsequent outcry from enraged conservationists persuaded him to change his mind and redesignate it as a conservation area, the new terms of reference turned a blind eye to commercial exploitation – at a sad cost to its wildlife.

Serengeti boasts a population of phenomenal diversity. Brindled gnus or blue wildebeests have been variously estimated to number between 300,000 and 500,000. Thomson's and Grant's gazelles number 500,000 as well, and zebras nearly 200,000. There are over 300 species of birds. In addition to these are roan antelopes, kongoni or Coke's hartebeests, giraffes, buffalo, and black rhino, as well as such predators as lions, leopards, cheetahs, hunting dogs, and hyenas.

In early June at the beginning of the dry season comes the renowned migration of the mixed herds of gnus, gazelles, and zebras in a slow procession stretching as far as the eye can see. They wind their way westward in search of water, attended closely by prides of lions waiting to attack the inevitable stragglers, mostly the aged and infirm.

Of the three zebra species, the mountain variety is restricted to the arid parts of southern Africa. So it is only Burchell's and Grevy's zebras that are found in these more northerly areas, the former in the lusher grasslands and the latter in the more arid parts. Although both species are sociable and remarkably similar in their general habits, Burchell's or the common zebra is a family animal, one stallion consorting with a family of some five to 20. Grevy stallions tend to be loners. Where their territories overlap, neither species is averse to forming large mixed herds with the other, but they do not interbreed.

Although by preference grazers, zebras have been known to browse on leaves or even to dig up roots, bulbs, and tubers. While neither species willingly strays far from water, Grevy's zebras seem to need less than their cousin. It is a remarkable thing that even when their diet is inadequate, zebras usually appear fat and well groomed.

Being wooded, the more northerly parts of the Serengeti provide an ideal habitat for such confirmed browsers as elands and giraffes. In spite of its large size and great height, the giraffe is a timid gentle creature. It has only two natural enemies – lions and humans, although leopards will attack the young.

Left: the mass migration of wildebeestes during the dry season is from the open plains of short grasses to country that is more wooded and better watered.

Because of their ability to see great distances and to run at speeds of up to 35 miles an hour, giraffes are usually only in danger when they are drinking. This is because they have to spread their legs very wide apart in order to reach the water, and they cannot get back on their feet quickly from this awkward stance. Recent research in the Serengeti has revealed that giraffes lie down to rest at night, sleeping for only short periods of up to six minutes at a time and remaining watchful the rest of the time.

As a rule one of the least aggressive of animals, the giraffe has two methods of defense or attack if needed. It kicks predatory enemies with its front legs, or it uses its long neck and thickly boned skull like a mallet against another giraffe.

Right: a close-up of a giraffe feeding in the Masai steppelands of Tanzania. The tallest animal in the world, giraffes can reach the top of bushes and high into trees for food.

Some Savanna Birds

The African savannas are the habitat of a great multiplicity of birds which live a precarious life because, no matter where they choose to nest – be it in trees, in the grass, or in a shallow saucer scratched out of the soil – they are always at risk from hungry predators. Many birds, therefore, have developed a strong pair of legs for fast running skills, or have learned to build safe nests, some of which are marvels of engineering ingenuity.

The commonest of the savanna birds are the many species of weaver. One of these, the quelea or red-billed dioch, is estimated to number some 100,000 millions. Because this bird eats nothing but seeds, it has a disastrous effect on the farming economy of the new African countries, many of which are poor. Any solution is made difficult because queleas are so numerous and such fast breeders that their predators are overwhelmed. Also endangered very often are the bushes and acacia trees in which the several varieties of sociable weaver birds build their communal nests, which can be as big as haystacks. The weight of the grass used for these elaborate constructions, combined with the weight of the birds which sometimes number as many as 400 in a single tree, has been known to bring down the trees. Be that as it may, the intricacy of weaver nests is remarkable and serves well to deter such enemies as snakes, monkeys, and the larger forms of bush baby. The design of weaver birds' nests varies from one species to another, though all are based on the ingenious knots that the birds tie in the grass. Some of the nests are equipped with guard rails to prevent the eggs from rolling out; others are placed near such undesirable sites as a hornet's nest.

Other members of the weaver family are the variously hued bishop birds, one of which is a bright red and another a vivid yellow. Both males and females are drab of plumage outside the mating season, but the males grow colored feathers when they start mating in the rainy season.

The eggs and young of another family of birds, known occasionally as weaver finches and containing such species as the mannikins and waxbills, can easily be mistaken for the true weavers. In fact, the violet-eared waxbill is itself fooled by the similarity between its own chicks and those of a true weaver called the queen whydah, and rears the young queen whydahs after their eggs have been deposited by their parents in the waxbill's nest. In adulthood the queen whydah looks nothing like a waxbill. Hornbills use another method of protecting their young. After mating, the females go into a tree hole high above the ground and the males, with their help, seal the hole up with mud. This rapidly bakes to a cementlike hardness in the heat. Only the tiniest opening is left. It is too narrow for predators to enter and just big enough for the male to pass food in to the female and her chicks when they hatch. This kind of feeding continues during the female's confinement which lasts until the chicks are about eight weeks old in some species. Then the female demolishes the plaster and the family departs together. In other species the mother leaves sooner – possibly when the young are only four weeks old – and helps her mate feed the young. In these cases, the half-fledged chicks, young as they are, repair the damage caused by their mother's departure. They replaster the hole with a mixture of rotten wood, droppings, dead insects, and saliva. This is an amazing example of instinctive behavior.

A tree bird that spends a good deal of its time on the ground is the secretary bird. It gets its name from the long feathers that dangle down the nape of its neck, which have been likened to quill pens tucked behind the ears of a 19th-century clerk. This bird, which feeds on snakes and other reptiles, large insects, small mammals, nestlings, and eggs, kills snakes by battering them to death with its strong feet and wings.

Below: a weaver hovers near its completed nest. Weavers spend a great deal of effort on their nests, which are large and heavy.

Above: the secretary bird is a long-legged predator found only in Africa south of the Sahara. It is mainly gray with black thighs and wing quills.

Right: a weaver nest in progress, this one on an acacia tree. Sometimes these remarkable structures are the work of a pair, sometimes of many. Weavers nest during the rain season and roam the plains looking for seeds during the dry period.

Ground Nesting Birds

In the more open grasslands, the scarcity of trees for nesting purposes has led to the presence of many ground birds. Some of them, like the kori or giant bustard, are so big that it is hard to imagine them nesting comfortably in the branches of a tree. This bird weighs up to 50 pounds and is some 3.5 feet in height and 4.5 feet in length. In fact, the kori can fly well if unwillingly. It has well-developed thigh muscles, broad feet, and three short stout toes pointing forward, which help it run swiftly. In all four African bustard species, the male has perfected a highly ritualized and spectacular courtship display, strutting with studied steps before the female, fluffing out his brilliantly white wing, neck, and tail feathers, and inflating the air sacs in his throat. Males do not participate in the hatching and rearing of the young.

Other great runners are the guinea fowls. Like the bustards they are gregarious, nest on the ground, and feed on insects and vegetable matter. While breeding, the mating male and female draw away from the rest of the guinea fowls, only rejoining them when they have mated. The vulturine variety is the most spectacularly marked species in the family with bright blue plumage and black and white spots and stripes. Unlike its close cousin, the crested guinea fowl, which shares the same habitat, it is totally devoid of head and neck feathers.

The crowned cranes, with their long legs, great

Right: the kori bustard undergoes an amazing transformation during its courtship ritual. From a dull gray-and-brown bird (left), it becomes a dazzling mass of white as it turns over its back and tail feathers to display the white undersides (right).

Left: a vast colony of carmine bee eaters inhabit a sandbank near Botswana's Okavango Marshes. Although these brilliantly colored birds prefer bees as food, they also eat other flying insects.

wingspan, black velvety skullcaps, and sunbursts of bristly head feathers, are at once more noticeable than either bustards or guinea fowls. The crowned crane is a good flyer, but nonetheless nests on the ground in clumps of grass, marshy by preference. Another crane that may be found in these areas is the delicately colored demoiselle variety, the smallest of all the cranes, but this species migrates from southeastern Europe. Cranes are shy and suspicious, especially when nesting, and the males help in the hatching and rearing of their chicks. Perhaps the best-known attribute of the cranes is their exuberant dance in which the birds, with wings half spread, circle each other with short swift strutting strides, every so often leaping high in the air – some species as high as 20 feet – and occasionally bowing low to their partners. Although these complicated gyrations are a basic element of their courtship ritual, cranes perform them all through the year and some authorities maintain that they are simply an expression of sheer high spirits. Like bustards and guinea fowls, cranes feed predominantly on vegetable matter and insects. The crowned variety has a habit of stamping its feet as it eats to flush the insects from the ground.

Egyptian plovers, on the other hand, have been observed to go so far as to enter the mouths of crocodiles to prod out food. This action is useful to the crocodile because the bird takes leeches and debris from its gums and parasites from its skin.

Another example of this kind of association, although somewhat less beneficial to the host, is that existing between the carmine bee eater and some larger birds like the ground hornbill and the kori bustard. The tiny, brilliantly colored bee eater rides on the larger birds' backs on the lookout for any insects disturbed by their tolerant hosts as they proceed through the grass.

177

More Small Mammals

Not all the terrestrial wildlife of the African savanna is composed of animals as large as elephants, ostriches, rhinos, giraffes, and big cats. There are many other species hopping or scuttling, slinking or slithering, wholly or partly obscured by the grasses. For instance, there are many species, possibly numbering several hundreds, of rodents alone. They provide a varied menu for predators, which are also represented by many species smaller than lions, leopards, and cheetahs, to whom small prey is unattractive unless the big animal is experiencing severe hunger. Nor are the predators restricted to the cat family, such as the serval, caracal lynx, and wildcat. Dogs are present in the shape of various species of jackals and foxes, and there are also striped weasels or zorilles, genets, and mongooses, including the strange suricate or meerkat.

The root rat is a 9-inch-long burrowing rodent that has devised a heating system for its home by the simple method of depositing its droppings, which radiate warmth as they ferment, under its nest. The root rat has long silky hair of a chestnut color. The smaller naked mole rat is a member of the only distantly related family of African mole rats and is distinctive in appearance. As its name suggests, it is bald all over except for a few strands of hair straggling from its pink raw-looking body. In addition to being naked, it also lacks external ears and is completely blind, but this is not of great importance because it stays in its burrow all its life.

The springhaas is another distinct species of rodent that measures about 1 foot in height. Despite its name, which means "springing hare" in Afrikaans, it is not a hare. Nor, despite its appearance and the fact that it moves in large leaps, is it a kangaroo. It is just as much a rodent as a mouse or a rat is, although it constitutes a family all of its own, and zoologists do not know which rodents are most closely related. Like the mole rats, it is a burrowing animal. When it goes to sleep in the morning after a night of activity, it takes the sensible precaution of sealing all the entrances to its burrow with plugs of earth. When it emerges in the evenings, it sometimes does so with a great bound – perhaps to outwit any expectant predators that may be lurking around the burrow's entrance. The springhaas has enormous eyes that are highly sensitive to the slightest movement, a useful asset to such a timid animal. The springhaas' diet consists mainly of bulbs, shoots, and grain.

Forming not merely a family but a whole order all to themselves are the hyraxes or dassies, referred to in the Bible as "conies." These strange creatures, of which there are six species including the rock and the tree hyraxes, resemble marmots and guinea pigs, but they are not even remotely related to them nor to the rabbits with which they also have some features in

Right: the springhaas or springhare is a hopping animal with long hind legs and very short front legs, much like a kangaroo. It can leap about five feet at one bound, but when running away from an enemy, it depends as much on dodging and swerving as jumping.

common. Odder still, their tooth structure is partly like that of both the hippopotamus and the rhinoceros, and their embryonic brain shows similarities to that of the elephant, although hyraxes are never much bigger than 20 inches long. Zoologists remain puzzled

Above: mole rats are burrowing rodents with the short dense fur, tiny weak eyes, and short strong feet associated with true moles. **Below:** the burrows of mole rats are sometimes so extensive that the ground collapses when something big goes over the area. Usually the burrows are dug about six inches under the surface.

about these biological misfits even today.

The habits of hyraxes are just as much a hodge-podge as their anatomy. Timid yet inquisitive, the rock hyraxes are diurnal but will often come out on a bright night, while tree hyraxes are essentially nocturnal but will occasionally come out during the day. Even their names are somewhat misleading because tree hyraxes live in the rocks in certain areas, and are more diurnal than nocturnal. Two habits that remain constant in all hyraxes, however, are a compulsion always to leave their droppings in the same place, by the entrances to their homes in the rocks, and the practice of spraying the surrounding rock with urine, which turns white when it dries. Hyraxes are the prey of leopards, caracals, mongooses, and particularly Verreaux' eagles. The flesh and skin of tree hyraxes are highly prized by local inhabitants, so humans also number among their predators.

The Big Cats

With such a wealth of prey in the African grasslands, it is only to be expected that there are numerous predators – and most of them are big cats. They come in all sizes, from the mainly insectivore dwarf mongoose, a scant 1 foot in length, to the great cat, the 9-foot-long lion. Lions can kill animals as large as buffaloes and giraffes, although their staple fare is made up of the more defenseless species such as antelopes and zebras.

Above: a lioness has no mane and is smaller than the male, but has the same coloration of tawny coat with black-tipped ears and tail. A female lion is mature between the age of three and four and bears a cub about three-and-a-half months after mating.

The lion is as much the embodiment of the popular image of African wildlife as zebras, elephants, and giraffes, although until quite recently it was present throughout most of the Old World. Even today it can still be found, if very rarely, in one small area in northwest India. Of all the cats, lions are the only species that can be said to be genuinely sociable, living in groups varying in number between two and 30. Courting males and females show apparent affection to each other and cubs are shown some affection by the males as well as by their mothers, but there is usually an uneasy peace within the male-dominated group. Females are the hunters and food providers; the much larger males, over 400 pounds in weight and one and a half times as heavy as their mates, are the protectors of the herd. They claim first pickings of any meat that their mates bring home. Lions kill only when they are hungry, and prefer by far to wait for food to turn up than to expend much energy hunting for it.

The leopard, which occurs throughout most of Asia as well as in the tropical rain forests and the widespread open woodlands of Africa, is beautifully camouflaged by its beautiful coat. Its sandy fur, mottled with dark rosettes, enables it to merge virtually unnoticed into the background of sunlight-dappled foliage. While smaller than both the lion and the tiger, the leopard is nevertheless sizeable, possessing a heavy frame and a body length of possibly 4.5 feet. It uses its 3-foot-long tail much like the Old World monkeys do, primarily as a balancing organ in the trees where it spends a good deal of its time resting or lying in wait for prospective victims. It also stores its surplus catches of meat in the branches, often as high as 18 feet above the ground, against future need. Unlike lions, leopards are loners that form brief liaisons with females only during the mating season. They are the stealthiest of all the cats, quieter, craftier and more aggressive than lions. Their typical prey consists of the smaller species of mammals such as impala, monkeys, warthogs, and at times domestic

Right: lions spend the greater part of their time sleeping and resting, and males like to stretch out for a doze in a tree.
Below: young cubs fight playfully, although sometimes it can get serious. Males are chased away from the pride at the age of two or so, and they roam until they can win a pride of their own.

animals. They also eat fish and birds such as francolins and guinea fowls. Once they have tasted human flesh, certain leopards become a peril to humans thereafter. Despite this and their occasional attack on domestic herds, leopards on the whole are valuable in keeping such crop destroyers as baboons in check.

Cheetahs might be thought to resemble leopards at a glance, being of more or less the same length and having tawny coats covered with spots. Closer examination reveals that the pattern of the cheetah's coat is entirely different from the leopard's, being an irregular sprinkling of black dots instead of black-outlined rosettes. The cheetah is also much slighter in build than the leopard, although it is a couple of inches taller at the shoulders. Long-legged and graceful, cheetahs are built for speed, and that speed has given it the designation of "the greyhound of the cats."

Above: a cheetah in a crouch does not look as graceful as usual. **Right:** after a kill, an adult cheetah rests while a young cub finishes its meal. Cheetahs hunt their prey by chasing, unlike most cats which stalk by stealth. Their slenderness aids speed.

Some characteristics of the cheetah are more canine than feline, for example partially unretractable claws only slightly curved and without sheaths, generally diurnal habits, and a reputedly affectionate disposition, but it is faster than any dog. In fact it is the fastest living quadruped, reaching speeds in excess of 60 miles an hour. However, the cheetah is strictly a sprinter and can only make a burst of such speed for less than 500 yards. Its hunting style, therefore, is to stalk its prey within striking distance, sprint rapidly, and bring down the animal by biting at the neck, usually severing the vital jugular vein. Death is quick, and the cheetah will either eat on the spot or drag its kill a short distance to cover before eating.

Although the cheetah's prey is similar to that of the leopard, the fact that their habitats do not often overlap means that these two predators are hardly ever in competition for food in those parts of Africa where both are found.

182

Below: any one of these animals that are found in East Africa is likely to fall prey to a cheetah, a predator of wide tastes. To the 25 species illustrated may be added a large number of others from grassy plains ranged by cheetahs in other parts of Africa.

CHEETAH

GRANT GAZELL

ORIBI

SABLE ANTELOPE

OSTRICH

Above left: leopards are surefooted climbers and use their skill often to get into trees. There they might rest, look out or lie in wait for prey, or make a meal of a kill out of the reach of ground scavengers. Leopards are also good jumpers and swimmers.

Left: a leopard at wait in a tree is so well camouflaged that few animals which come under attack from it are aware of its presence. The leopard comes out of hiding like a shot, which also helps take its prey unaware. This large cat is on the hunt constantly, and often adds birds and monkeys to its diet.

A Cheetah and Its Prey

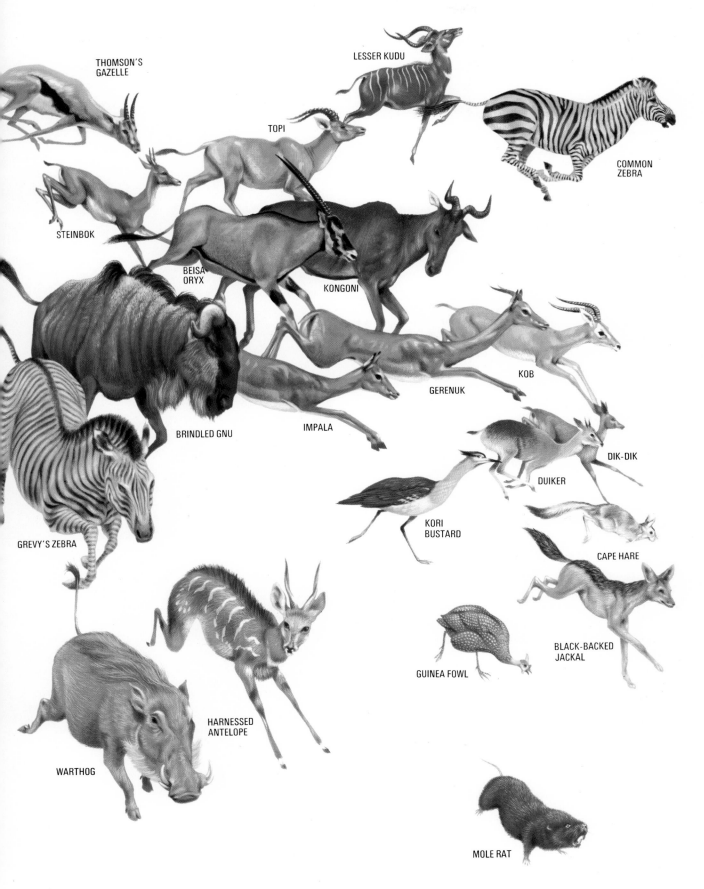

THOMSON'S GAZELLE

LESSER KUDU

TOPI

COMMON ZEBRA

STEINBOK

BEISA ORYX

KONGONI

GERENUK

KOB

BRINDLED GNU

IMPALA

DIK-DIK

DUIKER

KORI BUSTARD

CAPE HARE

GREVY'S ZEBRA

GUINEA FOWL

BLACK-BACKED JACKAL

HARNESSED ANTELOPE

WARTHOG

MOLE RAT

Small Predators

Big cats, hyenas, and jackals are not the only predators that reptiles, birds, and smaller African mammals have to fear. There are plenty of other carnivores with ever-ready appetites waiting for all of them. These include smaller cats, such as servals and caracal lynxes, and ratels, zorilles, and suricates. In addition there are wild dogs such as the bat-eared fox and the African or Cape hunting dog.

It is misleading to speak of African hunting dogs in anything but the plural, for they are pack animals of the tightest knit kind. They keep perpetually on the move except when the cubs are too young to travel, shrewdly choosing the uncertain light of either dawn or dusk to hunt for food. They hunt boldly, bounding toward a herd of gazelles or gnus, for example, to scare them into flight. The pack runs after them, soon singling out an individual animal for group attention. The pack hounds it, if necessary for mile after mile, until the hunted animal is exhausted and caught. The dogs all then bite at it, ripping pieces of flesh from its body until it falls, and eating it at once, often while it is still living. A dog pack can consume an impala in 10 minutes.

Adult hunting dogs are considerate of the others in their pack, allowing the younger animals to feed first as a matter of course. They also look after the cubs and those remaining behind to tend them, as well as the lame and the orphaned. After meeting their own food requirements, adult males bolt lumps of unchewed meat and, on returning to home base, disgorge them for their dependents.

Of all the strong smelling mammals, perhaps none has a more pungent secretion than the zorille, an inhabitant of the open country. This animal bears a close physical resemblance to the American skunk, although it is slightly smaller and lighter in build. Its black and white coat is an example of warning coloration. The zorille is nocturnal, hunting at night for reptiles, hares, rats, insects, and birds and their eggs. Also to be found in the open savannas is the white-naped weasel, a rare species sometimes called the snake weasel both because of its slender sinuous body and its practice of killing and eating snakes. A close relative of the zorille, the white-naped weasel hunts at any time of day.

Another creature known for its ability to exude an offensive odor is the African civet, which can be found resting during the day in an abandoned aardvark burrow. About 4 feet in length including the tail, this omnivorous animal with a vulpine face eats a varied diet of small mammals, insects, birds, reptiles, fruit,

Right: the blotched genet is one of six species living in Africa. Like the others, it looks like a mixture of a cat and a mongoose. It is distinguished by its large dark spots on a yellowish coat.

and tubers. A fatty substance from the civet is used in the manufacture of perfumes because of its excellent fixative qualities.

The closely related, somewhat smaller genets are more nocturnal in their habits than civets. The blotched, or large-spotted species, can jump great distances. They inhabit the wooded areas of savanna, and are very much at home in trees. Even the common genet of the drier, more open grasslands is at ease in trees.

Below: something has probably attracted this suricate's attention and, being an intensely curious creature, it is trying to investigate. This smallest of the mongooses likes to sunbathe when it can.

Members of the same family as civets and genets are mongooses and suricates. The large networks of burrows that the gregarious suricates excavate in the dry sandy plains, and the way they stand sunning themselves in groups outside the entrances, make them resemble the herbivorous prairie dogs of the American grasslands; but suricates are not related to prairie dogs. They hunt a variety of small animals by means of their keen sense of smell and kill them with a swift bite in the neck. Unlike most other animals, even highly aggressive ones, suricates do not give an advance display or warning.

187

The Eastern Highlands

Near the equator in eastern Africa and bordering the Great Rift Valley is a range of mountains that includes Mount Kenya and Mount Kilimanjaro. Farther north lie the spectacular Ethiopian Highlands. Both these mountain ranges support many unique species of which some, like the rock hyraxes, also are encountered in the savannas.

In the Ethiopian Highlands live two species of ground monkey, the hamadryas baboon and the gelada baboon, though the gelada is strictly speaking not a true baboon. The hamadryas was widespread throughout the Nile Valley in ancient times, and was held in reverence by the ancient Egyptians. This accounts for its other name of sacred baboon. It is often depicted on temples and monoliths as one of the attendants of Thoth, the Egyptian God of letters and learning. It was also mummified, entombed, and associated with sun worship. The hamadryas has a long cape of silvery-brown hair that flows down its back from its head and shoulders. This feature, together with the long muzzle typical of true baboons, has led some observers to describe it as looking like a trimmed French poodle. Like the olive baboon, it has prominent swellings on its buttocks, but the hamadryas' are pinky-red instead of gray-green. Hamadryas baboons move in troops, in their case of up to 100. For hunting purposes this large company is divided into smaller groups consisting of one male and about half a dozen females; they forage during the day and recongregate with the others in the evenings to sleep.

The gelada organizes itself into quasi-military formations much the same as the hamadryas baboons, although their groups can consist of as many as 400 individuals. Within each smaller division, females are hierarchical. The more important ones protect their inferiors from – or deprive them of – the attentions of the males, with the result that the more dominant females generally bear the young. Gelada baboons have a mane of long hair like the hamadryas, but otherwise are different physically. They are not only slightly bare-chested, but also have a short caved-in snout. This mobile muzzle is important in communication. In rage, fear, or jealousy the gelada turns over its lips in such a way that the upper one covers the nose and the lower one the chin.

The Ethiopian Highlands are also the home of a very rare representative of the ibex family, the walia ibex, and an obscure member of the dog family known variously as the Simenian jackal, Abyssinian wolf, Simienen fox, or Semien fox. This large carnivore, which has a face like a fox, is on the verge of extinction, hunted down because of its alleged destruction of domestic stocks. This could be an unjustified accusation inasmuch as this animal seldom touches sheep, feeding almost entirely on the small mammals of the high plateaus.

In the forests on the lower slopes of the mountains around Lake Kivu between Zaire and Rwanda dwells the mountain gorilla discovered in 1901. This shy

Above: mountain gorillas are very shy and comparatively rare. They live in family groups in the remote forests bordering the Rift Valley between Zaire and Tanzania, roaming the forest floor by day in search of leaves, stems, and other plant life.

Left: two dominant male gelada baboons from Ethiopia's Simien Mountains fight over the control of a group of females. Such fights may change the order of command within the troop, but the general structure will remain the same.

creature is not a distinct species from the more numerous lowland gorillas, but varies from them largely in minor anatomical characteristics such as color and skull formation. Mountain gorillas consume as much as 50 pounds a day of vegetation, preferring the choicest parts of vines, ferns, bamboo shoots, and other plants. They usually get enough moisture from this food to do without drinking. One of the few studies of mountain gorillas in the wild, completed in 1967, revealed them to be the gentlest of animals. The heavy mature males sleep on the ground, unlike their lowland relatives, but the others of a family group bend branches of a tree into a crude platform.

Africa's enormous antelope population is represented in these highlands by the large mountain nyalas and the tiny klipspringers and steinboks among others. Mountain nyalas favor the woods and heathlands between 9500 feet and 12,500 feet above sea level. Klipspringers, which are found nimbly negotiating the rocky slopes up to about 13,500 feet, are beautifully adapted for their habitational needs. They walk tiptoe on strong legs which are equipped with cylindrical hoofs whose tissues, like those of the chamois and ibex, are of a rubberlike consistency and aid grip as well as cushion shock. They are also able to jump great lengths with uncanny accuracy.

Swamp and Lake Dwellers

Besides being liberally supplied with swamps, central Africa also has a string of large lakes dotted along the Great Rift Valley. These include Lakes Victoria, Kyoga, and Turkona (formerly Rudolf) in the north and Lakes Malawi and Tanganyika further south. Turkona, Malawi, and Tanganyika are among the largest and deepest in the world. These wetlands are the home of a varied range of mammals, birds, reptiles, and amphibia. They are attracted by the dense growth of papyrus reeds, Nile lettuce, and other aquatic vegetation, by the swarm of edible insects, and by the rich picking of fish.

Those amazingly varied creatures, the antelopes, have two representatives especially adapted for an aquatic life. These are the lechwe and the even more water-loving sitatunga. Both these species have long hoofs and flexible ankles that allow them to splay out their hoofs on the spongy ground and distribute their weight more evenly. Although not very agile on dry ground, both the lechwe and the sitatunga are marvelous swimmers. Both spend a great deal of time in water, so much so that they are considered to be semi-aquatic. Lechwes live in the shallows of flooded rivers during the rainy season, feeding on submerged shoots

and grasses by immersing themselves belly-deep. They sometimes go deeper, spending almost the whole day immersed up to their necks in water. Sitatungas, which are about 3 to 3.5 feet in height, will go into 4 feet of water to feed, often submerging completely to get at the grass. They also hide from enemies by going into deep water, keeping all of their body except their nose under the surface. Despite their name, the much larger waterbucks are not as well suited to aquatic conditions as either the lechwe or the sitatunga, and so inhabit lakesides.

Still bigger are the buffaloes, widely distributed throughout the region from dense forest to open plain near pools for them to wallow in and mud for them to cake themselves with. This huge beast, of which the

Above: the monitor lizard sometimes catches and eats lake fish. **Left:** hippopotamuses nearly submerged in a pool that is almost concealed by a dense mat of floating plants. The egrets perched on their backs are feeding off the many parasites found there.

plains variety weighs up to 1800 pounds, is the only species of wild cattle found in Africa. Like most cattle, it is generally placid. If disturbed, however, it can become extremely savage, so much so that even lions will think twice before attacking it. In fact, there are reports of buffaloes getting the better of lions and killing them. Buffaloes do not see very far and are hard of hearing but possess a good sense of smell.

In addition to the elephants and white rhinos living in the vicinity there is the hippopotamus, whose low-slung belly nearly touches the ground as it lumbers along in the moonlight, going by time-honored pathways through the grass toward its grazing grounds. Although its name literally means "river horse," this animal is closely related to the pig. Usually found in groups of up to 15, but occasionally many more, hippos spend most of the day immersed in swamps, rivers, or lakes, or basking on the river banks. The hippo can weigh up to 4 tons, and this great bulk requires as much as 130 pounds of vegetable matter a day to sustain it.

Sharing the same habitat is the crocodile which, like the hippo, is equipped with eyes, ears, and nostrils on the top of the head and snout that enable it to breathe, smell, and hear while keeping almost totally submerged. As a rule an uneasy truce exists between the two animals but, should there be a confrontation, it is usually the hippo that gets the better of it.

Although crocodiles take the trouble to bury their eggs in pits by the rivers and the females carefully dig out the young at their first sound, the eggs are often stolen by Nile monitors. These 6-foot-long lizards also feed on the eggs of a wide range of water birds, including herons, pelicans, and spoonbills.

Standing in the marshes like statues are shoebills, water birds that patiently wait for fish or frogs to come within their range. Like storks, they can stand motionless for hours. It is thought that they sometimes use their broad hooked bill to dig up lungfish.

Two Southern Deserts

The southwest of Africa is largely desert or semidesert. The best-known of these areas, the Kalahari Desert, is not totally devoid of vegetation, however, and could more accurately be classified as subdesert steppe. The Karroo plateau, which makes up the greater part of the southwestern tip of Africa, is an arid region whose prevalent rocks and stones are covered in a blanket of brilliant flowers after the rains. The Namib Desert, on the other hand, is a desert in the truest sense of the word, consisting of gravel in the north and enormous sand dunes, some of them 1000 feet high, in the south. This desert, which runs in a narrow strip for 1200 miles along the Atlantic coast, has been formed by the climatic conditions of the adjoining sea, whose cold current has made it a cold desert like the Chilean and Peruvian coastal deserts. It attracts species similar to those found in the South American region, such as southern fur seals and penguins. The African penguin is the black-footed or jackass variety, which gets its name from its braying. There is also a commercial guano industry like South America's.

The Namib's apparent barrenness supports an unexpectedly rich and varied animal life including such typical desert dwellers as scorpions, web-footed geckos, sidewinding vipers, and Namib plated lizards. In the stonier parts to the north are klipspringers, rock hyraxes, rock hares, and Hartmann's mountain zebras. These zebras are a race of mountain zebra now numbering only a few thousand and in danger of extinction unless proper measures are taken for their full protection.

desert sands meet the sea are an ideal habitat for such wading birds as flamingoes, while the beaches themselves provide ample food for shore species like the oystercatcher. This bird's garish orange beak that looks like a chisel is well suited not only for prising stubborn limpets off rocks and jemmying open the

The nearness of sea and desert produces a wide range of birdlife in the Namib, of which some are the sandgrouse, tern, and falcon. The salt flats where the

Opposite below: a Temminck's courser shields its eggs from the sun. Keeping their eggs shaded is a problem for desert birds.

Below: white-backed vultures crowd around the carcass of a cow that has died in the Kalahari Desert. White-backed vultures are one of 15 species of Old World vultures, of medium size with a ruff of long feathers around their neck. They are found throughout Europe and Asia as well as in the dry open areas of Africa.

shells of bivalves that constitute the main part of its diet, but also for digging into the sand for worms.

The Kalahari Desert is surprisingly well populated by those antelope species that have low water requirements and such other adapted animals as suricates, zorilles, and ratels.

Jungle Animals

The tropical rain forests of the Congo Basin in Africa do not cover as vast an area as those of South America and lie much farther north in relation to the rest of the continent. Naturally, much the same conditions prevail as in the Amazon Basin, the dense foliage producing an even but dim light at ground level. This maintains a remarkably stable temperature and humidity. From jungle floor to treetop, the lush vegetation provides a rich harvest for a highly varied animal life.

Although the environment between the closely growing trees and shrubs favors the smaller species, there are nonetheless many representatives of the giants – such as elephants, hippopotamuses, and buffaloes – to be found crashing through the bushes. These, however, are small in comparison to their relatives in the savanna. The forest elephant, for instance, is only 9 feet in height as against the grass-land variety's 14. A pygmy elephant also exists in the swampier parts of the jungle. It is not more than 6.5 feet high and bears tiny tusks, but miniature though it may be, it is supposed to be particularly belligerent. There is also a pygmy hippopotamus about 30 inches tall, half the height of the distinct swampland species and, at 600 pounds, only about one fifth the weight.

The giraffe also has its forest relative in the okapi. This curious creature has an elongated neck and a sloping body from shoulder to tail that gives a general appearance of similarity to the giraffe, but it is not marked in the same way at all and is much smaller. Instead of dark patches over its whole body like the giraffe's, the okapi's body is a deep auburn color with darker brown haunches and upper limbs that are slashed with white stripes. It also has white legs. The okapi's neck, though supple, is no longer than that of an antelope and its ears are large in proportion to its head, probably contributing to its acute sense of hearing. A browser like its cousin, the okapi possesses a similarly prehensile tongue, which is useful for plucking leaves from trees or for washing hard to reach parts of the body such as the eyes.

The various forest species of antelopes, finding they cannot graze in the relative absence of grass in these areas, often share the okapi's diet of foliage. Such antelopes include the brown-and-white striped bongo which, at over 4 feet in height at the shoulders, is the largest of the forest antelopes; the much smaller duikers with their tiny backward-pointing ears which help prevent them from getting tangled up in the branches; and the royal antelope which is the smallest living hoofed mammal, being no bigger than a rabbit but with longer legs. Closely related to the antelope is the water chevrotain or mouse deer which is the smallest cud-chewing mammal. It bears an uncanny resemblance to the totally unrelated agouti of South America, a rodent. Although the chevrotain is naked of horns or antlers, the male has exceptionally long canine teeth, and these tusks protrude well below the lower lips. They make sharp weapons. Like most forest antelopes with the notable exception of the bongo, the water chevrotain is exclusively nocturnal.

There are also two species of pig that have adapted to the tropical forests of Africa, the bush pig or red river hog and the giant forest hog. Bush pigs are also primarily nocturnal creatures living for preference near water and being adept swimmers. By day they rest in thickets or reed beds, and by night they roam in gangs of up to 20, tunneling destructively in the undergrowth to feed not only on roots, berries, and other plant life, but insects, eggs, and sometimes snakes.

The giant forest hog was only discovered recently, having first come to light in 1904. It is the largest living pig, but has smaller tusks than its close cousin the warthog. Unlike the bush pig, the giant forest hog does not root for its food, relying instead on leaves, fallen fruit, small mammals, birds, and grass when it can get it. However, the regular movement of this heavy animal through the forest does in time beat visible tunnels in the thick bush.

Left: bush pigs, also known as red river hogs from their reddish-brown color, have a coat of short bristles and a disproportionately large head. Males can get to be 300 pounds in weight, females 200 pounds.

Right: two pygmy hippos. This species of hippopotamus lives in the West African countries of Liberia, Nigeria, and Sierra Leone. It is 5 feet long and nearly 3 feet at the shoulder.

Left: a rare picture of the bongo, an antelope that lives in the deep equatorial forests from Zaire to the Aberdare Mountains of Kenya. Its coloring and markings are an excellent camouflage.

Left: the rare okapi usually travels singly or in small family groups. They keep to well-trodden and familiar paths through the thickest forests of Zaire.

More Jungle Animals

The giant pangolin, the four-toed elephant shrew, and the crested guinea fowl are present over large parts of the African forests. So also is the Congo peafowl which, while it does not have the glorious train of the Indian variety, compensates for this by displaying not only its tail but also its wings. This bird was first discovered in 1936. The Gaboon viper, which is just as deadly to humans as to its prey, has a body camouflage that renders it almost invisible against the leafy forest floor. This snake is the biggest living true viper, reaching lengths of 6 feet and weighing as much as 50 pounds. It is not the sole representative of its clan in the forests, however, since the rhinoceros gaboon viper is also found on the forest floor, and the green tree viper, which has a prehensile tail, is present in the trees, waxing fat on tree frogs and small mammals.

Prehensile tails are possessed by many arboreal animals, another African forest example being the tree pangolins which are small cousins of the Cape and giant species. Some tree dwellers have adapted their tails in different but equally useful ways. The scaly tailed flying squirrels steer with their tail as they glide from branch to branch collecting fruit, seeds, leaves, flowers, and insects. Their bushy tails appear to be much like the tail of the true squirrel's, but the underside is equipped with two rows of horny scales that they press into the tree trunks when climbing. This gives them a better grip. The African brush-tailed porcupine has a long tail ending in a clump of bumpy bristles with which it makes a noise like a rattle as a way of frightening off attackers when it is threatened.

There are also several unusual species of rats and mice living in the forests. One is the African climbing mouse which nests at ground level but climbs trees in search of seeds, using its long prehensile tail both to balance and to grip with. Another is the giant pouched rat, an animal which, despite its large size of about 3 feet including its tail, is generally harmless. When

Below: the green tree viper freezes when it is threatened, and its color provides a perfect camouflage among the leaves. When lunging at prey, it grips the branch with its prehensile tail.

Above: an elephant shrew eating a cricket. Elephant shrews, which get their name from their long mobile snouts, depend on their sense of smell for finding food in the forest undergrowth.

Left: the large casque on the hornbill's beak is an air-filled chamber that may help to modify the sound of the raucous cries the bird utters. Hornbills are the largest fruit eating birds.

Below: Donaldson's turaco, one of the green birds of the species. Unlike most green birds, their color comes from a single pigment, turacoverdin. All turacos have crests, some of them pronounced.

eating it crams its cheek pouches so full of fruit and seeds that, when it returns to its burrow, it has to force the food out of the pouch by squeezing it with its forepaws.

The trees are alive with the sound of parrots, hornbills, and turacos. There are some 19 species of turaco widespread throughout the African continent. These birds are closely related to the cuckoos but, at up to 2 feet in length, much larger. Those inhabiting the South African brushland are rather plain looking, gray and brown with white markings. They have a distinctive call, however, which sounds like a loud "go-away, go-away." Most other turacos live in the deep forest and are strikingly colored, with green or blue bodies and bright red markings on their wings. A curious feature of the turaco is the mobility of its outer toe, which it can point at will either to the ⌐spreys do.

Turacos are very agile in the trees, climbing creepers and scampering along branches, and some are equally swift ground runners. Even larger than the turacos are the hornbills, of which the casqued variety has a donkeylike bray and a large horny cowl over its forehead.

197

The African Primates

The tropical African forests are an ideal habitat for primates, the majority of which are diurnal tree dwellers. This animal group contains the prosimians, which are a suborder of monkeylike creatures, and the monkeys and apes. Both monkeys and apes have grasping hands whose fingers end in flattened nails instead of claws, and binocular vision eyes that enable them to judge distance accurately. These features make them efficient climbers. Their diet is a mixed one of fruit, leaves, and insects or small animals.

The three kinds of prosimians present in the African jungle are nocturnal rather than diurnal, and consequently have the enormous eyes of many night-time animals. This gives them an appealing babylike appearance. Of the three, the bush baby is the most acrobatic, chasing insects through the trees with enormous bounds. The four different species of bush baby are by no means restricted to the tropical forests and can be found almost anywhere in Africa where there are trees. Bush babies have a habit of urinating regularly on their hands and feet. This is thought to give them a better grip, but the main function is probably to mark their territory.

The potto and its very rare cousin the angwantibo are slow deliberate climbers, more dependent on stealth than speed in catching their insect prey. In both these animals the forefinger is greatly reduced, giving their hands a large span. The thumb and remaining fingers form a kind of pincer somewhat like that of the chameleon's feet, and the grip of their hands is not released even when their owners are asleep.

The large number of tree monkeys can be divided into the three main groups of colobus, guenon, and mangabey. Colobus monkeys inhabit the high branches of trees and perform the most hair-raising leaps. They feed almost exclusively on leaves, possessing complicated stomachs especially adapted to deal with this rather tough diet. Colobus monkeys have beautifully marked, long, silky fur, which became a fashion rage in the 1920s. Thousands of these monkeys were killed for the fashion trade, and the red, green, and black and white species are still all in some danger of extinction.

The guenons are a large group of small monkeys, the majority of which are forest dwellers although some species do inhabit the grasslands. Some are green, others blue-gray or black-purple, and some have distinctive markings such as blue-and-white

moustaches, white fanlike beards, or red tails. These monkeys live in troops, keeping together by means of twittering calls and barks.

The mangabeys are larger than the guenons with longer legs and more pronounced muzzles. They often form a mixed group and travel with the guenons. Although the two types of monkey have a similar diet, they do not compete for exactly the same kind of food because the mangabeys' larger more powerful teeth allow them to feed on hard-skinned fruit and nuts that the guenons cannot pierce. The long muzzle and large teeth of the mangabey somewhat resemble the drill and mandrill, both members of the baboon family, and they are in fact closely related. The mandrill's face is the most spectacularly colored of all primates, and in fact of all mammals. On either side of the bright red nose are exposed areas of blue skin, and this pattern is echoed on the genital area and hind-

Above: a dwarf bush baby or galago. This animal is so tiny that it would easily fit into an average man's palm. Bush babies grow rapidly and become independent quickly. Particularly sensitive to their surroundings, they readily find their way in the night.

quarters. The drill and mandrill are both ground animals, their short limbs and heavy bodies being better suited to life on the forest floor.

The two apes of the Ethiopian region are the gorilla and the chimpanzee, and they are also to be seen to some extent on the floor of the forest. This is particularly true of gorillas, the old males growing so heavy that climbing becomes almost impossible. The chimpanzees, however, are largely arboreal, making night nests or sleeping platforms at relatively high levels by bending leafy branches over. Chimpanzees are sociable animals, and though they live in loosely knit groups, there is a male hierarchy. Status seems to be established by the most spectacular show of hooting and throwing rocks or tearing off and waving branches and young saplings. When in heat, females mate with several males, often in quick succession. With regard to their young, however, females exhibit

Left: the skin of the male mandrill's face and hindquarters is the brightest colored of any mammal. The nose is brilliant red and the enormous cheek swellings along the muzzle are vivid blue. There is a yellow band that looks like a beard under the chin, and the rump has blue patches with pink pads on each side.

Left: the potto has a bearlike look and wooly brown fur, but is one of the lower primates. It has several spines on its back once thought to be used for defense.

Right: the Mona monkey is one of the guenon species, inhabiting all types of forests from Ghana to Cameroon but preferring mangrove forests. Colorful like most of the guenons, it is reddish brown on the back with a yellow crown and white undersides.

Below: Colobus monkeys often leap distances that seem impossible for a small animal to clear. They seldom come down from the highest part of the tree, where they live in family groups of up to 20.

a high degree of maternal care, even adopting orphaned babies. A young chimpanzee usually stays with its mother for about the first six years of its life, and may help to care for its younger siblings. Chimpanzees are omnivores, eating everything from seeds to grubs to the meat of other mammals, and including even honey.

Highly intelligent, this ape uses sticks and stones as weapons and, by improvising with what comes to hand, manufactures and employs a number of tools. For example, it uses masticated leaves for soaking up drinking water and grass stems for extracting termites from their nests.

Gorillas are the largest of the apes but, despite their enormous strength and legends about their viciousness, they are shy gentle animals in great need of protection as their natural forest and mountain habitats are cleared for cultivation. Their greatly feared displays of chest beating are a show of strength when mature males meet or when they come unexpectedly across humans, but they seldom act on their threats. More vegetarian than their smaller cousins, they live in family groups consisting of between 16 and 30 in all. This includes one mature male known as a "silverback" because of the grayish tinge to an older male's fur, several immature males known as "blackbacks," and females with their young.

200

Above: chimpanzees never move far away from trees, even though they spend part of their day on the ground. The common chimpanzee lives in the forests north of the Zaire River while the smaller and rarer pygmy chimpanzee or bonobo lives to the south of the river. Other chimpanzees are found from the Niger basin to Angola. Sometimes neighboring groups join forces for a period.

201

Chapter 6
The Oriental Region

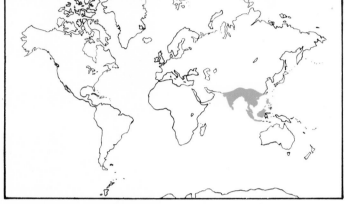

The Oriental region embraces tropical Asia, which includes the southern part of China, India, Burma, Thailand, Laos, Cambodia, Vietnam, and the Malay Peninsula on the mainland, and the islands of Sri Lanka, Singapore, and the Philippines. The Indonesian islands of Sumatra, Java, Borneo, and Bali, and a few other small islands are also a part of it, Bali being the easternmost. The southeastern area abuts the transitional zone between this and the Australian regions.

Although there are high mountain and deep ocean barriers, there are also many areas of contact and passage routes all around and the animal life of the region shows links with that of the Palaearctic, Ethiopian, and Australian regions. The most important meeting points are in the north where a number of tropical species have colonized the Eurasian steppes and mountains.

The fate of the monkey-eating eagle of the Philippines is in serious question. It has been killed in large numbers to supply a demand for stuffed specimens, and this killing has gone on without legal restraint. This true eagle is about 3 feet in length, brown on the upperparts and white on the underparts. It has a crest of long narrow feathers.

203

Man's Impact

Many of the people who live in the Oriental region believe that even the lowliest living creature has a soul. This belief, which is shared by Hindus and Buddhists alike, means that in many parts of the region all animals are treated with great respect. In fact, certain animals such as the monkey, the cow, and the peacock are considered sacred in various places, which has led to their careful and strict preservation. For centuries as well, great centers of civilization existed side by side with jungle societies whose people were primitive farmers, nomadic hunters, or simple food gatherers, with little interference by the city dwellers. All this worked to the advantage of wildlife until recent times. Then came the introduction of western technology and the population explosion, both of which brought drastic changes.

Modern means of transportation such as the train and the car has meant the destruction of animal environments to make way for tracks and roads. Modern firearms made hunting safer and faster and, when used in warfare, caused the slaughter of animals as well as humans. The pressure of increasing numbers of mouths to feed put more and more land under cultivation, destroying the homes of many animals and forest dwellers in particular.

Today, the Oriental region is the worst in the world as far as endangered and nearly extinct animals are concerned. Of the 25 most seriously threatened animals on earth, 10 of them are in southern or southeast

Above: these terraced rice fields on Bali in Indonesia are typical of the age-old methods of agriculture that allowed the development of communities without destroying the environment. **Below:** zebu cattle lounge at their comfort in the middle of the street in New Delhi, India. Cattle roam the streets at will because the Hindus revere the cow as Mother Earth's representative and the bull as a link with the god Shiva. They are never killed.

Asia. These include the Indian, Sumatran, and Javan rhinoceros, the tiger, the Indian lion, the kouprey, and the tamarau.

The cheetah is more than endangered: it is extinct locally, the last three having been killed on the same night in 1948. These sleek, speedy predators, had long been on the decrease, however. Their decimation started with their use by the nobility of India to hunt antelope in packs in the same way that dogs are still used today in Britain to hunt foxes and hares. Some princes had packs of several hundred cheetahs which, because they would not breed in captivity, had to be replaced constantly with newly captured ones. The fewer and fewer that remained in the wild had less and less food to live on because their main prey, the blackbuck antelope, was also being hunted to the point of extinction.

The Oriental region's three species of rhinoceros were the victims of an enduring popular belief that the use of their horns and other parts of the body could give special powers to people. The horns were and still are thought of as a sexual tonic. In addition, Chinese pharmacists use every part of the rhino in their medicines, including the hide, the meat, various organs, the blood, the bones, and even the urine. A market for the rhinoceros has existed in China for many hundreds of years and arose in other countries as well – at one time in Europe too. Trade reached its peak just before World War II when a rhino was worth almost its weight in gold. The small Sumatran species was easiest to hunt and disappeared the fastest, after having once been widespread throughout Borneo, Sumatra, Burma, Thailand, and the Malay peninsula.

The kouprey was the last large mammal to be discovered in the world, having come to light only in 1937. Relatively rare to start with, it was found only in two areas of northern Cambodia, in eastern Cambodia, and in western Vietnam. Much hunted by

Above: the single horned Indian rhinoceros owes its scarcity largely to the popularity of its horn for medicine and magic, but also to the fact that it has only one calf in three years.

soldiers who were forced to live off the land during the long guerrilla war in the region, this true wild ox is now on the endangered list.

Animals of the Philippines have suffered heavily since the end of World War II mostly because it has proved difficult to enforce the prewar game hunting laws. The tamarau or anuang, a buffalo living only on the island of Mindoro, is one of the most endangered. Although it has become nocturnal in order to escape the many hunters who stalk it for food or sport, its numbers have dwindled to about 100. The monkey-eating eagle is still worse off, being near extinction. For some reason, owning a stuffed specimen of this bird has become a status symbol in the Philippines and it is killed wantonly to supply the demand.

Two animals that are on the threatened species list partly because of their popularity in zoos are gibbons and orangutans. Unfortunately for both of these members of the ape family, hunters have found that the best way to capture a baby is to kill its mother. Without proper care and deprived of their mother's milk, many babies die before the zoos get them. It has been estimated that, in the case of gibbons, perhaps 100 animals die for every one baby delivered. Now getting rare for another reason connected with human demand is the big-headed tortoise of Thailand and Laos. It is captured in large numbers for sale as pets. The giant frog of Thailand owes its precarious position to still another aspect of human greed: people want its flesh as a delicacy for the dinner table.

Other animals in grave danger today in the Oriental region include the wild ass of the Gujarat peninsula of India, the sloth bear of the Deccan plateau forests of India, the Ceylon elephant, and the Burmese and Siamese thamin or Eld's deer.

Oriental Region: Southern Asia

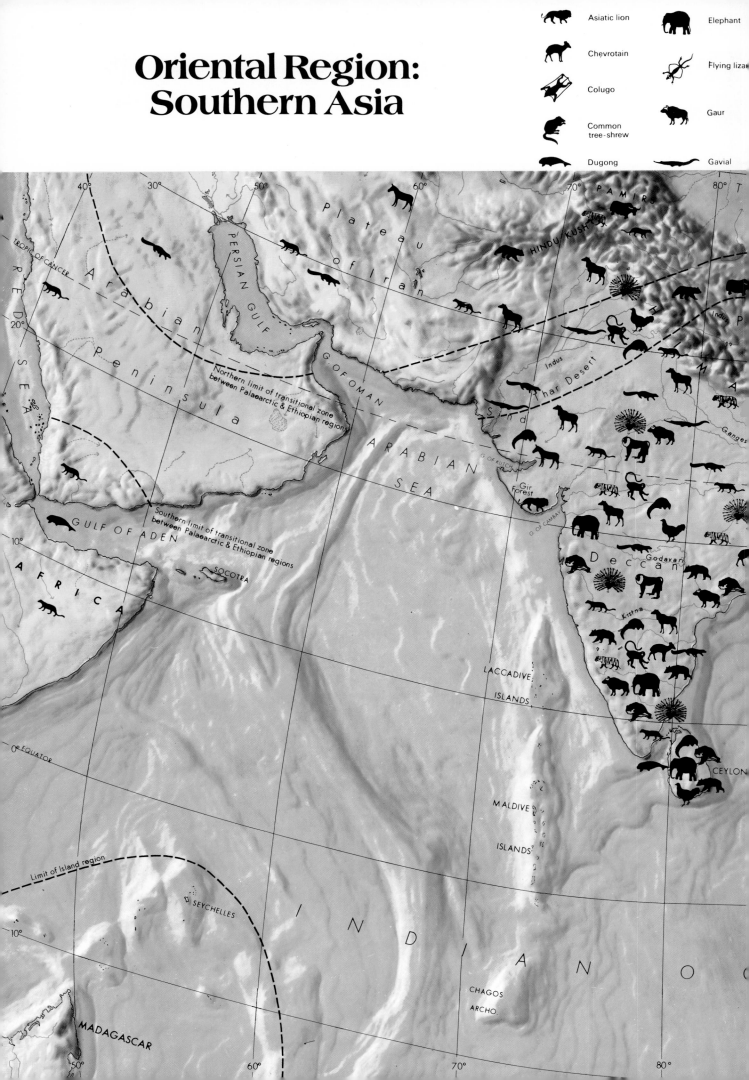

Legend (top right):

Asiatic lion		Elephant	
Chevrotain		Flying lizard	
Colugo		Gaur	
Common tree-shrew			
Dugong		Gavial	

Map labels:

Plateau of Iran · PAMIRS · HINDU KUSH · HIMA...

Persian Gulf · Indus · Thar Desert · Sind · G. OF OMAN · G. OF KUTCH · Gir Forest · G. OF CAMBAY · Ganges · Indus P...

TROPIC OF CANCER · 40° · 30° · 50° · 60° · 70° · 80° · T

Arabian Peninsula · ARABIAN SEA · Deccan · Godavari · Krishna

Northern limit of transitional zone between Palaearctic & Ethiopian regions

Southern limit of transitional zone between Palaearctic & Ethiopian regions

RED SEA · GULF OF ADEN · SOCOTRA · AFRICA

LACCADIVE ISLANDS · CEYLON

0° EQUATOR

MALDIVE ISLANDS

Limit of Island region · SEYCHELLES

INDIAN OCEAN

10° · 10° · 20°

CHAGOS ARCHO.

MADAGASCAR

50° · 60° · 70° · 80°

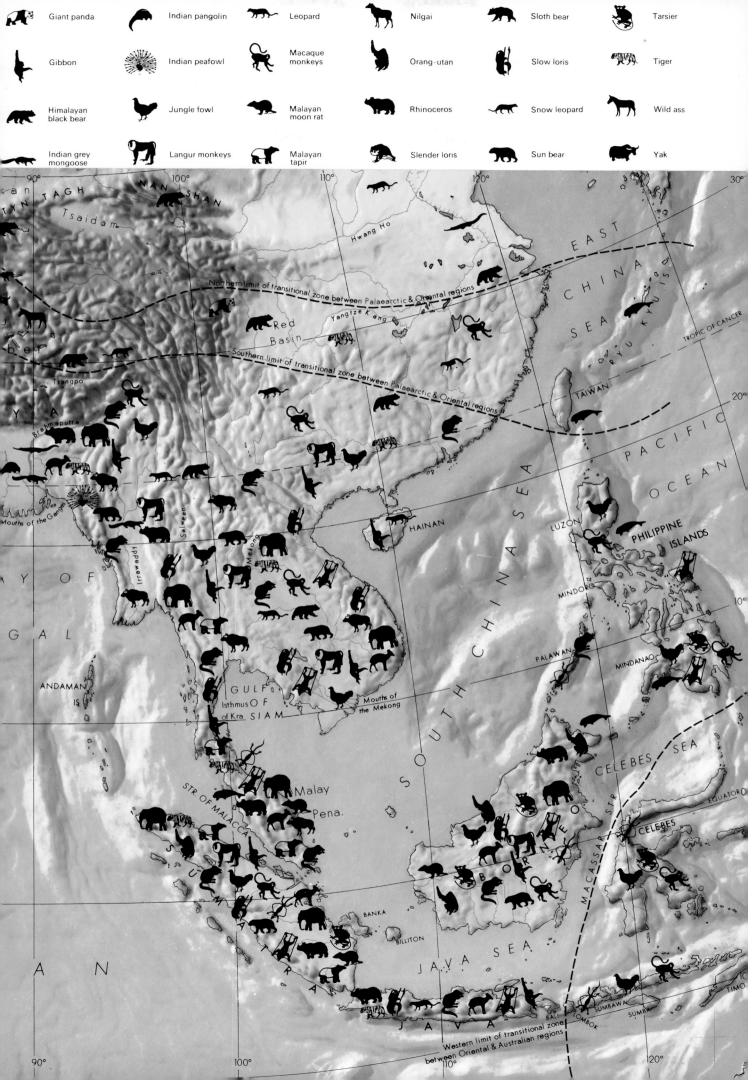

Giant panda Indian pangolin Leopard Nilgai Sloth bear Tarsier

Gibbon Indian peafowl Macaque monkeys Orang-utan Slow loris Tiger

Himalayan black bear Jungle fowl Malayan moon rat Rhinoceros Snow leopard Wild ass

Indian grey mongoose Langur monkeys Malayan tapir Slender loris Sun bear Yak

ALTYN TAGH NAN SHAN

Tsaidam

EAST CHINA SEA

Tibet

Tsangpo

Red Basin

Yangtze Kang

Northern limit of transitional zone between Palaearctic & Oriental regions

Southern limit of transitional zone between Palaearctic & Oriental regions

RYU KYU IS

TROPIC OF CANCER

HIMALAYA

Brahmaputra

TAIWAN

Mouths of the Ganges

Salween

PACIFIC OCEAN

Irrawaddy

Mekong

HAINAN

LUZON

MINDORO

PHILIPPINE ISLANDS

BAY OF BENGAL

ANDAMAN IS

GULF OF SIAM

Isthmus of Kra

Mouths of the Mekong

SOUTH CHINA SEA

PALAWAN

MINDANAO

CELEBES SEA

STR OF MALACCA

Malay Pena.

BORNEO

MACASSAR STR

CELEBES

EQUATOR

SUMATRA

BANKA

BILLITON

JAVA SEA

BALI LOMBOK

SUMBAWA

SUMBA

TIMOR

JAVA

Western limit of transitional zone between Oriental & Australian regions

90° 100° 110° 120°

The Himalayas

With the expansion of reliable air travel to what were once inaccessible reaches of the world, vacations in the Himalayas are today easily possible if expensive. Tourists can go to such relatively unknown places as Kashmir, Nepal, Sikkim, and Bhutan. This widening of travel has, however, aggravated the already serious threats to local wildlife.

Birds such as the beautiful western tragopan, a member of one pheasant family, are on the verge of extinction, and there are strong possibilities that the horned tragopan may already have disappeared. The survival of another species of pheasant, the monal, is put into question partly by the fact that its brilliant crest feathers are worn in their caps by some of the local militia. So far the more numerous wall creepers,

Above: blood pheasants in the snow 14,000 feet up in Nepal. These and other pheasant species are among the most colorful birds of the high forests of the Himalayas and nearby Asian ranges. In fact, the whole pheasant family is known for colorful plumage.

accentors, choughs, buntings, forktails, redstarts, and nutcrackers are holding their own.

Mammals such as the tahr, a goat-antelope, and the bharal or blue sheep are getting rarer. Another scarce mammal is the snow leopard or ounce. Although closely related to the common leopard, this elegant creature is a distinct species, different in color and markings and even more dissimilar as far as habits are concerned. About 3.5 feet long in the body, it is usually grayish or whitish on the back, though sometimes the color is more creamy. Its rosettes are dark and indistinct. The snow leopard's coat is thicker than the common leopard's, being about 2 inches long on its back and 4 inches on its belly and underside. The tail is about 1 yard long. Not only is this animal hunted

widely for its fur, but also it has to compete with wolves and sometimes bears for ever diminishing stocks of urials, hanguls, musk deer, gazelles, and wild boar.

Below the high peaks of the Himalayas lie dense forests of rhododendron in the west and bamboo in the east, which merge into tropical forest in the foothills. The range of the red or lesser panda of southern China's bamboo forests extends into the mountain ranges of northern Burma and Nepal. In both the

Right: the satyr tragopan is called that because of the male's horns, which resemble those of a goat. He uses these blue horns during the courtship ritual, spreading them wide, but they are otherwise not in evidence.

Left: there are three species of monal pheasants inhabiting the Himalayas. The colorful males are a shimmery green, blue, and purple on top with flashes of red and velvety black beneath. Some have yellow tails. The hens are mostly brown.

bamboo forests and thickets of rhododendron live the large surefooted takins, close relatives of the musk ox, which are used as food by the Chinese.

The tropical forests of the southern Himalayan foothills were once abundantly filled with wildlife. There were langur monkeys, Asiatic elephants, rhinoceroses, tigers, mongooses, and civets among the mammals. There was also a wide assortment of deer including the barasingha or swamp deer, hog deer, chital or axis deer, sambar, and Indian muntjac, known as the barking or rib-faced deer as well. As the forests have been cleared over the years to make room for more rice terraces and paddy fields, the original animal occupants have been robbed of their preferred habitat.

The Indian Plain

South of the fringe of the Himalayan tropical forest lies a plain that extends from west to east across the whole Indian subcontinent. This plain is formed by the valleys of the Indus, Ganges, and Brahmaputra rivers. The Indus and Ganges run from adjacent central points in Tibet, the Indus east and then southwest and the Ganges southwest and then southeast, both meeting to flow into the Bay of Bengal.

This plain falls into two distinct sections, the eastern part being very wet and the western extremely dry, merging into the Thar Desert. Only a few thousand years ago, this Great Indian Desert did not exist, being a thick tropical forest instead. Fossil evidence shows that water buffaloes, rhinoceroses, and elephants lived in it. Then the climate became much

Above: a female entellus langur rests in the fork of a tree. The langur monkey has a black face that contrasts with its whitish head, and body fur that is gray washed with buff or silver tones.

hotter, drying up the original rivers. The water table dropped and the lush vegetation died. Today the region is sandy throughout, but there is more vegetation than in the stonier Sahara.

Despite the dryness, there is an extensive animal population although much of it is rapidly disappearing. Many species migrated from other regions. According to a recent survey by an Indian zoologist, 56.4 percent of the mammals come from the Palaearctic region and 41 percent from other parts of the Oriental region. Only 2.6 percent of the desert animals are indigenous.

One species of gerbil, which migrated from other areas, was only discovered in 1965 and is now known as the Indian gerbil.

Among the species that have managed to adapt to the dry plains from their former woodland lifestyles are the bonnet macaque monkey, the chousingha or four-horned antelope, and the nilgai or blue bull. Bonnet macaques, which get their name from the cap-like formation of hair on their crowns, are widespread. The four-horned antelope gets its name from its two pairs of horns. This timid little antelope is a close cousin of the nilgai, the largest Indian antelope. Although once a popular target for hunters of old, this clumsy looking blue bull is twice fortunate today: it is considered by present day Muslims as not worth spending bullets on, and it is looked on as sacred by the Hindus because of its superficial resemblance to domestic cattle.

No such good luck has come the way of the swift-footed blackbuck, an antelope with spectacular spiral horns some 18 inches in length and a strange habit of jumping high into the air when running away from danger. Although this animal has been brought to the point of extinction in its native land, a few specimens were introduced into Texas some years ago and the herds there now number in excess of 5000.

Both the nilgai and the blackbuck obtain most of the water they require from their diet of leaves and grass. So also does the Indian gazelle or chinkara, sometimes known as Bennett's gazelle.

Preferring the somewhat more vegetated steppes and savannas that separate the Great Indian Desert from the rain forests are two species of deer and two of monkeys. One deer is the sambar, which is similar in shape to the European red deer but larger in size.

Above: leopards often take the remains of their kill into the trees in order to eat at leisure – and without having any ground scavengers around.

Left: rhesus monkeys perch nonchalantly on Swayambuth Temple in Katmandu, Nepal. They fear no harm from humans in many towns and cities of southern and eastern Asia because they are held sacred.

The other is the chital or axis deer, also known as the spotted deer because of its white-spotted coat. Of the two monkey species, the rhesus macaque is the most familiar of all the monkeys in the world. It has been widely used in medical and space research, in the first instance giving its name to the Rh factor in blood, in the second being among the first living creatures to be rocketed into space. On the other hand, the rhesus is considered sacred in some districts and is accordingly fed and protected. Even more venerated by Hindus is the entellus langur, a species of leaf-eating monkey also known as the sacred langur and hanuman. In Hindu beliefs this langur is connected with the monkey god Hanumān, so gaining its status as sacred.

The Asiatic lion, once widespread, is now confined to the Gir Forest in Gujarāt. This lion is now protected, but is still killed by local people because it feeds on the domesticated cattle that graze in the forest. In the arid region of northwest India known as the Little Rann of Kutch live the 700 or so remaining wild asses or hemiones. The Indian variety, known locally as the ghorkar, is paler than those found in equally sparse numbers elsewhere in Asia.

211

The Wet and Wooded Plains

In contrast with the parched Indus plain, the areas surrounding the Ganges and Brahmaputra rivers in the east of the subcontinent are extremely wet. Assam, the state immediately east of the Brahmaputra, is in fact one of the wettest places on earth. It is seasonally lashed by monsoon rains and has a mean annual rainfall of 472 inches. More than that, it is inundated every summer by enormous quantities of water created by the melting Himalayan snows. The terrain of this area varies from the grassy hills of north Bengal, which was called the "land of golden gardens" by 13th-century invaders from Burma, to the mixed swampy and wooded plains of Assam and the land around it. This wet area is rich in gorgeous flowers which, in addition to rhododendrons, azaleas, and wild roses, include orchids of incredible variety –

Above: orchids are abundant throughout the tropical regions, and India is no exception. All orchids have the same symetrical structure of flower, but vary greatly in petal shape and color.

from the famous lady's-slipper to the rare honey-scented kapauphul.

The whole of this region is particularly well stocked with deer, some species of which it shares with the Himalayan foothill area. Also still occasionally to be found is a race of the swamp deer, known in India as the barasingha, a word meaning "twelve points." This name does the barasingha's magnificent antlers an injustice inasmuch as they generally have from 14 to 16 points, and on occasion as many as 20. In common with so much of this region's wildlife, however, the barasingha has become very scarce, and it is possible that no more than 3000 remain in the marshes and open woodlands. Scarcer yet by far is a race of brow-antlered deer from the swamps of the neighboring state of Manipur, although this animal

has been protected by royal edict since 1891 and by government legislation since 1937. It is thought that less than 25 of these deer remain. The shins of their legs are horny and elongated, which helps them maneuver the thick mat of vegetation that invariably covers Lake Logtak, their last stronghold. How long they will be safe there is open to question because the rest of the lake outside their habitat was opened for shooting in 1953.

Considerably more abundant and widespread than either the barasingha or Manipur deer is the short-legged stocky hog deer, a cousin of the chital but with solitary habits. Another rare mammal of this area is the pygmy hog.

In contrast, birdlife is still rife in this region. There are francolins, black drongos or king crows, red-cheeked minivets, and red-cheeked bulbuls, among others. Favoring the more marshy areas are herons, the huge sarus crane which is looked on in India as a symbol of marital harmony, and the bald-headed, red-faced, red-whiskered marabou or adjutant stork that seems to walk with a military strut. While the rivers

Right: a group of chitals or axis spotted deer. These deer are found in the forests and forest edges, living in large herds. Their spotted bodies provide good camouflage in dappled sunlight.

Below: a black-headed bulbul that has been trapped for banding purposes. This Asian songbird is common in suburban, and even urban, gardens throughout its range. It is also popular as a pet.

still abound with gray pelicans and many kinds of teal and duck, one species no longer found is the pink-headed duck.

Inhabiting the waters of the rivers themselves are two large and unique aquatic animals. One of them, the Gangetic dolphin or susu, is a mammal. The other, the gavial or gharial, is a reptile and a specialized member of the crocodilians. These two animals, although poles apart genetically, have adapted similarly to deal with their diet of freshwater animals, predominantly crustaceans and catfish. Both possess long, narrow, beaklike jaws, ideal for probing the muddy river bottoms for food, and an array of about 120 strong sharply pointed teeth for trapping fish. The susu, which can measure up to 10 feet in length, is more or less blind, having lensless eyes, but its acute sense of smell is much more of an asset in the murky waters than good sight would be. The susu finds its way and its prey by a kind of radar system.

The fearsome looking gavial, which can grow to lengths exceeding 20 feet, is a scourge to fish, dispatching them with a quick sideways snap of its jaws.

Wildlife
of the Forest

Although Assam was once densely covered by luxuriant tropical forests from north to south, much of the forestation has been burned down or cleared to provide living space and timber for an ever growing population, and to make way for rice paddies, tea plantations, and other food cultivation. Nevertheless,

Right: tigers at their kill. This large striped cat is becoming increasingly rare as its habitat shrinks due to human expansion. In addition, there is much poaching to obtain its valuable fur.

Below: gaurs live in small herds that, except for the mating period, are composed of cows and calves. The bulls live separately, either singly or in small herds. These huge wild cattle have been domesticated, and in this state are known as gayals or mithans.

even today nearly a quarter of Assam is still forested. These woods provide an environment for a host of woodland species, of which some are widespread and others unique. The primates include the comparatively recently discovered and already endangered golden langur and the hoolock or white-browed gibbon; the reptiles include deadly snakes like Russell's viper; other mammals include the spotted linsang, which is related to the mongoose and genet.

Oddly enough, the wet forests of Assam are also the haunts of some species that would generally be considered too bulky to find movement among the thickly packed trees an attractive way of life. In fact, however, the area is the last stronghold of the great one-horned Indian rhinoceros. In addition to the rhino, there are ferocious Asiatic or water buffaloes with their 6.5-foot-long horns, and two more of the largest living Asian herbivores. These are the gaur and the Asiatic elephant.

The gaur, which favors the hillier regions of Assam, is at a height of 6 foot 4 inches at the shoulders the largest of living wild cattle, topping even the water buffalo by some inches. Despite its size, this animal, which is a close relative of the much smaller domesti-

cated gayal of Burma, is both very timid and very nimble on its feet when it feels threatened. Its legs are marked with white, just as though it were wearing white stockings.

The Asiatic elephant is smaller than the African bush elephant, the bull seldom achieving a shoulder height of more than 10 feet. It also possesses smaller ears, a less wrinkled trunk, a more domed forehead, and a trunk terminating in one "finger" instead of two. It is also more tractable and for many centuries has been tamed, trained, and exploited in all manner of ways, having been used as a beast of burden, a means

of transport, and a hewer of trees. The elephant's life span is about 70 years. Such a large animal has few enemies, but the Asiatic elephant seems to be in fear of the rhinoceros.

The most numerous of the three endangered Asiatic varieties of rhinoceros, the single-horned great Indian rhinoceros, itself numbers only some 900 in all. Of these, 400 lead protected lives in the Kaziranga Wildlife Sanctuary, a swampy 250-square-mile area just south of the Brahmaputra river. The Indian rhino is an inoffensive, retiring animal on the whole. On the rare occasions that it does go on the offensive, it does not use its single horn but slashes at its enemies with the sharp tusks in its lower jaw – a feature not shared by the African rhinoceros species. Like the African black rhino, however, the Indian variety is equipped with a pointed prehensile upper lip with which it browses among shrubs and bushes.

The delta of the Brahmaputra river in west Bengal is also a haunt of the 10-foot-long mugger or marsh crocodile. Unlike the gavial, the mugger is a true member of the crocodile family. In dry periods it will make long journeys overland in search of its diet of fish, birds, and mammals, including human beings.

The Deccan Plateau

South of the river plains lies the large triangular Deccan plateau which slopes gently eastward from the mountain range known as the Western Ghats to the Eastern Ghats. In contrast to the dry conditions of the plains to the north, the western side of the plateau gets heavy rainfall. Consequently it is covered in a lush mantle of monsoon forest, which in turn supports a richly varied animal life. The eastern side of the Deccan plateau is much drier except where the mountains are too low-lying to form an effective barrier against the southwesterly monsoon rains. The mean annual rainfall varies between 20 and 24 inches, and the landscape consists of thorn bush and acacia and jujube trees, with a predominance of grassy savanna.

Like the plains, these monsoon forests are well stocked with deer, all of them small varieties adapted to forest life such as axis deer, sambars, and muntjacs. In contrast to these diminutive animals are found Asiatic elephants and Asiatic buffaloes.

There is also the sloth bear which, like its Asiatic black cousin and the sun or honey bear, has a black coat with yellow patches on the snout and chest. The sloth bear's coat is much longer and shaggier. These animals spend their days sleeping in the trees or on convenient rocks and are active only at night. They have an awkward shamble on the ground and are slow moving like a sloth, from which they derive their name. Their diet consists of honey, fruit, and insects such as termites, ants, and bees whose nests they are adept at tearing apart with their large curved front claws. Sloth bears have long snouts that help them

Below: sloth bears can reach a size of 6 feet and a weight of up to 250 pounds. They move much faster than their name implies. Because of poor eyesight and hearing, sloth bears can be caught unaware and, when so started, react in a panic by attacking.

palm wine, and so get aggressively drunk. Sloth bears are unpredictable at all times, sometimes attacking humans and at other times ignoring them.

Among the small predators inhabiting these tropical forests is the widespread rasse or small Indian civet. This animal is so solitary that it associates even with others of its own species only for the purpose of mating, and then the female brings up her offspring alone.

The foxlike Asiatic wild dog or dhole, like its cousin the African hunting dog, is a fierce pack animal that ranges far and wide for its prey. Its habitat is extensive, stretching into Russia, Malaysia, Korea, and southern China. It usually feeds on deer and pigs although local villagers have reported that a dhole pack will go for anything including water buffaloes, sloth bears, and Himalayan black bears. Tigers and

Two civet species of the Oriental Region. The masked palm civet **(above)** is about 4.5 feet long and depends less on meat in its diet than the Indian civet or rasse **(below).** The Indian civet is carnivorous, eating such animals as snakes, birds, and frogs.

Above: the Asiatic species of chevrotain or mouse deer is known for its habit of creating tunnels through the grass or dense forest undergrowth. Chevrotains have a coat that is marked with both spots and stripes.

probe inside the nests, and they are able to seal off their nostrils while they suck up the insects. The noise they make while feeding can apparently be heard hundreds of feet away. Like the common palm civets and toddy cats or musangs of Burma and Malaysia, they sometimes steal the contents from the jars of sap the local inhabitants use to make their

leopards, which are probably the Indian forest's most notorious predators, are supposedly fearful of these canines and give them a wide berth.

The abundant and widespread leopard is one of nature's survivors, thriving even near humans. They are not afraid to enter villages, sometimes carrying off a chicken, dog, or possibly a sleeping person.

217

Unusual Animals of the Deccan

The forests of the western Deccan are the habitat of many unusual species. Of squirrel species alone there are giant flying squirrels, tiny striped palm squirrels, and large Malabar squirrels. There are also Malabar civets, brown mongooses, porcupines, spiny mice, and bandicoot rats. Among the several primates are the rare grizzle-bearded lion-tailed macaque, the Nilgiri langur, and the more primitive slender loris and tree shrews. Strangest of these forest creatures is a member of that family said to look like "animated pine cones," the pangolins, some species of which also live in the Ethiopian region.

To these mammals and many more must be added a great number of reptiles and a host of tree birds, some noisy and extravagantly colored. There are, for example, parakeets, barbets, and mynahs or Indian grackles, these last being far more accomplished at reproducing human speech than any parrot. Ground birds also abound, the most famous and beautiful of

Above: the Malayan pangolin is one of the smaller members of its family, being under 3 feet in length. It is a tree dweller.

Right: the India or blue peafowl is commonly known as the peacock. It is famous for its showy train or tail, which accounts for two thirds of its body length of up to 7.5 feet. The female of this species is the least colorful of the three species.

which is the Indian peacock with its huge train that becomes an enormous iridescent fan when it is spread to attract the drabbly feathered peahens. Of course this unshowy coloring is excellent camouflage for a female guarding eggs in a ground nest. Also to be found living on the forest floor is the bantamlike Indian jungle fowl, the ancestor of the domestic fowl.

The giant or Malabar squirrel, which measures over 3 feet in length, is a rodent of beautiful and varied coloration. Some are shiny black with light yellowish brown underparts. Others are deep red or shades of brown or bay, and still others have stripes or spots. Known locally as "tree dogs," they build large leaf-

lined nests of twigs high up in the trees. There they rear one or two young at a time, although several litters a year are reported. Malabar squirrels feed mainly on fruit, nuts, insects, bird's eggs, and bark of certain trees. The local species of flying squirrel, the nocturnal petaurista, is another giant, reaching nearly 3 feet in length. It sails rapidly down from branch to branch when gathering food or to escape from pursuing predators.

The Asiatic striped palm squirrel, an attractive little rodent that looks a bit like a chipmunk, is plentiful in these forests. Palm squirrels show little

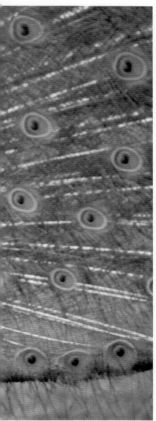

Above: a cobra and a mongoose square up for a fight – and it will probably be the mongoose that wins. This small relative of the civet and genet is known for its ability to kill snakes even twice as big as itself. It attacks the snake behind the head with such speed and tenacity that it seldom fails in the kill.

Above right: the red jungle fowl is one of four species, but is the one from which the domestic chicken came. Like domestic cocks and unlike its distant pheasant relatives, the male has a fleshy comb on the top of its head. It is a very cautious bird that stays carefully hidden in the forest.

Right: the flying squirrel calculates its flight pattern for taking off and landing and is able to land accurately at the spot it wants to. Just before reaching its destination, it puts its tail up, causing its head and body to also rise vertically. This brings its four feet into position so that it can cushion the force of the impact on touching down.

Above: a striped palm squirrel is only about 7 inches long in the head and body, but has a bushy tail of about the same length. Females may bear three times a year, giving birth to litters of from one to four. Babies grow to half the size of their parents by the time they are about two months old.

Right: the Nilgiri or John's langur has a yellowish crest that marks it as one of its colorful family. Langurs do not pay as much attention to rank within their groups, the dominant male usually behaving with benevolence. They spend a good deal of time on the ground after sunrise.

fear of humans, frequently living around forest settlements and becoming fairly tame when encouraged. They forage on the ground and in the trees during daylight for seeds, nuts, young bark, buds, and other small food items.

The lion-tailed macaque, which inhabits the forests in the mountains of the southwest, is unlike most monkeys in its preference for climbing down one tree and up the next rather than hopping from one to another. This highly intelligent monkey is also dissimilar from many of its near cousins in being shy and retiring.

The Nilgiri or John's langur is another monkey with the same restricted habitat as the lion-tailed macaque. Much more agile than macaques, langurs feed on leaves exclusively, processing this rough and monotonous diet in stomachs especially divided into three parts. Unlike the macaques, they do not possess

Above: the classification of tree shrews has long baffled zoologists. Some say they belong with true shrews, others that they are lower primates. Although there is still no full agreement among experts, tree shrews are usually put in a separate order.

cheek pouches for storing and carrying food.

A much less well developed local primate is the Madras tree shrew. Various species of tree shrew are to be found all over the Oriental region and, like lorises and tarsiers, are classed by the majority of zoologists as members of the prosimian suborder. Madras tree shrews are at first glance very like squirrels, having the same manner as a squirrel of sitting up and holding their food in their front paws to eat. However, they feed mostly on insects.

The slender loris has a curious though appealing appearance with matchstick legs, long slender fingers, small body, round little ears, and an expression that could be described as earnest and worried looking. It has the huge lambent eyes typical of nocturnal animals. When disturbed, the slender loris sways from side to side, growling and chattering. Although in the wild it feeds almost exclusively on insects, small birds, and lizards, in captivity it usually develops a partiality for fruit. Like bush babies, slender lorises take particular care of their bodies, scraping and combing their soft fur with their lower incisors and scratching themsleves with the special cleaning claws on their hind feet. Also in common with bush babies, they urinate constantly on their hands and feet to mark their territory.

Above: the slender loris measures about 10 to 15 inches long and has brownish gray fur with black circles around the large eyes. It has the ability to use its paws like clamps and cling to a tree branch in one position for a long time, like the pottos.

221

Other Deccan Animals

In the eastern part of the Deccan, human activity has helped change open woodland into short-grass savanna, and many of the animals that originally lived there have either become extinct or been driven to refuge elsewhere. Most of the remaining species are not in any way unique to this area. There are, for instance, gazelles, four-horned antelopes, nilgais, black-naped hares, and Indian gerbils. Several predators also roam the land, such as leopards, jungle and Bengal cats, hyenas, and wolves. There is also the little Bengal variety of fox, a low-slung, big-eared mammal that moves smoothly as if on casters on the hunt at night for small mammals and reptiles, insects and amphibia. Insect eaters include hedgehogs, bats, shrews, and the Indian pangolin.

However diminished the mammal population of this area may be, there is no shortage either of birds or of reptiles, particularly the latter. The profusion of

Above: the male paradise flycatcher helps in the incubation and feeding of its offspring. Flycatchers, of which the male is brightly colored, are adept at catching insects on the wing.

grain and seeds and the contour of the terrain also encourage the presence of many small seed-eating field birds, including the baya, manyar, and Bengal varieties of the weaver bird. Also found in these grasslands is the gorgeously hued little red avadavat, whose name is a corruption of the town of Ahmadabad from which they were first exported. The mannikin likes this open country because it feeds mainly on the

seeds of grasses. Among the insect-eating birds are pipets, chats, and drongos. Shrikes, which usually eat grasshoppers, crickets, and other large insects, have some characteristics of larger birds of prey, sometimes killing small vertebrates or even birds the same size as themselves for food. Their melodious calls seem out of keeping with their nickname of "butcher bird," which derives from their habit of storing their excess catches by impaling them on twigs, thorns, or spikes of barbed wire fences.

Among the larger birds of prey and scavengers encountered in this area are falcons, owls, buzzards,

Above: this shrike or butcherbird may decide not to eat the cricket it has caught and, if so, will probably impale it on a spike of the cactus it is perched on to save it for a later time.
Below: the male avadavat molts its bright plumage after mating and becomes more like the female, though it always retains a larger and more vivid patch of red on the rump. Avadavats are popular as cage birds and seem to do well in the captive state.

222

habitat – especially because the breeding pairs require a large territory in order to survive.

There are many venomous snakes in India, and they are responsible for numerous human deaths. In fact, out of the 25,000 people killed annually by animals in India, 20,000 die from attacks by poisonous snakes. The fact that the cobra is revered by Hindus probably accounts for its survival in spite of its being so highly venomous. The king cobra can reach lengths of 16 feet. Its smaller cousins the blue and banded kraits are only a quarter of that size but equally poisonous. No less dangerous are Asiatic coral snakes and some of the vipers. These include the saw-scaled variety which, when disturbed, issues an audible warning by scraping its scales together.

Harmless snakes are even more plentiful than venomous ones, some of them, like skunks, defending themselves by foul-smelling emissions from their anal

Left: a cobra with its neck inflated rises from the basket of a Bombay snake charmer. The street performer is taking an obvious risk because cobras cause many human deaths in his country.
Below: a Wagler's pit viper. There are 60 species of pit vipers, among which are some of the most dreaded snakes in the world. Pit vipers concentrate on hunting warm-blooded animals because they can detect such animals by means of the pits on their head.

vultures, and kites. In the more populated areas the pariah or black kite is much in evidence. It has become a fearless raider in towns, often seen perched on rooftops or telegraph poles or circling overhead.

The great Indian bustard, a large mainly vegetarian bird, is now officially classified as endangered. This is due in part to its being an easy target for hunters, but even more to the increasing encroachment on its

glands. There are also primitive burrowing snakes equipped with a flattened, spadelike scale at the end of their tail, and tiny blind worm-eating snakes. One of the most unusual is the egg-eating snake. It can distend its mouth and throat so much that it can swallow eggs four times the size of its body's circumference. Inside its throat are bony projections of the spine that break the eggshell on the way down.

223

A Varied Wildlife

Between the Indian subcontinent and China lies a large peninsula stretching some 1800 miles from north to south, bounded by the Szechwanese mountains on the north, the Bay of Bengal on the west, and the South China Sea on the east. Its southern extremity forms another narrow peninsula, the Malayan.

Geologically much younger than the Indian subcontinent, this region consists essentially of three distinct types of country: marshy lowlands, hills and mountains densely covered with tropical forest, and a large area of tall-grass savanna or open woodland.

The grassland is the home of large ungulates and other herbivores and is eminently suitable for them, the grasses providing ample food and the trees safe shelter. Because the soil is so poor, it is not likely that they will be driven out to make way for cultivated crops or timber.

The deer population of these areas is of wide variety, ranging from the tiny chevrotain (not a true deer) up to the large sambar, sometimes known as Aristotle's deer. Unique to this part of the world is the thamin or Eld's deer, one of two species known as brow-antlered deer. This animal, about 3 feet high at the shoulders and weighing about 220 pounds, has delicate lyre-shaped antlers that are popular among trophy hunters.

The wild cattle to be found in these partly tree covered grasslands include large herds of water buffalo, gaurs, and two species not encountered elsewhere, the banteng and the kouprey.

The banteng is a close if smaller relative of the gaur,

Above: the Thamin or Eld's deer of Manipur State in India is extremely rare today, and those living in the area from Thailand to the South China Sea island of Hainan have been greatly reduced in number; those of Burma are not endangered as yet.
Below: bantengs are found in Burma, Vietnam, Java, Borneo, and Bali. They have been fully domesticated on the islands of Java and Bali, where they are the common form of livestock.

and has the same white markings that look like stockings on its legs. Physically this animal resembles European domestic cattle more than its relatives among the wild cattle, and also provides meat pleasing to humans. Despite its wariness and excellent sight and hearing, it is now almost extinct in certain areas.

Little is known about the kouprey, of which there are only between 70 and 200 left. What is known about them has caused a certain amount of disagreement among naturalists. They possess lyre-shaped horns similar in construction to and almost as big and spreading as the buffalo, and their general coloration is similar to that of the water buffalo. But other features are closer to different cattle. For instance, they are almost as big as the gaur and, like that animal and the banteng, are white-legged. They also have the dewlaps found in domestic breeds, particularly the domesticated zebus of India. These mixed characteristics have led some zoologists to the conclusion that the kouprey is a hybrid rather than a species in its own right.

The birdlife of this area's open woodlands is colorful, diverse, and interesting, ranging from the huge

Above left: looking somewhat like a twig among leaves, this leech is ready to attach itself to any passing animal for a meal of blood. Leeches of southeast Asia are known to attack humans.
Above right: this sunbird demonstrates some of the brilliant coloring that makes them likened to hummingbirds. There are 104 species, half of which live in Asia and half in tropical Africa.
Below: one of the sunbirds that lacks bright plumage is known as a spider hunter in Southeast Asia. It is not known to eat spiders.

sarus cranes and giant ibises to the little sunbirds. Although not even remotely related to the hummingbirds of the New World, they share some common characteristics such as dazzling coloration and a diet of small insects and flower nectar. They are even able to feed on the wing occasionally but, being less adept at flying than hummingbirds, generally prefer to perch on or beside the flower from which they are feeding. Closely related to the sunbird is the little spider hunter which, in spite of its name, has the same diet as its cousin. It thrives on the nectar of banana blossoms. This long-billed, 6-inch bird constructs a unique cup-shaped nest from vegetable fibers, which it stitches to the underside of a broad leaf so as to give the nest a roof.

There are many other species of bird including lapwings, nuthatches, bulbuls, and parakeets as well as several varieties of mynah. One of these is the crested mynah, locally called the "buffalo blackbird" from its liking for riding on the backs of these animals to feed on their parasites. Another is the black-necked variety of mynah.

Above: a red-crowned parakeet. Parakeets are called by many different names, both popularly and scientifically, so that it is difficult to be exact. There is also much confusion as to which members of the parrot family should actually be called parakeets.

Forest Dwellers of Southeast Asia

From Szechwan, China, in the north to the southern-most ends of Thailand, Cambodia, and Vietnam runs a series of roughly parallel mountain ridges. Although these highlands never exceed much more than 6500 feet, their peaks are covered with heather, vegetation more typical of temperate zones than of tropical climates. Even at lower altitudes of from 5000 to 6500 feet the forests are still untropical in character, generally consisting of pine trees. Below this height, however, is the typical tropical jungle consisting of an amazing variety of trees, vines, bamboos, and epiphytes or air plants such as orchids and bird's-nest ferns. Plant fertility is so great that areas once cleared for cultivation and then neglected will revert to a state of wild growth after only a couple of years. An example of this can be seen in the ancient city of Angkor, which until the 14th century was the capital of the Khmer Empire in what is now Cambodia. Abandoned for some unknown reason, it was so totally overgrown by thick tropical forest that it was only rediscovered at the turn of the 20th century.

The ruins of Angkor provide an ideal refuge for wildlife, although the animals are sometimes killed as a measure to protect the city's ancient temples. Large millipedes, brilliant butterflies, and strange lizards are found among the ruins. Lizards of one species are known colloquially as "bloodsuckers" because of the

Above: millipedes live in cracks, leaf mold, and moist soil, all of which are available in Angkor. Although some species have no eyes, their general body surface is probably sensitive to light.

Above: the reticulated python is one of the largest snakes in the world and the largest of its species, reaching a length of 33 feet. Pythons are able to consume animals of the size of a medium-sized deer, but usually are satisfied with smaller prey.

Below: a stone ruin in the ancient Khmer city of Angkor, also called Angkor Thom. Believed to have been a city of one million people, Angkor took up five square miles and had a wall and moat Now a great tourist attraction, the ruins shelter many animals.

way they change from green to dark red when locked tooth to neck in combat with one another. The golden tree snake now and then glides down from the trees to the ground while the paradise tree snake, a close relative found more frequently in Malaya, turns the underside of its body into a kind of parachute and floats to earth. Also inhabiting the trees are other gliding animals, such as flying lizards and flying frogs, and many nongliding reptiles including the green whip snake and the pit vipers. Pit vipers, which are nocturnal, are members of the same family as

rattlesnakes. They have specialized nerve complexes, situated in pits behind their nostrils, that are especially sensitive to heat. These enable the snake to detect the animals it preys upon by their body warmth. Two dangerous snakes that live on the forest floor are the deadly 5-foot-long Russell's viper and the reticulated python. This python attains lengths of over 30 feet, making it a rival to the South American anaconda as the world's largest snake.

There are also bats galore, both insect-eating and fruit-eating. The kalong, whose wingspan can exceed 5 feet, is the largest bat in the world. Known as flying foxes, kalongs live almost entirely on fruit, sucking out the juice of mangoes and guavas and ejecting the pulp. Fruit-eating bats are great travelers, often flying as far as 30 miles to feed on newly ripened fruit elsewhere.

The trees are also the home of the colugo, sometimes known as the flying lemur although it cannot fly and is not a lemur. These animals, of which there are but two species, are the only living members of an order whose name means "skin-winged." At night they glide from their resting places high in the trees to feed on the fruit, flowers, leaves, and buds of lower trees. At dawn they climb back up to the treetops by means of their sharp curved claws.

227

Predators of the Forest

The abundance of prey in the tropical forests of southeast Asia, including many species of deer, cattle, tree, ground and flying squirrels, and a large number of primates, naturally attracts a wide variety of carnivorous predators. Many of these are feline – leopards including the very rare, very beautiful clouded leopard, leopard cats, Temminck's golden cats, and jungle, fishing, and marbled cats. Nonfelines include the sun bear, wild dogs, mongooses, linsangs, bin-

turongs and small masked civets, although in general these smaller predators eat other food besides meat.

In addition to the animals that require substantial quantities of meat, there are those whose staple fare is predominantly insects. Among these are many species of shrew of which one, the tiny musk shrew, is called the "money shrew" by the Chinese because its rapid high-pitched call sounds like chinking coins. There is also the eastern mole, earless and almost sightless, which burrows deep with its specialized claws in search of worms and grubs.

The black panther is another predator of the humid forests. It is not, as is sometimes supposed, a distinct cat species, but merely the black or dark form of the common leopard. In fact, this animal has the same

Above: the black panther is in fact a leopard with different coloration from the more familiar tawny and spotted one. Sometimes the black and spotted ones are born in the same litter.
Left: there are 170 species of shrews and they live everywhere except in the polar regions and Australasia. They are the smallest mammals alive and, because small bodies lose heat more rapidly than large, they must keep constantly on the move to keep stoking themselves with food as the only way to keep warm.

Left: the leopard cat is much smaller than the leopard after which it is named because of its spotted coat. Its spots are solid rather than rosette, however. This cat resembles the leopard in its habits as well as in its appearance.

Right: the golden cat has several variations of color including gray, rosettes, and stripes. Found both in India and Sumatra, it also lives in other parts of Asia as far north as Tibet.

Below: in contrast to the subdued coloring that gives it its name, the clouded leopard has sharply defined markings on its face. It is thought that this might have a hypnotizing effect on prey.

pattern of rosettes although they are hard to discern against the black background of its coat. It also leads the same lonely nocturnal life as leopards.

The clouded leopard is not a very near relative of the true leopard, although it also is a skillful climber and leads a solitary night existence among the tree branches in the thickest fastnesses of the jungles near river banks by preference.

The richly hued Temminck's golden cat is one of the few unpatterned members of the cat family, but even it has black stripes on its cheeks and lines above its eyes. The rare marbled cat, like Temminck's golden cat, is about 2 feet long. Fishing cats frequent the swampier areas. Some experts claim that the fishing cat has never been seen to catch or eat fish, but the theory that it does gets some support by the fact that the animal has slightly webbed toes. Most common of all the small wildcats in these areas is the jungle cat, which inhabits the drier less thickly wooded areas of the forests. No bigger than a domestic cat, these felines will go for anything from an insect to a small deer.

Almost as much tree lovers as the cats are several varieties of civet. One of these, the spotted linsang, is catlike in more ways than one. It has claws that can

Right: the masked civet is found from Borneo north to China. It is an excellent climber and is also good at catching fish.

Below: the binturong or bear cat often reaches 5 feet in length. In spite of its ferocious appearance it is more of a vegetarian than a meat eater. Its bushy tail makes up about half its length.

be retracted into sheaths, and it hunts by stalking its prey stealthily until it can make a lithe leap at an opportune moment. Civets are as a rule much less restricted to a meat diet than cats, and will eat almost anything when very hungry. This is particularly true of the strange binturong, which is sometimes called the bear cat. The binturong is not only the largest member of the civet family but is also the hairiest, its fur being in demand for human wear. It is also the only Old World placental mammal with a fully functioning prehensile tail, useful for braking when the animal decides to descend head first from a tree.

There are also some representatives of the closely related mongooses in these forests, including the crab-eating mongoose. Snake-eating mongooses often attack reptiles much larger than themselves, seizing them by the neck with a speed that shocks them, then killing them. Mongooses are not immune to snake venom, however.

The sun bear, at a mere 4 feet from its nose to its

2-inch tail and only 100 pounds in weight, is the smallest living bear. Like the Asiatic black and sloth bears, its black coat is relieved by a yellowish muzzle and a yellow crescent on its chest. The chest marking is thought to resemble the rising sun, and so gives the animal its name. It is also sometimes known as the honey bear because of its extreme fondness for that food, its long tongue and flexible lips being well suited for extracting the contents of bees' nests.

Above: the crab-eating mongoose attains a head and body length of about 2 feet with a tail of almost the same size. Although it is not aquatic, this species gets much of its food from water.

Right: the Malayan sun bear is also known as the bruang and the honey bear, the last name coming from its liking for honey. Its habitat is in tropical and subtropical forests, it is a good tree climber, and it does not hibernate like most other bears.

Oriental Primates

The primate group is very well represented in the Oriental region. There are monkeys, apes, lorises, tarsiers, and some dozen and a half different species of tree shrews, ranging all over the region from the western coast of India to the East Indies and the Philippines and inhabiting forest and scrubland.

Tree shrews show definite differences in habit and behavior from one species to the next. Some are aggressive loners, others are social animals that live together in sexually mixed groups of between eight and 12. The widespread common tree shrew lives either alone or in pairs. The female builds a separate nest for her young, suckles them only once every 48 hours, and returns to sleep with her mate in between. The babies, usually twins, remain content for this long period because they gorge themselves at each feeding. Although the majority of the species are tree dwellers, a few like the terrestrial and Philippine tree shrews, nest in holes on the ground.

The lorises of the Oriental region are members of the same family as the potto, angwantibo, and bush babies of Africa. The tarsiers, however, form a family unique to the islands of the south China Sea. There are three species of tarsier: the western of Sumatra and Borneo, the eastern of the Celebes, and the Philippine of those islands. They live mainly in the lower shrub layers of the forests and are amazingly accomplished acrobats, jumping as much as 6 feet in one bound in their branch-to-branch search for small vertebrates, insects, and insect larvae. The adhesive suction pads

Above: the Philippine tarsier is a nocturnal primate that feeds mainly on insects. Its powerful legs can launch its tiny body on leaps that carry it up to six feet. Its name comes from the fact that it has a lengthened tarsus or ankle section on its hindlegs.

Above: the proboscis monkey lives only in Borneo and is named from the large bulbous nose of the male. This nose can be as long as 3 inches and makes the animal look startlingly human.

on their fingertips allow them to cling to the smoothest of surfaces. These 6-inch-long, 6-ounce animals have huge astonished looking eyes that serve their nocturnal life well. In addition, tarsiers are able to swivel their heads in a wide arc of 180°. Tarsiers do not seem to build nests like others of their species, but instead sleep clinging vertically to stalks, stems, and thin tree trunks with an almost inextricable grip.

Slow lorises are close cousins to the much smaller slender loris. These animals, of which there are two species, occur in southeast Asia, Sumatra, Java, and Borneo. The lesser variety of the species is much more restricted in range. Although just as tenacious of grip as tarsiers, lorises are slow and deliberate. They move silently among the tree tops, often along the underside of the branches, stalking insects and small vertebrates with a hand-over-hand action.

The monkey population of this area is varied and in some cases striking. Among the noisy and aggressive macaques are the short-bodied, long-tailed crab-eating macaques. They live in groups of between 14 and 70, about 20 being most common, with two or three females to every male. The almost tailless Celebes monkeys are generally regarded as related to the macaques although they are known variously as black or Celebes apes, while local residents refer to them as baboons and consider them sacred. Among leaf-eating monkeys are the widespread silvered leaf monkey, the capped langur, and the douc langur of Vietnam which was much reduced in number during the recent war.

Probably one of the most interesting and strange looking of all animals is the proboscis monkey whose nose is distinctive and startling. A native of the forests of Borneo, it is related to other species such as

232

the pig-tailed langur and snub-nosed monkeys. Only the males develop the large nose, which becomes so long that it hangs down over the mouth and chin. It also flushes and swells when the normally placid 4- to 5-foot-long animals are angered.

Two of the four types of ape live in the Oriental region: the gibbon, of which there are seven species, and the orangutan of Sumatra and Borneo, which is now endangered.

The highly vocal gibbons, whose shrieking, chattering, and booming is amplified by special inflatable vocal sacs in the throat, are the least highly developed of the apes. Living almost exclusively among the trees, they usually travel by swinging hand over hand from branch to branch, often leaping distances of as much as 50 feet without mishap.

Above: orangutans are the only great apes found in the wild outside Africa. They now exist only in Borneo and Sumatra, although they may once have been common throughout Asia. Orangutans seldom come out of the trees.

The orangutan, which is Malayan for "man of the woods," is the only non-African great ape. It leads a family life very similar to that of the gorilla and chimpanzee, but is more like the gibbons in being better suited for a life in the trees. Orangutans are not well adapted to walking upright although they occasionally do. These gentle animals have been brought to the edge of extinction in the wild even though trade in them is illegal and reserves have been established. Zoos, in which this popular animal breeds fairly well, will not buy from illegal traders, but poaching seems to go on nonetheless.

Malayan Animals

The Malayan peninsula and the islands of the neighboring archipelago, while the home of many animals found elsewhere in southeast Asia, are also the habitat of several unique species. One is the Malayan tapir, whose nearest relatives live in South America. Remnants of a much wider distribution which once extended across North America and Europe, these two isolated groups have diverged remarkably little over the ages. The main differences between them are superficial: the Malayan tapir's coat is black with a white saddle over its hindquarters, while the three South American species are a uniform deep brown, with minor variations depending on the species.

Two other creatures unique to this area are the otter civet and the Malayan moon rat. The otter civet is a true civet which, through adaptation to suit its river habitat and predominantly fish diet, has come to resemble the otter, although lacking the otter's well-developed webbed feet and powerful tail. Unlike otters, however, it sometimes climbs trees looking for fruit which balances its diet.

The Malayan moon rat is a whiskered insectivore whose narrow body and long mobile snout allow it to search in crevices for its insect food. Despite its name and somewhat ratlike appearance, the Malayan moon rat is in fact a gymnure or hairy hedgehog, a subfamily confined to southeast Asia whose members all lack the sharp spines of true hedgehogs. Also unlike true hedgehogs, the moon rat, which is the largest living insect eater, has a splendid 8-inch-long ratlike tail. Under its base are anal glands that produce a repellent odor, said to be like rotting meat.

At least four kinds of badger are also found in this region. These include the hog badger, the Malay badger, the Philippines badger, and a variety of ferret badger. The hog badger is sometimes known as the sand badger, and although more like the common Eurasian badger than the others, has longer legs and a more piglike snout. The Malay badger or teledu is smaller, and is covered in long brown fur with a skunklike white stripe running the length of its back from head to tail. It also possesses the skunklike ability to defend itself against enemies by squirting an offensive fluid from its anal glands for relatively long distances. The stinking badger, as it is sometimes called, also has webbed toes on its forefeet to aid in burrowing. But the ferret badger, though looking even more like a skunk than the teledu, lacks its defense mechanism.

Of the two particularly endangered species of the already depleted Asian rhinoceros, the Sumatran rhino is the smallest member of its family. Like its African cousins it bears two horns, and unlike its Asian relatives it has a smooth hide from which

sprout clumps of coarse hair, giving rise to its local name of "buffalo rhinoceros." It is estimated that some 150 of these are scattered through the dense forests where they are still threatened by hunters seeking their horns. The single-horned Javan rhino-

Above: like its cousins in South and Central America, the Malayan or Asiatic tapir is stoutly built, weighing between 500 and 700 pounds. It has a short trunk, a stub tail, and bristly fur.

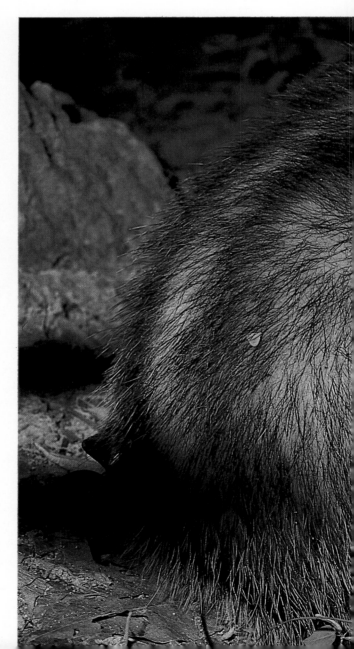

ceros is even rarer – only 40-odd survivors inhabit a special reserve in western Java. Like its larger Indian cousin, this species is covered with dark gray granular skin that is thickly folded to look like armor plating.

The silver-whiskered Bornean wild boar is the staple food of the area. These wild boars are reputed to undertake occasional mass migrations, after which they may appear in regions where they have not been seen for many years. They are ferocious.

Also present in these areas are the three species of tarsier – the only entirely carnivorous primate – as well as orangutans and monkeys such as the pig-tailed macaque, which is sent by humans to climb up coconut palms and collect the nuts. The birds include such widely differentiated species as hornbills, known for their huge bills, and spider hunters.

Inhabiting the tropic seas around Malaysia are not only the dugong, a sea cow related to the manatee of the New World, but also an abundance of marine reptiles. These range from the highly poisonous sea-snakes to the migratory green turtle whose eggs and flesh are considered great delicacies, and the hawks-bill turtle whose horny plates provide the tortoise shell used in ornaments and combs.

Above: a female green turtle works laboriously at night to dig a sand pit in which she will conceal up to 1000 eggs to hatch. In spite of an aquatic life, sea turtles lay their eggs on land.

Below: the hog badger resembles the European badger, but has a longer tail and a snout like a pig's, which gives it its name.

Between Two Regions

Strung out like stepping stones between the Oriental region and Australia lies a series of islands. East of Malaya are the large islands of Sumatra, Java, and Borneo, and a maze of smaller islands between them and New Guinea. These islands include the legendary Moluccas – the "spice islands" whose plant life includes the nutmeg and clove trees that made Europeans fight over possession of the islands once they were discovered in the 15th century. In the 19th century they became the center of another exotic trade – supplying feathers for the hats of women who

he was struck by the amazing difference in their animal populations. Although these islands lie close to each other, they are separated by a deep water trench. Of course, birds could fly across and mammals were often transported from one island to another by human beings, but in the main the animals on either side of this channel are strikingly dissimilar. The Oriental and Australian regions are still divided through this channel by an imaginary line known as Wallace's Line. To the west of the line are found carp and other Eurasian freshwater fish; such typically Oriental birds as bulbuls; and mammals such as porcupines, macaques, and civets. To the east are the colorful birds typical of the Australian region, the cockatoos and birds of paradise, whose tail-feathers were so much a part of 19th-century fashion, as well as the curious large-footed brush turkeys or megapodes

wanted to be in the fashion swing.

These islands are interesting biologically as well as romantically, in that they provide a link between the typically Oriental animals and the very different fauna of the Australian region. It was while collecting animals in this area that Alfred Russel Wallace, 19th-century British naturalist, realized that the world could be divided into regions according to the animals that lived there. He began speculating on why these regions should contain different fauna – a train of thought that led him to the theory of evolution. His moment of truth came while traveling between two minor islands of Indonesia, Lombok and Bali, when

and pouched mammals or marsupials such as the furry cuscus and the long-clawed tree kangaroo.

In addition, these islands and the neighboring Philippines are the home of several unique animals. Celebes is the habitat of several species of monkey that are rather baboonlike in appearance as well as the moor macaque, which differs from the macaques of the mainland in having a thick coat of long black hair and no tail. Unique varieties of squirrel and civet exist there along with the babirusa, a long-legged almost hairless pig with spectacular curled tusks. A miniature relative of the buffalo found only on Celebes is the anoa, which is so small that it more nearly

Above: the huge Komodo dragon is a monitor lizard that lives on the Indonesian islands of Komodo and Flores. Its heavy body is grayish brown with red circles all over, and its powerful tail is about the same length as the body and head put together.
Left: the anoa is a dwarf buffalo which, at a height of about 3 feet, is the smallest of all cattle. In spite of its size, it has a reputation for aggressiveness. There are only two species and both of them are found on the Indonesian island of Celebes.

resembles an antelope than a buffalo. An animal unique to the Philippine island of Mindanao is the very rare monkey-eating eagle, a powerful bird that preys on mammals, birds, and reptiles of all sizes.

Island life has apparently encouraged the evolution of insects of ever-increasing size. There are a number of giant iridescent birdwings, the most majestic of all butterflies, and each island sports its own distinct species. There is also a giant beetle whose larvae are considered locally to be a delicacy. Another animal of giant proportions is the Komodo dragon, the largest living reptile, which is actually a lizard.

The existence of the Komodo dragon had been reported by Malayan fishermen for years, but these rumors had been discounted until 1912 when a pioneer Dutch aviator landed accidentally on Komodo Island and found himself surrounded by enormous dragon-like reptiles. He had little more success than the Malayans in getting his story accepted by scientists when he returned to Java. Nevertheless a Dutch officer was sent to the island to investigate, and he returned with the remains of two of the beasts. After this confirmation of their existence, hunters arrived to try to exploit the reptiles for trade, but the Sultan of Bima intervened and issued orders protecting these animals.

Although they are about 10 feet in length, weigh up to 350 pounds, and are voracious and strong, Komodo dragons do not attack human beings. They do, however, hunt mammals as large as pigs and are also scavengers. They have been known to eat a whole deer, bones and all, so freshly killed deer is often put out as bait to attract the huge lizards.

Chapter 7

The Australian Region

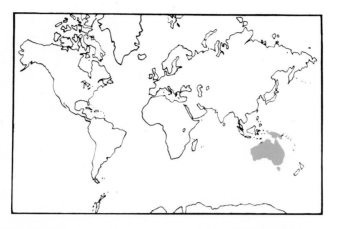

Australia, Tasmania, New Guinea, and the Celebes, Moluccas, and Lesser Sunda Islands that neighbor it make up the Australian region, although the smaller islands form a transitional zone between the Australian and Oriental regions. Like the Islands that are treated separately, this region is completely cut off from all others by sea. Most authorities agree that it has probably been separate for a period of 200 to 500 million years. This long isolation has meant that the animals of the region have had a different evolutionary pattern from animals in other parts of the world. That is why Australia has many unique animals, especially among its mammals.

Almost all of Australia's mammals are marsupials, ranging in size from the tiny flat-skulled marsupial mouse that is only 3.75 inches including the tail to the large kangaroo that reaches a height of 6 feet. Neither marsupials nor monotremes, which are the other indigenous mammals of the region, have the same method of nourishing their unborn young, nor of giving birth to them, as the more common placental mammals found elsewhere in the world.

The bearded dragon or bearded lizard is found all over Australia except in the northwest, but it is most numerous in the eastern part of the continent. It is unusual among lizards in that it can remain active at lower temperatures than most of its family as the result of being able to store heat from sun bathing. A bearded dragon living in a dry region will have richer coloring than one living where it is damp. It will use color changes as a way of self-protection.

Man's Impact

Humans made their first appearance on the Australian mainland some 20,000 to 30,000 years ago with the coming of the people now called the aborigines. Before that the land had not felt the tread of any human foot. It is even possible that these first human invaders saw the last of the giant marsupials, including the giant kangaroo and marsupial lion.

These human newcomers subsisted largely on a simple diet consisting of lizards, grubs, and wild berries, and did not consume more than the land could amply yield. One of the few meat dishes in their

Below: after the European rabbit was introduced to Australia by early settlers, a method of control was looked for because of its effect on grasslands and crops. It was not until an epidemic of myxomatosis was deliberately started that the rabbits died off.

cuisine seems to have been roast emu, which was cooked in a sealed heated pit. The bird's head was left attached to its buried body, sticking up out of the ground like a periscope.

The next wave of human inhabitants came in the late 18th century with the arrival of British prisoners sent as settlers. They brought their own familiar staple crops and livestock at such an accelerating rate that many of the native animals and plants soon dis-

appeared. In New South Wales alone about one third of the woodland was destroyed in the first 100 years of the Europeans' presence, giving way to farms and grazing lands. Of the 52 species of marsupials once present in this state, 11 of them are now extinct.

Another early blow to the ecosystem was the introduction of the prickly pear from South America toward the end of the 18th century for the purpose of providing red dye for soldiers' uniforms. The red dye came from cochineal insects that lived on the cactus. The plant thrived to such an extent that it soon ran rife, covering some 60 million acres of land, and another South American insect, the cactoblastis, had to be brought in especially to inhibit its further spread.

Later on the wild gray rabbit was also introduced to Australia and, even more rapidly than the prickly pear, became a pest amounting almost to a plague. Foxes were therefore imported to combat the rabbits, but instead multiplied and became a menace in their

Left: the Australian water buffalo is an example of conservation by means of utilization. This animal, once indiscriminately shot for its hide alone, is now farmed for use in a thriving buffalo meat industry.

Below: early explorers of Australia's interior desert decided to use camels as pack animals because of their low water requirements. Some of them went wild and their descendants still live in the wild state.

own right. Finally, as a last desperate measure to curb the rabbits, myxomatosis, a contagious virus disease, was deliberately introduced. It spread like wildfire and the gray rabbit was brought to the verge of extinction, although it has now reestablished itself to some extent.

Horses, asses, water buffaloes, and pigs, introduced as domestic animals, have returned to the wild state in some areas of Australia. The camel has also become feral in the central Australian desert, after 20 of them were brought into the country in the 19th century as animals for exploration into the interior.

Although the smallest continent, Australia is a huge country almost as big as the United States of America. Fully one third of the country is arid and unsuitable for any form of land use. In spite of this, Australia ranks as one of the world's major exporters of wheat, wool, meat, and dairy products – an indication of the intense kind of use of domesticated stock

241

and available land that poses a threat to wildlife.

What European settlers gained on the introduction of certain animal and plant life, Australia lost on the damage to its indigenous fauna and flora.

However, it is possible that the first victims of the human presence were the Kangaroo Island emu and the thylacine, which were exterminated by the aborigines on the mainland. The doglike thylacine is in fact a marsupial, believed to have been displaced by the more efficient and aggressive dingoes brought over by the aborigines about 6000 years ago. The thylacine flourished to such an extent in Tasmania that 2268 were killed off between 1888 and 1914 because of its predatory activities. Reports differ as to its present status, but it is not yet extinct and is now protected by law. Besides these two instances, the aborigines had no adverse effect on the ecosystem.

Since the European presence, however, more and more of the original animals have become endangered. Two species of rat kangaroo, four of bandicoot, the

Below: although there is no real way to tell a wallaby from a kangaroo, it is generally accepted that wallabies are smaller. There are more than 20 species of wallaby of which several are in danger of becoming extinct. Five species live in New Guinea.

Above: a halfbreed dingo dog is used as a guard dog in a banana packing shed in New South Wales. In most of the world, domesticated animals now live where large wild animals once roamed.
Below: the rufous rat kangaroo is the largest of nine species of marsupial related to the kangaroo family. Not only are there far fewer of them today, but also their range is much smaller.

Nalpa bilby, the Toolach wallaby, the Tasmanian emu, and the white-tailed rat have disappeared for good. The Parma wallaby, which is extinct in Australia, survives in New Zealand where it was successfully reintroduced. In danger of extinction in the near future is a whole string of animals, including native cats, planigales, opossums, wallabies, and the rusty numbat among mammals and the Cape Barren goose, the Western whipbird, a variety of grass wren, the

mers have been killing them in the mistaken belief that they compete with domestic livestock for grazing land and food. In fact, kangaroos and sheep can easily coexist because they usually eat different types of grasses and herbs, and kangaroos need a little less than half the food a sheep does daily. Another reason for the kangaroo's wholesale slaughter is that its flesh is used in commercial pet foods. Although the export of all kangaroo products was banned in April 1973, intense pressure from importing countries – especially the United States – brought about a lifting of the ban. Today it is again illegal to export kangaroo products, but poaching seems to go on unchecked.

Left: the rare Cape Barren goose of southern Australia is now increasing in number after strict protective measures were taken. It breeds on offshore islands, especially those in the Bass Strait. It is believed to be a primitive relative of true geese.
Below: the saltwater or estuarine crocodile of Australasia and Southeast Asia established itself in the Philippines, Palau Islands, and Fiji, and even reached the Tuamotu Islands halfway to South America. It is now nearly extinct in Australia, however.

bristle tail, the helmeted honeyeater, and several species of parakeet, parrot, and scrub bird among birds.

Although the two big kangaroos, the great gray and red varieties, are not yet on the official list of endangered species, it is likely that they will be if stringent protective measures are not soon taken. There are several reasons for the serious threat to the great kangaroos. One is that Australian sheep far-

Kangaroo skin is also used for leather goods, which adds to the temptation for illegal trade. A third danger to kangaroos comes from hunters who kill them for sport, finding this giant marsupial easy to hunt with dogs.

In an even worse plight than kangaroos is another of Australia's big animals, the 20-foot saltwater crocodile of the northern tropical waters. It has been almost completely annihilated.

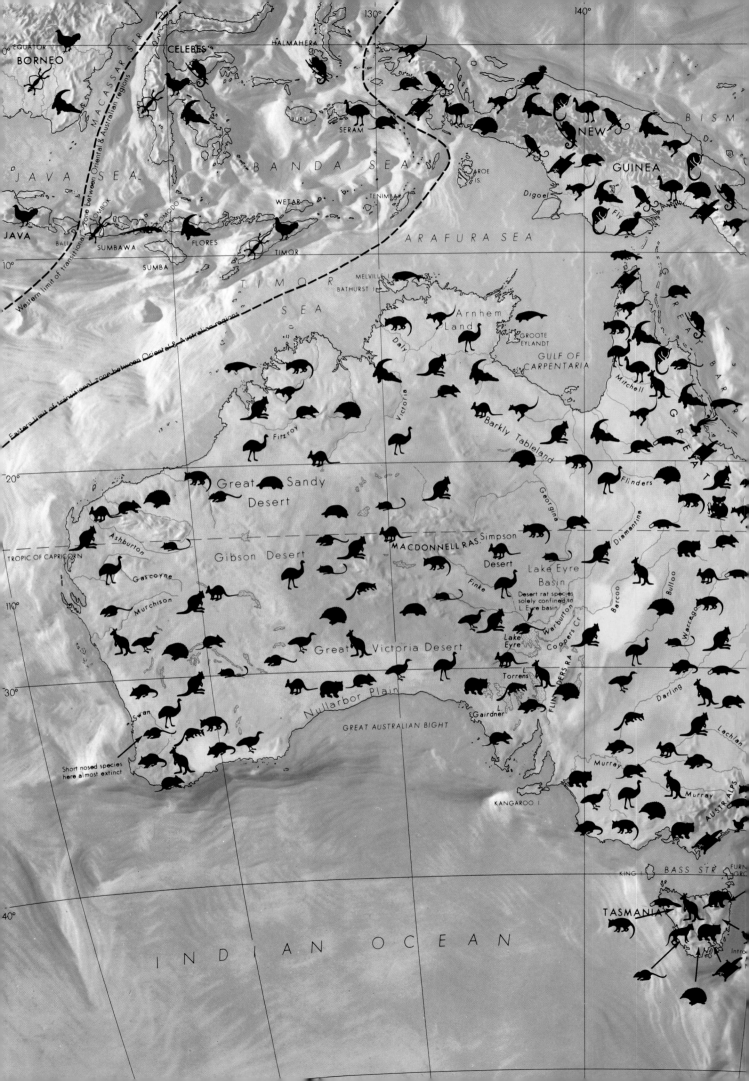

BORNEO

CELEBES

0° EQUATOR

120°

HALMAHERA

130°

140°

BISM

NEW

GUINEA

JAVA SEA

J A V A   S E A

Western limit of transitional zone between Oriental & Australian regions

SERAM

BURU

B A N D A   S E A

AROE IS.

Digoel

Fly

JAVA

BALI
SUMBAWA
LOMBOK
KOMODO
FLORES

WETAR

SUMBA

TIMOR

T I M O R
S E A

MELVILLE I.
BATHURST I.

A R A F U R A   S E A

Eastern limit of transitional zone between Oriental & Australian regions

10°

Arnhem
Land

GROOTE
EYLANDT

GULF OF
CARPENTARIA

Daly

Victoria

Mitchell

Fitzroy

Barkly Tableland

G R E A T   B A R R I

20°

Great   Sandy
Desert

Flinders

Georgina

Diamantine

TROPIC OF CAPRICORN

Ashburton

Gibson Desert

MACDONNELL RAS.

Simpson
Desert

Lake Eyre
Basin

G R E A T

Gascoyne

Finke

Barcoo

Bulloo

Warrego

110°

Murchison

Desert rat species
solely confined to
L. Eyre basin

Lake
Eyre

Warburton

Coopers Cr.

Great   Victoria   Desert

FLINDERS RA.

Darling

Lachlan

30°

Nullarbor Plain

L.
Torrens

Swan

Gairdner

GREAT   AUSTRALIAN   BIGHT

Murray

Murray

AUSTRALIAN ALPS

Short nosed species
here almost extinct

KANGAROO I.

KING I.
BASS STR.
FURN
GRO

40°

TASMANIA

Intro

I N D I A N   O C E A N

The Australian Region

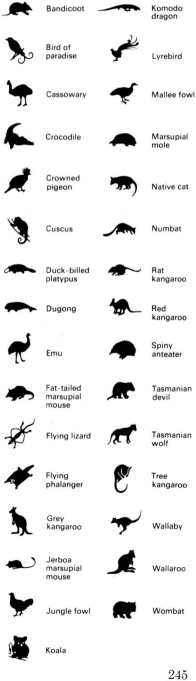

	Bandicoot		Komodo dragon
	Bird of paradise		Lyrebird
	Cassowary		Mallee fowl
	Crocodile		Marsupial mole
	Crowned pigeon		Native cat
	Cuscus		Numbat
	Duck-billed platypus		Rat kangaroo
	Dugong		Red kangaroo
	Emu		Spiny anteater
	Fat-tailed marsupial mouse		Tasmanian devil
	Flying lizard		Tasmanian wolf
	Flying phalanger		Tree kangaroo
	Grey kangaroo		Wallaby
	Jerboa marsupial mouse		Wallaroo
	Jungle fowl		Wombat
	Koala		

245

The Most Primitive Mammals

Probably the most striking characteristic of Australia's native mammals is that, besides the bats which were able to fly to this isolated land mass from other regions and a few rodents which were brought in deliberately or inadvertently, they are all either monotremes or marsupials.

Monotremes are the most primitive of the mammals,

a reptile's is small with a leathery thin shell and large yolk. Three other resemblances are poorly developed temperature regulation, the ability to go without food for long periods, and the presence of poison glands.

After hatching, the feeble bald infant struggles up its mother's body to her belly where it nuzzles about for food. This activity seems to stimulate the mother's mammary glands which then secrete milk. In the absence of nipples, the milk is exuded through slits in the belly or lower abdomen and forms droplets in the fur.

It is the male that is equipped with poison spurs on its hind feet, but these seem to function only during

classified as such because they suckle their young even though they lay eggs instead of giving birth to live babies. The word *monotreme* comes from Greek and means one hole. It applies to only two families, the echidnas or spiny anteaters and the duckbill platypus, both of which have only one orifice serving the multiple functions of intercourse, egg laying, and excretion. Monotremes occur only in Australia.

It is believed that these animals developed from the early part-mammal reptiles into a completely distinct order tens of millions of years before the marsupial and placental mammals arose at the beginning of the Cretaceous period about 135 million years ago. They certainly have several features more in common with reptiles than with more highly developed mammals. One is the single orifice that gives them their name. Another is the type of egg they lay, which like

Above: the spiny anteater or echidna looks somewhat like a hedgehog in shape and prickliness. Their habitats within Australia vary widely from humid jungle to freezing mountain to the hottest desert. They breed from June to September.

the breeding season. Thoughts vary as to their use. Some believe the spurs may be used to subdue a female during courtship and mating, while others think they are used to fend off a male encroaching on another's territory.

The spiny anteater usually lays one egg a year which hatches in 10 or 11 days. When the baby's spines are too developed for the mother to keep it close to her body, it is placed in a burrow. The mother feeds it every 36 to 48 hours and weans it at about three months of age.

The Australian species of spiny anteater is smaller and lighter than that found in New Guinea and its snout, though elongated and cylindrical, is shorter. Its little external ears are well hidden and its small eyes at the base of the snout are not very noticeable either. The long sharp pines that cover its squat body are about 2 inches long and are either all yellow or yellow with a black tip. When threatened, the spiny anteater will simply dig itself into the ground, a feat it performs with amazing speed.

On the other hand, the duckbill platypus is totally aquatic. This species of monotreme was first discovered in 1797, and when the remains of some of them arrived in Europe, they were thought to be a zoological hoax. Suspicion was founded on the fact

that many expeditions returning from Australia in those days brought fake mermaids and men-monkeys supplied by taxidermists in Far Eastern ports, and the strange looking platypus could easily fall into this category. For strange looking it is with its mole-like body and fur, its web feet, and its ducklike rubbery beak. It was not for another five years, in 1802, that the platypus was found to be genuine. Arguments continued even after that. One French naturalist suggested that the animal was a mammal that laid eggs, coming close to the truth. But the celebrated Lamarck disagreed. While granting that the creature possessed certain mammalian characteristics, such as a four-chambered heart and a diaphragm, he maintained that its absence of mammary glands disqualified it from being a true mammal. He called it a prototype mammal. It was left to a German anatomist in 1824 to discover that, although lacking nipples, the platypus did in fact possess mammary glands.

Left and below: the duckbill platypus has webbed feet that help make it aquatic. When on land, this egg-laying mammal can fold back the webbing on the forelimbs in order to walk or dig with them. Adults have no teeth. Instead they have a horny plate with which they crush their food of small marine life and fish.

Australia's Many Marsupials

Although still primitive in comparison with placental mammals, marsupials are much more highly developed than monotremes. For example, they give birth by bringing a baby out of the uterus, and the baby is born live. They also have nipples with which to suckle the young. However, marsupial infants at birth are tiny and undeveloped, still looking like embryos. Even in the larger species such as the red and gray kangaroos the baby usually weighs less than an ounce. Despite almost total helplessness, a baby marsupial contrives unaided to make its way to its mother's nipples within the pouch, in which it remains for as many months as it requires to develop fully.

The limited distribution of marsupials is very peculiar and long presented a puzzle to zoogeographers, who make a study of animal distribution. Most authorities now consider the problem solved on the basis of how the continental plates have moved since earliest times. They think that marsupials originated in South America in the Cretaceous period, soon spreading into North America. During the Eocene epoch about 40 to 60 million years ago, some must have migrated farther north and into Europe by way of the Arctic and the Bering Strait land bridge. At the end of the Miocene epoch about 10 to 25 million years ago, pouched mammals were extinct both in North America and Europe. Because they faced less competition from more advanced

placental mammals in South America, a few survived successfully there. Some of them moved across Antarctica, which was then attached to South America, and ended up in Australia. This migration could possibly have been as early as Eocene times or as late as the Palaeocene epoch about 60 to 70 million years ago. Once in Australia, conditions seemed to be ideal for their diversification. The factor most in their favor was the absence of competition from placental mammals, which evolved later. The habitat has suited marsupials so well that today, even after some 200 years of being hunted and killed, 176 species remain in the Australian region.

The pouches of marsupials are formed in a variety of ways, each one best suited to the particular species' way of life. In the species that jump or stand upright at times, like kangaroos, the pouch opens at the top so that the babies will not fall out. In species that

Above: marsupial babies in their mother's pouch. Whether kangaroo, opossum, wombat, or other marsupial, the function of the pouch is the same – it gives the poorly formed embryo a chance to develop more fully. Tiny marsupials cannot even suck at the teats for their nutrition; they are fed by muscular action of the nipple, which squirts milk into their mouth from time to time.

move on all fours, especially those that burrow such as bandicoots and wombats, the pouch opens at the bottom, which would be toward the rear of the animal. This makes it easier for the baby to reach the pouch from the mother's vagina after birth, and also gives some protection to the newborn from showers of earth as the mother digs with her front paws.

Other marsupials have only vestigial pouches or none at all, such as numbats and certain rats. In these cases, the young cling to their mother's nipples until they are able to be on their own.

Left: the Tasmanian wombat lives on the islands of Tasmania and Flinders. It is very like the common wombat of eastern Australia and differs from the hairy-nosed wombat of southern Australia only by being hairless on the muzzle between the two nostrils.

Below: a red kangaroo and its baby, called a "joey" by the Australians. Baby kangaroos are the size of a bean at their birth.

More Marsupials

The marsupials of Australia fill nearly all the niches occupied in other ecosystems by placental mammals. There are marsupial herbivores, insectivores, omnivores, and carnivores. There are marsupials that run, jump, and burrow. There are even marsupials of aquatic habits. In fact, though marsupials evolved earlier, some of them resemble the placental mammals they substitute for. This is because they have evolved to suit the same kind of habitat and diet of placental

Above: the numbat is also called the banded anteater but this is partly a misnomer. While the term "banded" logically applies to the white bands around its body, the term "anteater" is not appropriate because the numbat eats termites rather than ants.

mammals, though separated in both time and space.

Of course, it is impossible that every one of the niches occupied by the almost 4000 different species of placental mammal could be filled by the 248 species of marsupial, and among the more notable gaps is the absence of any marsupial "bats", "seals", and "whales". The nearest parallel are certain arboreal marsupials that glide on outstretched membranes like the placental flying squirrels and lemurs.

There are eight families of marsupials, of which six are found in Australia. The family known as the dasyurids includes the numbats, Tasmanian devil, marsupial mouse, and eastern and spotted-tailed cats. By and large these fill the roles occupied elsewhere by such meat-eating animals as weasels, martens, wildcats, and wolves. The numbat is sometimes called the marsupial anteater because it has the same kind of powerful claws and long sticky tongue that placental anteaters possess. Closely related to the dasyurids are the rarely seen but common marsupial moles, of

which there are two species in a separate family classification. With their tiny eyes and well-developed front feet, they are unbelievably like the moles of Eurasia, and are without doubt the most remarkable replicas of a placental mammal found among all marsupials.

The bandicoots of Australia, Tasmania, and New Guinea are shrewlike omnivorous animals that have earned their name from their striking similarity to the rodents of the same name in India.

The family called phalangers, all members of which live in trees, possess prehensile tails like tree-dwelling placental mammals. Among these are the sugar glider, looking much like a squirrel; the 6-inch-long feather-tailed glider that looks like a mouse; the bear-like kaola; and the cuscus, also called the Australian opossum. This largest of the phalangers is similar to the sloth and slow loris in movement. It slowly and stealthily stalks small roosting birds and lizards, but the main part of its diet is great quantities of leaves and fruit.

The wombats and the hairy-nosed wombats are the only two members of the vombatidae family. Although there was an ancestor as big as a hippopotamus, the present-day wombat reaches a maximum size of just under 4 feet in length. Its subterranean activities and largely vegetarian diet are combined with an appearance similar to a badger's, but with the teeth and jaws of a rodent. Both upper and lower jaws have teeth like chisels, which grow continually and have to be kept in check by constant gnawing. The habitats of the two genera of wombats differ. The common wombat prefers mountainous, or at least hilly, coastal areas and the hairy-nosed wombat likes sandy and drier areas.

Above: the cuscus is often thought to be a monkey from its appearance, but it is related to the kangaroo. During the day the cuscus sits almost continuously, doing all its food hunting at night. It has a repulsive odor, which may be a defense mechanism.

Right: the sugar glider looks much like a squirrel until it opens its gliding membranes to take to the air. With its skin outstretched in an unbroken line, it looks like a kite from below.

Kangaroos and Wallabies

Few people think of the animals of Australia without thinking of the kangaroo. What would probably surprise them is that there are 55 species in the family of kangaroos and wallabies. These include the small rat kangaroos that inhabit the undergrowth, and the tree kangaroos of northeastern Australia and New Guinea. That this family has diverged into so many species is due to the fact that there were virtually no other grazing animals in Australia until humans brought domesticated herds, and a radiation of species took place. This can be compared to what happened to the antelopes of Africa. The almost total absence of predatory animals large and strong enough to threaten kangaroos meant that they could fill the many different habitats of desert, grasslands, rocky country, and even forests. The picture changed when humans brought into the country the dingo, which preys on kangaroos, and sheep and rabbits, which vie with them for food. Three species of kangaroo have become extinct and several more are on the danger

Below: tree kangaroos are furrier and stockier than other members of their family. There are seven species, of which five live in New Guinea and two in the northeast section of Australia.

Below right: the red kangaroo is one of the two largest of the species. It is the male that is reddish; the female is blue-gray.

list. The great gray and red kangaroos are thought by some to be threatened although the number that can be shot annually is limited by law.

All kangaroos have especially well-developed hindlegs and small front limbs, although this difference is less marked in tree kangaroos. All have a pouch that opens forward as a way of keeping the baby inside when the animal propels itself forward.

The kangaroo's method of leaping on two feet is a characteristic of this animal, though it moves on all fours when grazing. When a group of kangaroos is startled, they break their normal silence by a coughing noise and a warning thump of the hind feet on the ground. The old male kangaroos or "boomers" and the females or "flyers" as they are known all rear onto their hindlegs and hurry across the open grassland in leaps that can be up to 25 feet long.

Kangaroos can form a tripod with their tails and hindlegs. When the males fight they grasp each other with their small forelegs and, using the tail as a prop, lash out with their hindlegs. The claws make these limbs dangerously cutting. When trained to box in circuses, kangaroos must first be broken of their kicking habit, which can be deadly to an opponent.

The great development of the hindlegs is also seen in placental mammals such as the rabbit and the hare, but none equals that of the kangaroo. Kangaroos also have acute hearing and sight.

Smaller kangaroos are known as wallabies, and there are many different kinds of them living in a variety of habitats. The rock wallaby has special foot

soles that keep it from slipping when it climbs the steep rocky slopes on which it lives.

Tree kangaroos are found in the northeastern forest regions of Australia and in New Guinea. They have comparatively larger front legs and smaller ears than other species and they use their tail only as a balancing organ. They also differ by browsing on fruit and leaves instead of grazing, although they sometimes leave the trees to graze on the forest floor at night.

As their name implies, rat kangaroos have a decidedly ratlike appearance with small ears and scaly tails. In some species this tail is slightly prehensile and is used to carry nesting material to the hollow log or rock crevice where these nocturnal animals hide during the day.

Rat kangaroos, which are the smallest member of the family, suffered badly from the introduction of the rabbit. Although the two animals are able to live together, even sharing the same burrows, the rat kangaroos come off worse if food or water become scarce. They are also far slower breeders and cannot recover from population setbacks as quickly as rabbits.

The smallest of the rat kangaroos is the musk kangaroo, which supplements its vegetable diet with insects. In this it is nearer to the possums from which the kangaroos are thought to have evolved.

Above: two gray kangaroos stop for a drink of water. Kangaroos can actually go without water for long periods of time, but will let nothing stand in their way once they catch sight of some.

Below: the ring-tailed wallaby, also called the yellow-footed wallaby, has a banded tail and yellowish feet and ears. It is one of the rock wallabies inhabiting the rocky southern areas.

Life in the Desert

Australia is usually thought of as a modern industrial country, highly developed agriculturally and technologically, so it may come as a surprise to learn that its interior is a huge desert having an area second in the world only to the vast Sahara of North Africa. In fact, of Australia's total area of almost three

tonous as it may seem, provides the red kangaroo with all of its solid sustenance as well as much of its water requirements. Kangaroos pant like dogs to cool themselves. They also continually lick their hands, chests, and arms, which lowers the body temperature as the saliva evaporates. In order to reach water in arid areas, the animal often digs a pit 3 feet deep in dried up river beds. By these means and because their activities are affected to some extent by temperature as well as light, kangaroos will venture out by day when it is not extremely hot. They are regarded in the main as nocturnal animals, however.

Left and below: the vast desert of central Australia is composed of different types of soil. In parts it is rock or stones, and in parts it is sand. Because the Australian desert region gets more rain than many other deserts, there are periods of flourishing plant life – which in turn supports the animal life.

million square miles, more than one million or 43.5 percent are classified as desert.

This desert is for the most part the least arid one in the world, however. There are occasional short sharp showers from either the northern monsoons in the summer or from the Southern Ocean in the winter. Owing to the comparatively flat and featureless terrain of most of the continent, and particularly the interior, there are no clearly delineated life zones: the grasslands of the east merge imperceptibly into savanna, which in turn gradually deteriorates into scrubland, semidesert, and then rock-strewn desert. Moreover, these lines alter with climate changes so that long periods of drought may turn grasslands into arid wastelands. Consequently, the varieties of wildlife are not confined to strictly marked boundaries.

Aside from the burgeoning lushness that briefly follows a fall of rain, the vegetation of the desert is sapless, meager, and stringy. It consists mostly of mulga, which is the aboriginal name for the local dwarf variety of acacia; mallee, the local name for dwarf eucalyptus; and spinifex or, as it is known in Australia, porcupine grass. This spartan fare, mono-

Opposite top: flowers bloom profusely in the bleak landscape near Alice Springs, Australia after a rainfall, and the desert is transformed by brilliant color. Experts believe that there is water under the desert, which could be brought to the surface.

Because of the relative abundance in desert conditions of insects, reptiles, and small rodents, it is reasonable to suppose that a number of marsupials that feed on such prey will make their home in the region – and so they do. A small corner of the southwestern part of the desert provides a habitat for the fat-tailed and crest-tailed mice and the marsupial jerboa, so-called because it has long hind legs. These animals, all of which are carnivores, live mainly on insects and lizards.

Another slightly larger marsupial that has a similar diet inhabits the central and driest part of the desert. This is the marsupial mole, which perplexed the zoological world when it was discovered in 1888. It resembles the South African golden mole so closely that some experts believed they were related. Even today little is known of this animal's habits. Observations in zoos suggest that it alternates abruptly between utter lethargy and sudden great activity, burrowing or digging and eating enormous quantities of worms and insects.

Occasionally to be found in the desert is the numbat or banded anteater. Unlike most marsupials it is

Below: a tiger snake eating a mouse. One of the venomous cobra species, this snake gets its name from the fact that many have brown and yellow bands around the body. Others vary in color, however. Its venom can be fatal to humans as well as to animals.

Above: the frilled lizard opens its 8-inch neck frill to display aggression when it or its territory is threatened. It walks upright, like some of the other lizards do, but it leaves tracks that have a strange resemblance to those of extinct dinosaurs.

diurnal, exploring the cavities of rotting trees to find the termites that infest such spots. Its numbers have been depleted by the dingoes that prey on it and by the humans who are destroying its habitat.

If only a few mammals find Australia's hot arid interior satisfactory to live in, the same cannot be said of reptiles. The area abounds with them and, while many are to be found in other zoogeographical regions, a large number are unique to Australia.

Surprisingly, many of Australia's desert snakes are species that are least able to adapt to desert conditions. Most of these are venomous and extremely deadly, such as the death adder, the tiger and black snakes, and the taipan, which is possibly the fiercest snake in the world. Australia is the only region to possess more venomous than nonvenomous varieties of snake, although there are no vipers.

There are several species of lizard that rely on their grotesque looks for self-protection. The frilled lizard, for example, threatens its enemies by hissing and raising its neck frill. This makes it appear much bigger and usually frightens off an aggressor. The bearded dragon changes color, bristles its pines, and enlarges its throat sac, which then looks like a beard

Above: both names of the moloch or thorny devil do this frightening looking orange and brown lizard an injustice. Moloch comes from the ancient god to whom children were sacrificed, and devil indicates evil. Yet this lizard is harmless.

256

and gives it its name.

The way that the moloch or thorny devil takes in moisture is interesting and, for a time, was mysterious. It is now known that water creeps along a network of tiny channels in the horny skin, reaching the angle of the jaws by this capillary action. The lizard is then able to drink it. This is why it reacts by opening and shutting its mouth as if drinking when any part of it is dipped into water.

If the thorny devil were a large animal instead of being a mere 6 inches long, it would be truly terrifying with its flinty eyes and sharp spikes. In fact, it is totally inoffensive except to the stingless ants it lives on. When alarmed, this animal makes a threat by drawing its head between its front legs to display a thorny hump that stands up on the back of the neck. Besides an infrequent dingo, there are few ground predators that threaten the thorny devil. Even the birds of prey are cautious about it.

Another bird of prey that is fairly widespread throughout the Australian region, with the exception of densely vegetated areas, is the wedge-tailed eagle. With its 7-foot wingspan, it is among the largest birds in the world.

Other birds of the desert include budgerigars, which add their bright plumage to the fast-dying brilliance of the sudden blossoming after a rain shower, emus, and mallee fowls.

Above: the shape of the wedge-tailed eagle gives this large bird of prey its name, and it is the only eagle with such a shape to its tail. It is found only in Australia where it has a wide range.

Below: a young black-shouldered kite puts on a threat display to ward off a carpet snake. The carpet snake is related to the pythons, and will crush or strangle the bird before eating it.

257

The Wildlife of Western Australia

Radiating out from the arid heart of the central desert, the land becomes progressively if slowly less barren. First it changes into mulga grassland, then mallee grassland. Then, to the southwest it becomes woodland, and to the north and east steppelike country and sparsely wooded savanna. As the vegetation grows more plentiful and varied, so does the animal population. Some species that are encountered are related to those that scratch out a meager existence in the desert. Others, like the echidna and the very few placental mammals native to Australia, for example, are completely different.

The false vampire bat, one of the largest bats in the world with its wingspan of some 2 feet, is also sometimes known as the ghost bat because of its pale coloration. This animal roosts in crowds in caves or cracks in the rocks by day, and swarms out to forage for reptiles and small mammals by night. These bats even include smaller bats in their diet. Although they belie their name and do not actually suck blood, they do inflict savage bites.

There are several species of rodent to be found in Australia. In addition to water rats, which might have reached these shores simply by swimming, there are a considerable number of other rats, including a desert rat confined solely to the Lake Eyre Basin, and many varieties of mouse. Among the mice is the Australian hopping mouse which, when it needs to

Right: the short-nosed bandicoot digs up the forest floor in search of grubs and roots on which to feed. They are beneficial to farmers because they eat insects that harm crops.

move quickly, will use its well-developed hind legs to hop. These little creatures have adapted to life in a dry climate by being able to forego drinking water entirely if necessary, instead utilizing the moisture that all seeds, even the most desiccated, contain. Like so much of the wildlife in this hot region, they prefer feeding at night.

Similar in appearance to a rat is the brush-tailed rat kangaroo that inhabits the grassy southwestern tip of Australia. Despite its appearance it is a marsupial, although it differs from other members of the kangaroo family in its teeth, of which its canines are large. It is also nocturnal, spending the day in a camouflaged nest of grass and leaves on the ground rather than in a burrow. Like all kangaroos it is strictly herbivorous. While it feeds it also gleans nesting material which it loops neatly in a bundle and carries away with its prehensile tail.

Besides these herbivores there are several families of marsupials that are insectivorous or carnivorous, and some that are omnivorous. One such is the short-nosed bandicoot, which inhabits the same area as the brush-tailed rat kangaroo. One of the larger varieties of the species, it measures up to 27 inches including its tail. The rat kangaroo exhibits great ferocity toward others of its kind, but is very timid when confronted by other animals, including humans.

There are at least three varieties of bandicoots in the west of Australia: the long-nosed, the rabbit or bilby, and the pig-footed. The pig-footed bandicoot may now be extinct, however.

Two varieties of dasyurids that live exclusively on meat are the widely distributed western native cat and the little northern native cat. The latter is confined to the steppes and thinly wooded savanna of the north.

The bird life of Australia is not as unique and distinctive as the mammals, although there are many colorful parrots and some flightless birds.

Members of the *megapode* (big foot) family of birds do not rely on their body heat to incubate their eggs, nor do they protect their nestlings. Depending on what kind of terrain they inhabit, they utilize other sources of heat. For instance, some deposit the eggs in

Below: the short plump tail that gives the fat-tailed marsupial mouse its name is not always of the same size. Because it stores reserves of fat, it is more swollen when the mouse is well fed.

safe hiding places in the rocks and let the heat of the sun hatch them. Those that inhabit volcanic areas lay them in places warmed by the lava. Those living in the forest dig holes, fill them with vegetation and lay the eggs on top of it; as the vegetable matter decomposes, it gives off the heat needed to incubate the eggs.

The mallee fowl, a megapode that inhabits the eucalyptus scrubland of the southwest, has to contend with extreme seasonal fluctuations in temperature. It requires ceaseless labor by the bird to keep the eggs from either frying or freezing during the two and a half months of incubation, and the main responsibility for their care falls to the male.

About four months before the first egg is due to be laid, the male bird digs out a round hole from 6 to 10 feet in diameter and about 3 feet deep with its enormous feet, like forest megapodes do. It then gathers every bit of vegetation it can find, fills up the cavity with it, and scoops out a hole for the eggs. Because the vegetation will not rot satisfactorily unless it is damp, it must wait for the rains to come before it covers the nest with a heavy layer of sand.

Every time the hen is about to lay, which she will do once a week for about six months, the cock has to

Above: this male mallee fowl is cooling the eggs inside its mound nest by removing some of the sand from the top. This bird uses its tongue to measure the temperature of the incubator mound, and does what is necessary to keep the temperature even.

Left: a male and female mallee fowl at the nest in which the female has laid her eggs. The hole in which the eggs are kept for incubation might be 15 feet in diameter and 4 feet in depth.

after the nest occupies 11 months. Consequently, the adult mallee fowls have no time to look after their chicks. Although many chicks die before they can get out of their stifling nest, they can run as soon as they are born and, because they possess some flight feathers at birth, they can fly within a week. This means they stand a reasonable chance against predators, of which the most dangerous is the infrequent fox. However, up to 50 percent of the chicks fall to predators.

Above: a mallee fowl chick emerging from its nest. By the time the last egg has been laid during the long breeding season, the first chicks will be hatching. They make their way out with great difficulty and immediately look for some shade in which to rest.

uncover the nest, expose the hole that has been prepared, and recover it after she has laid. The hen usually lays two eggs at one time.

During the entire period of incubation, the temperature within the nest must remain at a constant 92°F because variation by more than a couple of degrees spells disaster. The cock dances continual attendance, testing the nest's temperature with his tongue and removing, replacing, or adding sand as necessary to cool, to heat, to insulate, or to ventilate the interior.

From start to finish the job of building and looking

Koalas and Other Tree-dwellers

Along with the kangaroo and duckbill platypus, the animal that is most associated with Australia in the public mind is the koala bear. The koala is not a bear, however, but a tree-dwelling marsupial. Now in a more healthy state after nearly being made extinct for use in the fur trade, koalas live in scattered areas down the eastern coast. They thrive in a sanctuary of 20 acres outside Brisbane, but their natural range is much reduced.

Koalas are slow moving animals that seldom come

Above: the opposable digits on the koala's forelimb, seen clearly in this photograph, helps the animal grip the branches strongly.

Right: the koala lives both in lowland and mountain forests, but those forests must have eucalyptus trees because of this marsupial's total dependence on gum tree leaves for food and survival.

down to the ground. The first and second digit of the forelimbs and the first digit of the hindlimbs are placed in such a way as to allow a strong grip, which helps the koala cling to tree branches. They climb to the highest branches of the eucalyptus or gum tree for the tender shoots, almost their only food. Zoologists have noticed that koalas living in the Victoria forest avoid grayish or bluish gum leaves while those of Queensland select such leaves. It is also believed that the animal eats mistletoe, box, and tea leaves from time to time, but it must have gum tree leaves to survive. The koala's intestine is modified to help it digest eucalyptus leaves, which also make it smell like cough drops containing oil of eucalyptus. Its restricted diet means that the koala cannot easily be kept in captivity outside its native land.

As recently as 1924 two million koalas were killed for the export fur trade and another 600,000 suffered the same fate in 1927. Even before that, an epidemic disease at the turn of the century had killed off millions of the animal. Some authorities estimate that

their current number runs only in the thousands, even with strict protection. However, the happy discovery that many unsuspected small colonies exist in out-of-the-way places may change that assessment.

Koalas do not breed quickly. There is only one

breeding season a year, and the mother rarely produces more than one offspring.

The other arboreal marsupials of the eastern forests are both more mobile and less restricted in their diets than koalas. The sugar glider, one of three species of flying marsupials, is actually airborne while moving down from tree to tree in its quest for insects and nectar. Leadbeater's possum is similar in appearance to the sugar glider while lacking its gliding membranes. The ring-tailed possum, equipped with a prehensile tail, also has opposable digits somewhat like the koala's, which increases the safety of its passage through the trees.

The tiny pygmy possums are sometimes called dormouse possums because of their superficial resemblance to the European dormouse and their habit of sleeping for long periods during cold weather. Although no bigger than a mouse, this marsupial has a strictly meat diet, mostly of insects. In captivity, however, dormouse possums will eat sugar and honey. Like many other marsupials, notably kangaroos, and some placental mammals, the dormouse possum can make use of a reproduction technique known as delayed implantation. This phenomenon allows the fertilized egg to develop to a stage in which it is a tiny hollow ball of cells and then to remain as an embryo for an indefinite time. Development of this embryo will only continue to completion when the previous baby has left the pouch. If something happens to the older baby while it is still in the pouch, the implanted embryo will finish its development early, and save breeding time.

Arborial marsupials have few natural enemies besides domestic cats and the wedge-tailed eagle and, as a consequence, are still relatively numerous. Even Leadbeater's possum, which was long thought to be extinct, was rediscovered in the central highlands in 1961 in thick mountain ash forest. It had previously been known only from five specimens collected between 1867 and 1909.

Above: pygmy possums are apt climbers and often run down trees head first. They have a prehensile tail which also helps them in climbing.

Left: Leadbetter's possums, like koalas, have opposable digits on their forelimbs to allow stronger grip. Also like a few others of their own species, they have molars that are adapted for chewing leaves.

An Abundance of Birds

The birdlife of southeastern Australia is particularly abundant, not only in the number of birds but also in the number of different species. About 377 species have been recorded at one time or another, only 45 of them being oceanic. The most prevalent birds are the honeyeaters, of which Australia boasts 69 species. Of these, the red-headed and white-naped species are both only 5 inches in length. All the honeyeaters are similar in appearance if different in color, ranging from the more common drab brown to bright scarlet. Their long beaks curve down and their tongues are especially adapted to brush up the nectar that they mainly live on, though they sometimes eat soft fruit and insects. As nectar eaters they are also pollinators, and so contribute to perpetuating such trees as the eucalyptus and banksia. Although honeyeaters build the same kind of nests and lay the same kind of pinkish eggs with red spots, their habitats and feeding methods vary a good deal from species to species. Some live in the forest's undergrowth, others in a tree's outer foliage or trunks and branches. Some swoop from perches like flycatchers, a few hover like hummingbirds or sunbirds. One, the painted honeyeater, has largely given up eating nectar and substituted berries.

Another bird of Australia's open grassy woodlands is a creature almost as much a symbol of Australia as the kangaroo, koala, and duckbill platypus. It is the kookaburra, a member of the kingfisher family also known as the laughing jackass, laughing kookaburra or the bushman's clock. The less usual third name is a reference to its habit of regularly singing at dawn. This song is amazingly like human laughter, although a harsh scream like a bray often accompanies it. Kookaburras eat anything fleshy – insects, birds, and fish – and have been known to kill snakes by battering them against the ground while holding them in the beak like a vice. When dead, the snake is swallowed whole, head first.

Another unusual bird belonging to this region is the frogmouth, so called because of its wide mouth which often gapes open. Frogmouths are similar to nightjars, of which the white-throated species is found in the eastern Australian forests. They feed almost exclusively at ground level on centipedes and snails, geckos, small marsupials, and rodents, mangling their prey in their powerful bill before swallowing.

Vying with the Indian peacock in the beauty of tail

Left: a kookaburra in flight. Kookaburras are among the largest of the kingfishers, but they do not have the bright coloring of their relatives. There are two species and between them they cover almost all of Australia, Tasmania, and New Guinea.

Right: frogmouths sleep on a branch in the open during the day, dependent on their protective coloring to stay secure from enemies. They are either grayish or reddish brown with dark markings, which makes them blend into their background.

plumage are two species of lyrebird, the superb and its smaller cousin the Prince Albert. The male's tail is indeed lyre-shaped, with outer feathers giving the appearance of the frame of a lyre, and the feathers in between are as delicate as lacy filigree. Each male constructs several mounds during the mating season from April to October and visits them in turn, singing with loud melodious resonance and making dancelike movements. The mother bird, who may be but one of many mates of a male, builds a domed nest in a cave or tree hollow, lines it with her thigh feathers, and lays a single egg which will take six weeks or so to incubate. During the 10 days after hatching, the chick loses its down and begins to grow feathers. It leaves the nest after six weeks.

Also remarkable in behavior are the bowerbirds. There is a primitive species of these called the tooth-billed catbird because of its serrated beak. They are also known as stagemakers because of the male's habit of building a stage in some woodland clearing, using its bill as a saw. It then installs itself above on a song perch and bursts forth into song to attract a mate.

The male of other more developed species of bowerbirds has evolved a more elaborate courtship behavior. It builds a whole edifice. Some of the species, like the satin bowerbirds, fashion avenues walled on

Above: a male superb lyrebird shows off his tail feathers in a mating display. Superb lyrebirds are ground birds that live in mountain forests. They are rigorously protected by legislation.

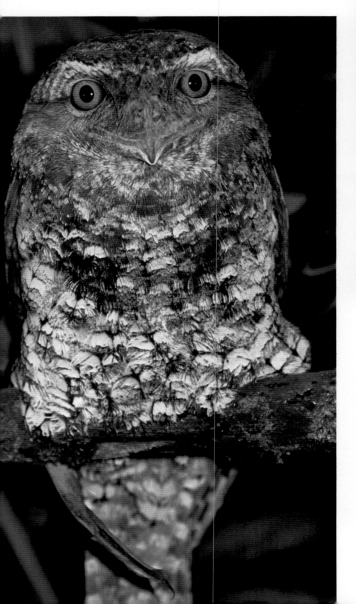

Above: a male satin bowerbird enticing a female into his bower. After mating, the female will build her nest elsewhere. Males are usually a uniform glossy black that looks blue-purple in the sun.

either side by twigs leading up to platforms of sticks. Some build columns up to 10 feet high, while others create mats out of sticks and ferns and festoon them with shells, seeds, or even the carapaces of insects. Satin bowerbirds clearly favor blue objects for their decorations. Some of the avenue builders also paint the inside walls of their bowers, using a mixture of saliva and masticated bark, charcoal from a bush fire, or dried grass. Certain of them even use wads of plant material held in their beaks like a paint brush.

Tasmanian Wildlife

Two hundred miles south of the southeastern state of Victoria across the Bass Strait lies the verdant land of Tasmania, a small nearly equilateral triangle of an island some 190 miles across at its widest point. During the past million years this island has been joined to the mainland four times and then cut off again each time by the rising seas that came at the end of the several Ice Ages. Tasmania's terrain is very varied considering its size. It contains forests, fast rivers and waterfalls, mountains, tree-lined lakes, pasture, and moorlands.

Although the island is not as rich in animal life as the nearby mainland, particularly in reptiles and birds, it possesses many mammals. Some of these are unique, having been driven from the mainland as a last refuge.

The reptile life of Tasmania consists of a mere 20 species, of which two lizards are unique to the island. It is devoid of tortoises, goannas, geckos, and pythons. Among the several venomous snakes are the tiger snake and the copperhead. The tiger snake is so called because of its grayish-yellow striations; one variety of this reptile is believed to be the deadliest snake in the world for its size. The copperhead, which can reach lengths of nearly 5 feet, also has a poison that can kill.

The lyrebird has been introduced into Tasmania and flourishes in Mount Field National Park, but there are 14 species of bird unique to the island. One of these is the Tasmanian native hen, which is aquatic by nature. Another is a species of parrot called the green rosella. There are also dusky and hooded robins and an abundance of black swans, perhaps Tasmania's greatest pride among its birdlife. Another

Above: an Australian copperhead devouring a frog, whose contorted limbs show the effect of the snake's venom. During the process of swallowing, the snake lubricates the frog with saliva.

Right: the black swan is native to Tasmania and Australia, but has been successfully introduced into other parts of the world. It has curly black feathers and a bright red bill.

Above: the Tasmanian devil has a large face on a short stocky body. Its jaws and teeth are powerful and its claws strong. In spite of its reputation for savagery, it is docile in captivity.

Right: a colony of gray-headed albatrosses on a steep hillside. All species of the albatross except four breed south of the equator, usually on the remote islands that are dotted around the southern seas.

species encountered in Tasmania and nowhere else is the yellow wattle bird, a honeyeater.

The mammals of the island include two varieties of marsupial mouse, two pygmy possums, the common wombat, and three dasyures in the Tasmanian devil, the eastern or native cat, and the tiger cat. There are also ring-tailed and brush-tailed possums and three kinds of kangaroo, the huge gray forester kangaroo, the red-necked or Bennett's wallaby, and the rufous-bellied pademelon that is the size of a domestic cat.

The rare thylacine and the Tasmanian devil are Australia's two largest carnivorous marsupials. The Tasmanian devil, despite its persecution by farmers as a chicken stealer, is still relatively common in the island's more inaccessible reaches. It is from 2 to 3 feet long including a 1-foot tail and can weigh from 12 to over 20 pounds. Its name comes from its reputation of being savage toward its prey, even animals larger than itself. It will feed on carrion as well as freshly killed flesh.

Both species of monotreme are present in Tasmania. The duckbill platypus' habitats are wide ranging on the island. It may be found both in tropical streams and chill mountain lakes as high as 6000 feet – in fact, anywhere that it can find freshwater crayfish called "yabbies," tadpoles, larvae, and earthworms. After it sieves these from the mud with its flexible bill, the platypus stores them in its cheek pouches before swallowing.

Tasmania has its own species of the other monotreme, the spiny anteater or echidna. The word *echidna* is Greek for viper and refers to the poison

spurs on the male's hind feet. The Tasmanian echidna is larger than its mainland cousins and its short spines are almost completely hidden by fur. Like the hedgehog to which it bears some resemblance, it can roll itself up into a ball when threatened. It can also do a quick disappearing act by burrowing itself swiftly into soft soil.

Tasmania's surrounding seas, particularly the Bass Strait, and its nearby islets have a thriving marine life. They contain some of the world's largest seabird colonies, which include the extremely rare Cape Barren geese, penguins, and albatrosses. On some of the Bass Strait islands live the short-tailed shearwater or muttonbird, whose migrations take it to British Columbia by the roundabout route of Japan and Kamchatka. These birds furnished the early settlers with food, the flesh of the fat young before they fledged being said to taste like mutton. Some 170,000 of them were consumed between March and August in 1790 alone. Annual slaughters took place until the early 19th century, but they are still the most numerous of the Australian birds.

267

Emus and Other Savanna Animals

Although preferring the savannas, the emu is widespread throughout the region. This bird, which is second in size only to the ostrich, migrates coastward during the drier seasons, leaving a wake of destroyed crops in its path. This annual trek reached such proportions nearly 50 years ago that it caused what was known as the Emu War of 1932, in which the troops were called out against the big birds. Although the soldiers did manage to shoot a few hundred of them, it was the emus that carried the day. In a subsequent campaign, the Australians wiped out the Tasmanian subspecies. For all this, the emu is so typical of the region as to be embodied, together with the kangaroo, in Australia's coat of arms.

The emu is a flightless bird that has a bluish, rather bare head and coarse drooping feathers on the body. Unusual as it is, the female tends to be a little bigger than the male. As is the case with all flightless birds,

Above: the male emu has the responsibility of caring for the chicks, which he guards for 18 months. He uses guttural cries very different from the female's call to guide and teach them.

it is the male's task to incubate the deep green eggs that are laid in clutches of about nine. During this eight-week period, the father bird loses about 20 pounds in weight. The male also tends the chicks, keeping the brood together by guiding them with loud grunting sounds. In experiments conducted on emu chicks, the male's stern grunts were recorded and played back to the chicks. They responded to the people holding the recording machine as if they were their own parents, following them around obediently. Emu chicks have brown and yellow striped plumage as a camouflage, but they are nonetheless much preyed

on by dingoes and wedge-tailed eagles. If they reach the age of 18 months, they are on their own.

Like the ostrich of Africa, the emu eats many non-food items, and its stomach has been known to include such indigestibles as glass marbles, nails, cartridge cases and, in more built-up areas, money. Such inedible rubbish is taken in by instinct rather than deliberately. Their normal diet consists of insects and such plant matter as grass, berries, and fruit.

Among other inhabitants of the grasslands are rodents and bats. The long-haired rats that live in the savannas of Queensland and the Northern Territory have a fluctuating population, their numbers at times reaching plague proportions. In such periods they

inflict great damage on gardens and crops. There are also three species of stick-nest rat, which was called the rabbit rat by early settlers because of its short blunt nose, big ears, and fluffiness. The stick-nest rat is a gregarious creature, living in colonies as a defense against predators. Their nests, which can measure up to 4 feet across, are constructed from twigs and are often reinforced by being built against rocks or around shrubs.

Left: like most flightless birds, the emu is a fast runner. It can sometimes reach a speed of 30 miles per hour in a sprint:

Below: emus congregate at a water hole. Living in small parties or sometimes large herds, emus roam the grasslands in search of food and water. In the dry season they raid the farm crops.

The Northern Coastal Strip

The northern and northeastern coastal strip of Australia, situated on the fringes of Queensland and the Northern Territory and reaching inland as far as the Great Divide, consists of a mixed terrain of dryish tropical savanna interspersed with many pockets of lush rain forest.

The most unusual geographical feature of the whole area is the Great Barrier Reef, an immensely long chain of coral reefs and islands stretching more than 1250 miles in length and roughly parallel with the coast of Queensland. It varies in distance from the mainland from a mere seven miles to more than 200.

The majority of the islands are uninhabitable and therefore, as would be expected, are a haven for many seabirds such as noddies, terns, and sea eagles. They are also rich in many forms of other marine life such as the green turtle. The surrounding seas are the home not only of colorful tropical reef fish like the golden demoiselle and the Venus tusk fish, but also of the vicious Moray eels and sharks; there are also several species of dolphin.

Coral reefs are formed by the skeletal remains of polyps, and some of the marine life of the region lives

Heron Island **(below),** off the east coast of Queensland, Australia, is a nature sanctuary in the vast coral structure known as the Great Barrier Reef. Parts of this reef, which is one of the natural wonders of the world, have been totally destroyed by the crown-of-thorns starfish **(right).** A sea animal that gets its name from the spines covering its body, the crown-of-thorns feeds on the living coral polyps that form the Great Barrier Reef.

on these tiny animals. For example, each crown-of-thorns starfish consumes about 65 square feet or so of living coral polyps a year. This starfish multiplied at a great rate in the recent past, but is now declining again. During the population upsurge, it was thought that the starfish would destroy the reefs completely, but many of them are recovering. Fossil records of the crown-of-thorns show that similar population explosions have occurred in the past, roughly every 100 to 200 years.

The Australian rain forests abound in animals that

feed on fruit and insects, especially many species of strange and resplendent birds. Bowerbirds are present in several different species, each with its own building pattern. The great gray bowerbird, like the satin bowerbird, contrives an avenue lined by two walls of twigs painstakingly paved with any or all of such items as shells, flowers, bones, feathers, and pebbles. The golden bowerbird constructs a pyramidlike room around the stems of saplings and bushes. This can measure 3.5 feet in height and 2 feet in diameter.

The majority of the 40 or so species of birds of paradise inhabit New Guinea, but two species live in the Molucca Islands and four in northeast Australia. Three of these four are known as riflebirds, while the fourth is called the manucode or trumpet bird. Although probably the most spectacular of all birds, the Australian birds of paradise are not as gorgeously feathered as their cousins of New Guinea. Nonetheless the males make a spectacular display during courtship, fluffing out their brilliant feathers, dancing and bowing and, in some species, doing acrobatics on their perches.

The largest birds to be found in these forests are the cassowaries of which there are three species. This flightless bird is largely black but its head and neck region is a patchwork of bright purples and blues on bare skin. Bright red wattles hang from the neck of the common cassowary. There is a large brown crest on top of the cassowary's head, partly as an aid to courtship display and partly as a means of pushing its way through the rain forest's thick undergrowth in its search for fruit and berries.

Above: the trumpetbird, which measures from 10 to 13 inches long, is named after its loud call. It is a plain colored species of the usually brilliant birds of paradise. In its courtship display, the male chases the female through the trees rather than gathering in a particular spot like those of ornate plumage do.
Below: the wings of the flightless cassowary have unfeathered quills which, along with its bony crest, enable it to push aside low branches and run through undergrowth without tangling.

271

Tropical Forest Life

In the tropical forests of north Australia and New Guinea, two kinds of marsupial occupy the places filled in South American and African forests by monkeys. These are the tree kangaroo and the cuscus. Tree kangaroos probably originated in New Guinea, where there are seven species. Although they are exclusively vegetarian in diet like other kangaroos,

these animals as intermediates between true kangaroos and arboreal phalangers.

The cuscuses that live predominantly in New Guinea are members of the possum family. They are as big as well-developed domestic cats and have faces something like the pottos, with large eyes and small ears. Cuscuses are slow-moving nocturnal animals having prehensile tails. They feed on a diet of insects, birds' eggs, fruits, and berries. The aborigines found the cuscus edible and easy to catch because of their lethargic habits.

The monotremes are represented in the New Guinean tropical forests by a genus of echidna that is

they differ from their ground-dwelling cousins by having forelimbs almost equal to their hindlimbs in length and strength. This adaptation came as a result of tree-dwelling habits in which greater security is allowed by four well-developed limbs. They are in fact able to leap great distances anyway – 20 feet with gravity behind them and twice that far if going from branch down to ground.

Two species of the gray kangaroos live in the more open parts of these forests as well as the musk kangaroo, so called because of its distinctive body odor. The musk kangaroo has one toe more on its back foot than any other kangaroo, which is a movable one at that. It also is unique among its family by being a mixed feeder, eating worms and insects in addition to vegetation. For this reason some zoologists place

Above: a black-headed python in the act of killing a bearded dragon. Pythons make a quick attack on their prey and seize it in their jaws. Then they wrap themselves around the animal and squeeze it to death. This snake can easily swallow an animal as big as an impala, which is between 30 and 40 inches in height.

larger and faster moving than the mainland genus.

Many of the forest snakes are among the world's most venomous. These include the brown tree snake, black-headed pythons, and boas. In fact, New Guinea is the only part of the world in which pythons and boas are found to live side-by-side. Among the lizards are the Queensland forest dragon and the frilled lizard, both capable of assuming a terrifying aspect when threatened, but both totally harmless. Geckos, which are represented in New Guinea by a species called the bent-toed gecko, were often objects of terror to the aborigines, some species being said to cause blindness if they were so much as touched. Like many species of lizard, geckos are able to break off their tail if it is caught by a predator. The piece of tail wriggles and keeps the attention of the predator while the gecko quickly escapes. This lizard is also able to clean its eyes with its tongue, which it does with mechanical regularity.

One of the aquatic animals of north Australia is the lungfish, of which the only other species are encountered in Africa and South America. It can grow to well in excess of 6 feet long, feeding on a wide range of food from mussels and shrimps to water plants. Unlike its relatives, the Australian lungfish cannot survive droughts by caking iself in mud and reducing its bodily functions.

The mudskipper occurs in the northern river estuaries and mangrove flats. They are strange looking creatures, somewhat like a cross between a tadpole and a fish but with two close-set bulging eyes nearly on the top of the head. Their pectoral fins are almost like limbs, enabling them to crawl, walk, and even jump over the mud as well as to climb over mangrove roots and into trees. They can remain out of water by taking air into respiratory chambers which diffuse oxygen into the bloodstream.

Left: the Australian lungfish is found only in Queensland in the northeast of the country. It has a single lunglike structure from which it gets its name.

Below: an enlargement of a mudskipper's head shows the gills through which it breathes out of water. They are kept moist by the tightly closed gill covers. Mudskippers may also absorb oxygen through their tail, which they often keep submerged.

New Guinea's Colorful Birds

New Guinea, which lies just across the Torres Strait from the northernmost tip of Queensland, is the second largest island in the world. Most of the island is covered by dense tropical rain forest, almost impenetrable because of a tangled undergrowth of vine, a slithery floor of mud and rotting leaves, and swarms of malarial mosquitoes. Otherwise there are a couple of small areas of savanna on its south coast and a backbone of high mountains. Part of these is permanently snow-capped and rises in Mount Carstensz to a peak of over 16,500 feet.

Although most of New Guinea's animal life is local species of other Australian animals, it is also the home of some unique birds. The crowned pigeon, for instance, of which there are three species, is the largest pigeon in the world at almost 3 feet in length. They are brightly colored with erect fan-shaped crests on their heads. Crowned pigeons inhabit the swampier parts of the forest floors, wandering around in small groups while pecking fruit and fallen seeds.

Related to them and sometimes even more brilliantly colored are the fruit doves and green pigeons. Not to be outdone in gaudiness are the pittas, a chubby short-tailed bird that is similar in appearance to a thrush. They have long strong legs that enable them to hop speedily on the forest floor, where they spend most of their time.

There are two species of the common cassowary that are restricted to New Guinea. One is the small Bennett's variety that has no wattle, and the other is the single-wattled cassowary.

Pygmy parrots, of which there are six species, are unique to the island. Measuring only between 3 and 5 inches in length, they are gorgeously colored, very often with green backs and red or yellow bellies sometimes edged with pale blue. These little birds, which are usually restricted to the low-lying forests, are all exclusively arboreal. They have comparatively long feet and short tails, and in some ways behave like woodpeckers. For example, they support themselves

on tree trunks by forming a tripod with their two feet and tail, nibble at the fungi, and then drill through the bark of the tree to get at the insects and larvae inside.

Another New Guinea parrot that inhabits the same steamy regions as its pygmy cousins is Pesquet's parrot. It is about 20 inches long with a head almost devoid of feathers, and it has a strong, comparatively long, and slightly curved beak to deal with its vegetarian diet.

Among the 19 bowerbird species, 11 are exclusive to New Guinea. These include Vogelkop's gardener, Lauterbach's bowerbird, Macgregor's gardener, the striped gardener, and Newton's bowerbird. The closely related birds of paradise that are modestly represented in Australia itself are widespread in New Guinea. The species known as Princess Stephanie's bird and the splendid astrapia are found at about 5000 feet, while the greater, the lesser, and Court Raggi's birds of paradise occur at lower altitudes.

The bird of paradise was so named by the Spaniards because of its fine feathers and brilliant colors. The first to be seen in Europe were the skins of several birds sent to the king of Spain by the ruler of the Moluccas, which arrived in 1522. The Spaniards named them birds of paradise because they thought them too beautiful to have originated anywhere but in a paradise. Reinforcing this idea was the fact that the skins came without the feet attached. The assumption was made that without feet the birds could never alight on tree or ground, therefore that they did not need to eat, and therefore that they must be visitors from a heavenly paradise.

Chapter 8

Antarctica

The South Pole, unlike its northern counterpart, is situated in the middle of a land mass larger than the United States of America. This land mass, the continent of Antarctica, is saucer-shaped with mountains around its rim. The plateau of the interior is covered by a permanent sheet of ice up to 12,000 feet thick which extends out over the sea in the form of ice shelves. The sea around these permanent ice shelves also freezes so that the continent's shape appears to wax and wane as the sea ice grows in July, August, and September – which is the antarctic winter – and melts and breaks up into pack ice during the polar summer. The only visible land is found around the coasts or where isolated mountain peaks penetrate the thick icy covering.

Fossil remains of subtropical plants and animals indicate that Antarctica was once warmer and possibly located away from the pole. Now, however, it is the coldest place on earth.

The crab-eater seal of the Antarctic is the most numerous of the seal species of the region, and perhaps of the world. They live on ice floes and can move across them with remarkable speed. In the summer they move closer to shore as the ice breaks up, but they are still difficult to study and many of their habits – especially in the matter of breeding – remain little known.

Birds of Antarctica

Antarctica is the most unwelcoming place on earth; temperatures as low as –126.4°F have been recorded, and winds of up to 90 miles an hour make life on this continent almost impossible. But, in contrast to the barrenness of its land, the antarctic sea bustles with life, especially during the six months of summer. Two phenomena occur to cause this profusion in a sea so cold that its temperature is at times even lower than the freezing point of blood. The first is the upswell of currents from the bottom which bring with them such nutrients as nitrates and phosphates, without which plants cannot live and grow. The second is the period of continuous light during the antarctic summer, which enables plants to photosynthesize. Summer conditions allow rapid multiplication of algae, and the surface of the sea becomes thick with minute, floating single-celled plants. This *phytoplankton* is the food of innumerable small, floating, shrimplike animals known collectively as *zooplankton* which, in their turn, become the food of fish, baleen whales, seals, seabirds, and penguins.

Two of the seabirds that share in this harvest are long-distance fliers – the wide-winged albatross and the Arctic tern which travels between the Arctic, where it nests, and Antarctica. The Antarctic tern, however, is found permanently in the south, as is the Dominican gull. A number of birds nest on the islands off Antarctica and even on the antarctic continent itself, including the snow petrel which has been found breeding nearly 200 miles inland.

Only two of the 17 species of penguin actually nest on this forbidding icebound continent, the small Adélie and the largest penguin, the emperor. Although penguins are usually thought of as creatures of the ice and snow, the majority of species are not. A number do breed on the islands surrounding Antarctica, but the jackass penguin, for instance, chooses 'he southern tip of Africa, the Magellanic inhabits the

Above: the snow petrel has a more southerly range than any other bird except the emperor penguin, and is always associated with ice. It is considered by many to be one of the most beautiful birds in the world.

Left: the Arctic tern breeds in the Arctic and winters in the Antarctic. Its migration is the longest known of any bird species.

southernmost coasts of South America, and one species, the Galápagos penguin, lives almost on the equator, nesting in the Galápagos Islands. Penguins are flightless birds, their wings having been adapted for use as paddles, and in the water they no longer seem ridiculous or clumsy as they do on land, but move with great speed and agility to catch the fish and squid which constitute the bulk of their diet.

These warm-blooded animals have bodies especially designed to keep them constantly warm despite the cold of their environment. Their tiny feathers, 70 to the square inch, are oiled to repel water, and they cover an inner heat-trapping layer of down. Below this is a thick insulating layer of fat or blubber which gives the animal its rather barrellike shape.

The small Adélie penguins are sociable birds and form large rookeries on the coast of Antarctica and the surrounding islands, where they claim individual territories and build primitive nests consisting of a few stones, which are designed more to prevent their eggs from rolling away than to protect or insulate them. The emperor penguins, on the other hand, make no nest because there is nothing for them to build nests with, breeding as they do further inland where nothing can be found but ice and snow. The female lays her solitary egg in the intense cold and dark of the antarctic winter, seemingly impractical but necessary so that the bird can hatch before spring. This means it will have the advantage of a full summer before it need fend for itself. It must attain adult plumage and acquire a sufficient store of blubber under its skin before the next long, hard winter. The egg, however, is not left on the ice but is taken up by the mother's mate as soon as it is laid and tucked into a position of insulation atop his webbed feet and under an enveloping fold of his abdomen. The male will continue to hold the egg there on his feet for the next 50 to 60 days, huddling together with the other brooding males for warmth while the females make their way to the coast to feed and fill their *crops*, special pouchlike enlargements of the gullet, with food for the emerging chicks. So strong is the male's brooding instinct that an egg laid down on the ice may be snatched up by a rival, and those males with no access to eggs will incubate round lumps of ice or snow.

The females return to the rookery with bursting crops just in time for the hatching of their offspring. How they find their own mates is a mystery, but sound may be a factor. The emaciated males make their way toward the sea and food, having fasted for the entire incubation period and losing about a third of their weight in the process.

By November the ice is beginning to melt and break up, and the chicks, which by now are like their parents about 4 feet high and up to 90 pounds, are borne northward on the ice floes. With luck their ice islands will last long enough for them to molt their baby down and attain their full mature plumage, after which they will take to the sea and begin their adult life.

Above: a pair of emperor penguins attends to the needs of their newly hatched chick. Emperors live on the Antarctic shore, the farthest south of any penguin, and they have to cope with the harshest living conditions of almost any animal in the world. They are the largest of the penguins, measuring about 3 feet in height and weighing up to 100 pounds. They feed on fish and squid that they catch in their long sharp-edged bill underwater.

Antarctica

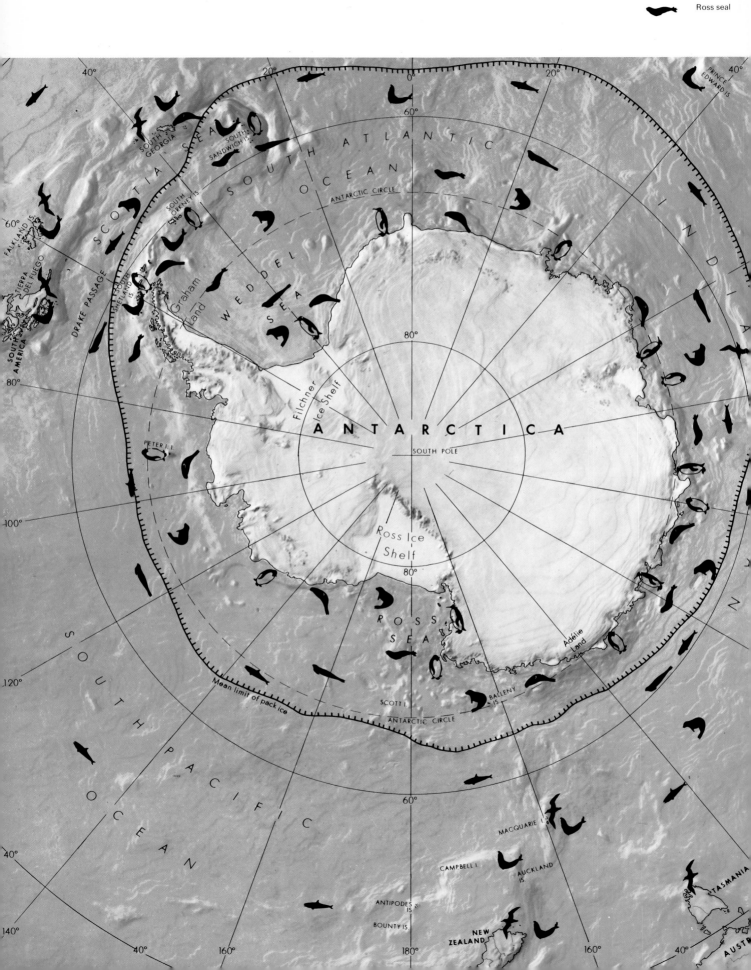

Killer whale

Leopard seal

Ross seal

Southern elephant seal

Weddell seal

Crabeater seal

Emperor penguin

Adélie penguin

Albatross

Above: Adélie penguins have the black and white tuxedo look
and the laugh-provoking waddle that people associate with all of
the penguins. They travel in huge crowds and sometimes behave
like a flock of sheep, all doing what the first one or so do.

Seals of the Southern Seas

The birds of the Antarctic are not the only creatures who feed on the mass of plankton which floats in the top five fathoms of chilly sea. A number of mammals also take advantage of this abundance of food, either by eating the tiny crustaceans themselves or the fish that have already eaten and processed the protein.

Whales and seals both inhabit the polar waters but whereas the whale lives its entire life in the water, seals must take to the land in order to breed and to molt. Five species of seal may be found on or around the coastal ice of Antarctica, including the southern elephant seal, an occasional visitor found more usually on subantarctic islands such as South Georgia. These enormous animals suffered terribly at the hands of sealers during the 19th century when, because the carcass of a large adult male can produce 720 pints of oil, the animal was practically exterminated to keep alight the oil lamps of Europe and America. The seals have, however, been pro-

tected since 1910 (although limited killing is still permitted on South Georgia), and their numbers have recovered. The elephant seal is so named not only because of its colossal bulk, but also because the males possess extraordinary inflatable noses which dangle down over their mouths like trunks. These are used to intimidate their rivals, establish and defend territories, and attract mates – by acting as resonating chambers to make their roaring more terrifying. Contact between competing males is not restricted to noise-making, though, and bloody fights often take place at the breeding grounds.

Of the four species of true seal which breed on Antarctic ice, the crab-eater seal is the most numerous, some estimates placing its population as high as 20 million. The animal escapes human persecution by breeding on the drifting pack ice so that its pups are inaccessible; the pelts of the adults, furthermore, are worthless because they are always scarred, although whether these wounds are inflicted by rivals or by the predatory killer whale is not known. The crab-eater

Below: in spite of their name, crab-eater seals do not eat crabs. They live on planktonic krill, which they strain from the water through their three-pointed teeth. Females are generally a bit larger than males, but both are slim-lined and lithe in body.

shelves, although recent research indicates that seals, like whales, dolphins, and bats, possibly use the sound vibrations of echoes as a kind of sonar system. The Weddell seal can dive to depths of 1800 feet and stay submerged for up to 60 minutes.

Their ability to hold their breath underwater is because seals have much more blood than human beings, and their blood has a much greater capacity for storing oxygen as well. In addition to this, their heartbeat slows during diving and the blood flow is cut off from all inessential organs, so that oxygen is only directed to such organs as the brain.

The Ross seal is another large-eyed hunter at sea floor level. It is a solitary creature, chubby with a

Above: the Ross seal is the rarest and smallest of the Antarctic seals, living on and around the pack ice far out at sea. Like the Weddell seal, it eats fish and squid. Its sharp curved canine and incisor teeth help it to hold onto its slippery prey.

Left: the Weddell seal has a spotted coat somewhat like the leopard seal, but it is much heavier in the body and has a smaller head. These seals show no fear of humans and therefore are easy to study. More is known about their habits than any other seals.

seal's diet, like that of some seabirds and the baleen whales, is made up exclusively of plankton. Its teeth are many-cusped and close-fitting, thus forming a sieve which retains the tiny plankton while the seawater is expelled from the sides of the mouth.

The darker colored Weddell seal has a different diet, mainly the squid and fish that inhabit the bottom of the ocean around the shores of Antarctica. This species, therefore, spends most of the winter below the ice, cutting breathing holes for itself with its teeth by fixing its lower incisors into the ice and using its upper teeth to make circular slashes – an operation which is very wearing on the teeth. Worn teeth can be a cause of death if a seal is thereby unable to keep its breathing holes open. The Weddell seal is equipped with large eyes to enable it to find its holes as well as to hunt in the murky depths below the ice

short, wide head, and it inhabits the zone of drifting pack ice around Antarctica. It has been so rarely sighted that very little is known about its habits.

The least attractive of the antarctic seals is the leopard seal which has a somewhat reptilian looking head, a slim, blotchy body, and sharply pointed teeth. Although its main food is fish and squid, it also preys on warm-blooded animals – the penguin is its chief victim, but it will also eat young seals, including its own, and has been reported as attacking human beings. Adélie penguins are terrified of the leopard seal and will teeter on the edge of an ice floe waiting for one of their number to lead the way into the water, for the leopard seal is often lurking under the ice waiting for them. Sometimes a seal will even take a "run" and heave itself out of the water and into the midst of the penguins hesitating at the edge of the ice.

283

Antarctic Whales

When Captain James Cook returned from his exploration of polar waters in 1775 he brought with him tales of seas swarming with seals and whales. These stories triggered off an unprecedented orgy of killing as whaling and sealing stations were set up on the previously untouched Antarctic islands. But it was not until the 20th century that modern whaling fleets, often accompanied by factory ships to process and store the catch, made whaling an efficient industry. These modern fleets are even equipped with radio and sonar devices and sometimes even with light aircraft or helicopters for spotting the whales. Their harpoons are fitted with explosive heads which explode on impact, blowing huge holes in the unfortunate animals. Although some measure of international protection exists in the form of a quota system administered by the International Whaling Commission, this depends for its enforcement upon individual governments and only covers certain species. Many whales of the Antarctic are still overhunted.

The whales are the only mammals which have completely emancipated themselves from the land; in fact, death usually results if by chance they are occasionally stranded on beaches. Therefore whales are not to be seen on the shores or the pack ice.

All the species of fin whale – the largest of the whales – spend the summer months in the Arctic or Antarctic seas, migrating from these icy waters in the winter to warmer waters nearer the equator. The reason for choosing these seemingly inhospitable areas are the vast amounts of small crustaceans, the *krill* as they are called by the whalers, which account for a high proportion of the abundant plankton. This is particularly true of the Antarctic, whose seas produce enough of these tiny, shrimplike creatures to provide the blue, rorqual, humpback, sei, and minke whales with sufficient quantities of food to fill their huge stomachs. When the stomach of a blue whale, the largest animal that has ever lived, was accidentally pierced by whalers, more than a ton of krill could

cascade onto the whaler's deck. (The blue whale is now protected and no longer hunted.) It seems strange that such large creatures should feed exclusively on such small prey, but their mouths and throats have been so adapted that it is difficult for them to swallow anything bigger than the very small fish which sometimes augment their crustacean diet.

This is because none of these animals possesses teeth. Instead their mouths are equipped with great curtains of *baleen* or whalebone, which hang down on either side from the upper palate and form highly efficient sieves. The whale opens its enormous mouth and in flow the krill; the seawater is then forced out of the sides of the mouth between the baleen plates by the action of the tongue, trapping the krill.

Right: the teeth of a killer whale are very large and conical in shape. It has 20 in each jaw, and when its mouth is shut, these teeth interlock. Other toothed whales have a like arrangement.

Below: the minke whale is the smallest of its species, measuring about 30 feet long. Like the other fin whales, it is gray or blue-black on the upperparts and light gray to white underneath.

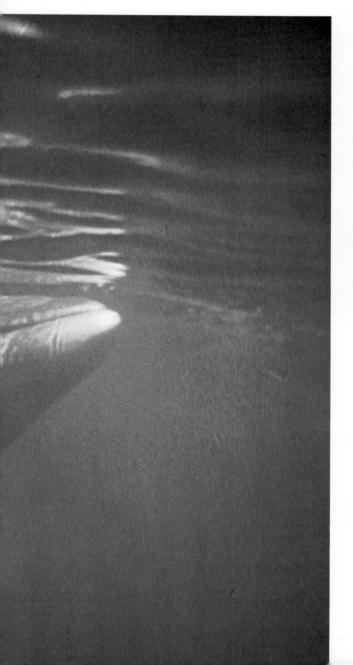

The killer whale, another species of the Antarctic waters, subsists on a very different diet from the larger baleen whales, feeding mainly on warm-blooded creatures – seals and penguins – as well as fish and squid. This comparatively small, neatly marked, black-and-white whale has a large dorsal back fin reminiscent of a shark's and a mouthful of very efficient pointed teeth. The killer whale is the terror of the seas it inhabits, for sometimes it hunts in packs and will apparently even attack animals larger than itself such as the fin whales, which it harries and exhausts by clinging to their lips and tongues. Even humans might be attacked by the killer whale; certainly it sinks small boats, and the British explorer Robert F. Scott, in the diary of his last expedition to

Antarctica in 1911, cites an example of killer whales trying to dislodge one of his companions from the pack ice on which he was standing, presumably with the intention of eating him.

Once in captivity, however, the killer seems to lose its aggressive instincts, and it will swim peacefully beside its trainer and even allow him to ride on its back or place his head in its mouth.

There have even been instances when killer whales helped men. In Twofold Bay, Australia at the end of the last century, a pack of killers was reported to have cooperated with whalers who were catching the humpback and minke whales as they swam through the bay on their annual migration from their Antarctic summer feeding grounds northward to their breeding grounds.

285

Chapter 9

The Island Regions

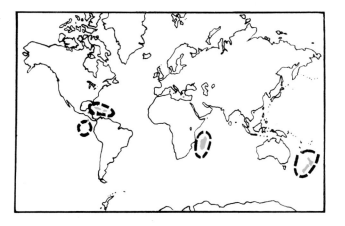

Although zoologists divide the world into six main regions according to the kinds of animals in them, some of the world islands, along with Antarctica, do not fit into these. While many islands have an animal life much the same as that of their nearest continent – as is the case with the British Isles, for instance – others contain animals that are remarkably different. These include New Zealand, Madagascar, the West Indies, and the Galápagos Group. A good example of the development of unique wildlife is Madagascar. This island lies only 260 miles from the east coast of Africa, but is the home of large numbers of lemurs and other animals not found on the mainland.

In fact, the islands mentioned contain an unusually large number of unique animals, which is not so surprising in the light of the fact that isolation is a prerequisite for the evolution of new species.

The ring-tailed lemur is one of the larger species of a family of animals that is unique to Madagascar. It lives in the grassy plains of the southwest of the island and, in contrast to the twilight habits of most lemurs, is more active in the daytime. In the social groups of about a dozen, the females are dominant over the males.

Life on Islands

Some islands are far older than others. New Zealand and Madagascar, for instance, probably broke away from the huge land mass known as Gondwanaland some 200 million years ago. Fossils show that this was before mammals existed and explains the lack of indigenous land mammals in New Zealand. Great Britain, however, was only separated from Europe at the end of the Ice Age about 7000 years ago and thus the animals on either side of the English channel are more or less identical.

Most of the smaller islands dotted on the world's oceans have never had a connection with a land mass, having been formed by volcanic action. Unprotected by any kind of vegetation when first thrust up, such islands are easily destroyed by the erosion of wind and waves, and many have had a short geological life. However, except for the very smallest, most have survived long enough to be colonized first by plants and then by animals. It is now known that there is a pattern to such colonization.

Winged and tufted seeds are often carried for vast distances on high air currents or by hurricanes, for example. Undigested seeds in a visiting bird's intestines can be eliminated by the bird and take root. In these ways a volcanic island can be vegetated.

Winged animals such as birds and bats frequently reach oceanic islands simply by flying to them, and birds may carry minute animals in the mud caking their feet or feathers. Moths and dragonflies have been carried along the path of the surface wind drift. So the islands can begin to get an animal life.

Some larger animals such as crocodiles, tortoises, and possibly certain mammals, may reach the islands by swimming or floating from relatively near habitats, while others may arrive on drifting flotsam carried out to sea by flooding rivers. Finally, a number of mammals, especially rats and mice, are brought by humans whether by design or not.

The animals most rarely encountered on oceanic islands are amphibians and freshwater fish which find saltwater an impassable barrier.

The formation of new volcanic islands and their colonization is still taking place today. As recently as

1963 the island of Surtsey rose out of the boiling sea southwest of Iceland. The island of Krakatau in the Pacific, which has existed in its present smaller form since 1883, has been studied in some detail. It was seen to have been colonized first by grass and primitive plants, then by insects and birds. Later came forest trees among vegetation and skinks and crocodiles among animals. Last came rats, conforming to the pattern of how oceanic islands get their animal life.

Above: a close-up view of red hot lava sliding into the sea on a part of the unstable coastline of Surtsey. This island appeared in 1963, formed by volcanic action southwest of Iceland.

Left: an aerial view of Surtsey. Steam rises where torrents of molten rock reach the sea.

Right: floating vegetation that broke free during the rainy season in Ecuador drifts down the Guayas River at Guayaquil. These plants and any animals riding on them will float out to the Pacific. In this way in the past, some land species of plant and animal colonized the Galapagos Group of islands.

Madagascar's Wildlife

Although it is the fourth largest island in the world, Madagascar is only a little more than twice the size of Great Britain. It measures 1000 miles from north to south and about 400 miles across. Yet within its confines it contains a terrain of wide diversity: lush rain forests in the east, a great central and western area of dry deciduous woodland, a patch of steppe and spiny desert in the southwest, and a chain of mountains down the center. These mountains average between 5000 and 6000 feet in height with some peaks topping the 9000-foot mark.

Between Madagascar and the east coast of Africa is the Mozambique Channel, a deep trench that has been in existence for about 200 million years. It has proved an effective barrier to animal movement between the continent and the island, leaving the island's native wildlife to evolve independently. The island is the unique home for more than 70 species of mammal and 125 of bird. Curiously, although the

Below: the flying fox is the largest of the fruit bats and has a wide range that includes the islands of the Pacific from Indonesia to Madagascar, where it is one of the few animals that lives on the plentiful fruit there. It is 1 foot long in the body.

woods and forests provide an ample supply of fruit and seeds, Madagascar has few animals that live mainly on fruit or seeds. It has been estimated that some 90 percent of all the island's species are unique to its forests. In view of the fact that these forests are

Above: the leaf-tailed gecko is a tree climbing lizard that is exclusive to Madagascar. A pattern of broken and uneven lines provides it with camouflage among leaves. It has big jaws on a largish head that gives it the nickname of "tree crocodile."

being cleared rapidly to make room for humans, the outlook for animals is not the brightest.

About half of the world's total number of 85 species of chameleon live on Madagascar, and they come in all sizes from the 1.5-inch-long dwarf to the 2-foot-long species. There are also about 50 species of gecko inhabiting the island, including the green gecko and the ingeniously camouflaged leaf-tailed gecko. Oddly enough, there are representatives of the iguanas in Madagascar although these lizards are otherwise found only in the New World and on some isolated Pacific Islands such as Fiji and Tonga. Their counterparts in Eurasia, Africa, and the Far East are the agamid lizards such as the common agama and moloch.

The tenrec family, of which there are 30 species in many guises, is confined to Madagascar. There are tenrecs that look like hedgehogs, those that look like shrews, and those that look like moles. The web-footed tenrec parallels the water shrew in its aquatic habits, and the rice tenrecs go underground like the moles they resemble.

The banded tenrec looks like a cross between a skunk and a hedgehog. It uses its spines for defense, but they have another use as well. When a party of these 6-inch-long animals venture forth into the night for food, the spines clatter together and this noise keeps all members of the group in touch.

Right: a chameleon in the act of shooting out its tongue, which is folded like a concertina, to trap an insect that has landed nearby. The head of most chameleons end in a pointed crest.

Below: the tenrec has a larger mouth in relation to its body than any other mammal. It eats mostly insects and worms but also some plant food, and the rice tenrec often feeds on rice.

More Animals of Madagascar

The three indigenous families of birds on the island are the mesites, the asities, and the vangas. Of these, the vangas have done the most to diversify their habits in order to make the best of whatever food and shelter is available – in much the same way as the honeycreepers of Hawaii and the finches of the Galápagos have done.

The mesites, which are also variously known as roatelos and monias, are ground birds related to the rails and the cranes. They are present in three varieties. These birds are so ill-equipped for flying that they even have to climb up the trees into their nests, which are loosely constructed platforms of sticks a few feet above the ground. The best-known of this family is the brown mesite which lives in the tropical forests along the east coast. Another mesite, Bensch's rail or monia, is unusual in that the female has several mates, all of which share in the building of the nest.

There are four species of asities inhabiting the humid forests on either side of the island. Two of them, Schlegel's asity and the velvet asity, are among the few species that live on fruit. The other two species are both known as false sunbirds, resembling true sunbirds to such a degree that they were originally classified with them. The main visible differences are that the asities are slighter in build and shorter of leg. Both have a long bill that curves down, and it was

Below: a hollow in a tree suits the kestrel for a place to incubate its eggs, since it does not make a nest. It also uses cliff ledges, crevices, or the abandoned nests of other birds. Kestrels are small falcons that, unlike other members of their family, hover in the air to look for prey and then attack on the ground.

Above: the harrier of Madagascar is also called the pied harrier because of its black and white coloring, although it is mostly black. Harriers differ from other birds of prey by roosting and nesting on the ground, sometimes building nests in colonies.

not until 1933 that the asity was distinguished from the true sunbird. The more common of these two species is the beautiful wattled false sunbird with its glittering blue upper plumage. The other is the small-billed false sunbird, now so rare because of the destruction of its forest habitat that it is known only from nine specimens in museums. These were collected originally from three localities near Tananarive. Some authorities think that the small-billed false sunbird is already extinct.

The vangas are the most remarkable family of birds on the island. Being closely related to the shrikes, they are sometimes referred to as vanga-shrikes. The 11 species of the vanga family, which subsist on insects and small vertebrates, look and behave differently. The blue vanga, for instance, keeps to the

branches of the trees to pick insects out, while Lafresnaye's vanga has the same habit as the flycatcher of adding to its insect diet with lizards and frogs. The minute tit-shrike is a fairly close model of the great tit. The helmet bird preys on geckos, chameleons, lizards, and small birds, while the foot-long sicklebill uses its long bill to probe for insects in the cracks of tree bark. The coral-billed nuthatch is so-called because it is so like the true nuthatches.

There are many birds of prey exclusive to Madagascar including Henst's goshawk, the Madagascar cuckoo falcons, fish eagles, and harrier hawks. Probably the rarest of the local avian predators is the Madagascar serpent eagle which belies its name twice over: it is not a true eagle and it is not known actually to eat snakes.

Of the various species of lovebird on the island, the lavender-headed variety is native to Madagascar.

The mammal predators of the island include the common mongoose and a species of wildcat that were introduced by humans. The indigenous carnivores are mostly of the civet family such as the Malagasy civet, the closely related falanouc, and the fossa which is a strange mixture of mongoose, genet, and wildcat. In fact, the 5-foot-long fossa is so catlike that it was classified with the cats for a long time. A solitary animal that comes abroad at dusk, it is the island's largest mammal predator and lives mainly on lemurs. One of the ways that the fossa defends itself is to exude a foul smelling glandular secretion.

Above: the common or Egyptian mongoose was introduced into Madagascar and has thrived there, as it seems able to do everywhere.

Below: fossas are fierce predators, attacking pigs and climbing trees after lemurs. It is possible that this catlike animal is a descendant of the same ancestor as cats and civets. It lives in the forests, free of any threat to its safety except from humans.

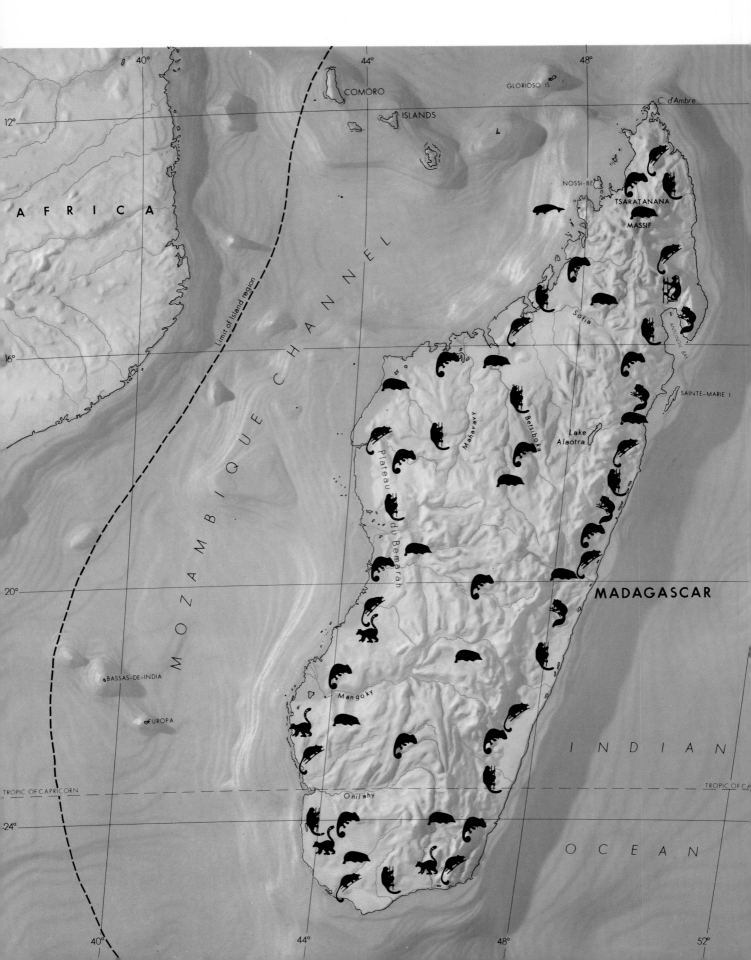

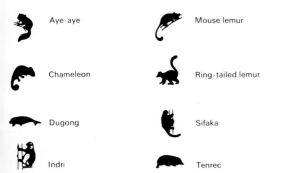

	Aye-aye		Mouse lemur
	Chameleon		Ring-tailed lemur
	Dugong		Sifaka
	Indri		Tenrec

Below: two Verreaux' sifakas at rest in their treetop habitat. When active, Verreaux' sifakas can make great leaps of over 30 feet at one jump, and they are known for making accurate landings even in the trees of cactuslike spines in the southern forests. They also inhabit forests of the northwest and west. Sifakas live in small groups of up to eight, each group claiming and defending a specific territory. They often sit and sunbathe.

Madagascar's Many Lemurs

Probably the best known of Madagascar's unique animals is the lemur. Many of these live in the forest, although the ring-tailed lemur lives among the rocks. Lemurs are related to the prosimians of Africa that include the bush baby and potto, and to the loris of Asia. Today, Madagascar lemurs are grouped into three families containing 21 species. Most lemurs have a monkeylike appearance, are the size of a domestic cat, and have long tails and foxlike muzzles. The lesser dwarf lemur, however, is about the size of a young rat.

The largest lemur is the indri, a black-and-white animal about 30 inches long. Indris live in family groups in the forests of east Madagascar. The young are born in November or December and are carried by the mother from birth. This lemur can be heard more easily than seen because it lives so high in the trees, spending the early morning sun bathing on the high branches. It is now increasingly rare.

It is likely that the lemur today differs only in minor respects from its original ancestors. However, they

Below: the indri is known by the local inhabitants as the "dog of the forest." This name comes from its doglike face and loud barking cry that echoes through the mountain forests it lives in.

also possess some of the characteristics developed by the higher primates. For instance, their brains have temporal lobes, if only in a rudimentary form, there is the vestige of a yellow spot on the retina of the eye, and they practice certain sophisticated social patterns characteristic of the higher primates.

Lemurs do not possess the binocular vision of the higher primates, but they do seem to have some color sense. Their sense of smell, on the other hand, is highly developed and is important in mating as in other activities.

The 16 species of true and dwarf lemurs vary in color from a bright chestnut through several shades of brown and gray to a stark black and white. The

Above: ring-tailed lemurs live in thinly wooded areas rather than in forests like most of the family. During the mating season, males use their bushy tails to waft their scent on the air.

ruffed lemur, which has a black and white coat, lives in the forests of the northern coast, being active in the early morning and at twilight. Like many of the lemurs, its numbers have declined as the tall trees in which it makes its home have been cleared.

The ring-tailed lemur – the one seen most commonly

in zoos – lives in tamarind trees although it does spend some time on the ground. It is one of the species that is active by day. Unlike their monkey relatives, these animals have an extremely limited breeding season. The fight for mates among males during this period brings their spectacularly striped tails into play. The tail is wiped across the forelimbs where scent glands are situated and then brandished at the rival male in a gesture of aggression.

The tiny dwarf and lesser mouse lemurs are nocturnal. Like their larger cousins, these animals are mainly vegetarian, eating fruit and leaves, but they supplement this diet with insects and birds' eggs.

The sifaka is one of the larger lemurs, a diurnal

Above: the lesser mouse lemur is one of the smallest living primates. By day it sleeps curled up in a ball, often twisting its tail around a branch for support. It feeds on insects and fruit.

bony fingers, the third one on each forepaw being almost as thin as a wire. The aye-aye searches for grubs in trees by tapping the wood with this long middle finger, listening with its large ears for the grubs inside, and tearing at the bark with its long incisors to make a hole in the wood. It then uses its long fingers to extract the grubs from the hole it has made. Aye-ayes are strictly nocturnal.

Below: the aye-aye looks so much like a squirrel that it was originally classed as a rodent. It is one of the rarest animals in the world, dying out as its northeastern forests are destroyed.

animal that is a superb leaper. It has a creamy white fur with chocolate markings on head and limbs. Like the indri, the sifaka is becoming more and more rare. Another fast vanishing lemur is the aye-aye, which differs so much from the others that it is classified in a separate genus. The aye-aye looks more like a rodent than a monkey and even has the same kind of incisor teeth.

The most unusual feature of the aye-aye is its long

Wildlife in Isolation

New Zealand, like Madagascar, was isolated from any other land mass for about 200 million years – long before mammals evolved. Unlike Madagascar, however, it was separated from its nearest neighbor by a distance great enough to be a serious barrier against mammalian migration. The only mammals that were able to reach the islands on their own were bats, of which New Zealand possesses two types.

New Zealand's total lack of idigenous land mammals meant that the ground habitats normally occupied by such animals would be taken over by others. In the case of New Zealand, the animals that adapted best to fill the niches are flightless birds.

Originally New Zealand had a few land animals, which were of only three types. There were the flightless birds of which one – the kiwi – has been adopted as the country's national emblem; three species of rare and primitive frogs; and some reptiles such as geckos, skinks, and the tuatara, the only species left of a group of reptiles which, apart from this lizard, died out 100 million years ago.

With the arrival of the first humans came the dog and the rat. The land mammal that suffered most from the dog was the enormous flightless bird called the moa. This bird, of which there were 19 species, belonged to the same group as the African ostrich, the Australian emu, and the South American rhea. With the dog as predator and helper to Maori hunters, moas were probably hunted to extinction before the Europeans landed in the late 18th century. Since then, however, the whole picture has altered. By 1950 there were 29 different kinds of mammals on New Zealand's two islands, imported from all over the world, and they included animals as diverse as mice, phalangers, and elks. Furthermore, the native New Zealand birds were joined by hundreds of foreign species from thrushes to mynahs, skylarks to kookaburras, and finches to peafowls. Some of these brought with them diseases that the indigenous birds had never been exposed to and to which they fell easy victims.

New Zealand's flightless birds include the kiwis, the takahe, the kakapo or owl-parrot, and the weka. The kiwi, a relative of the extinct moa, probably escaped its cousin's fate by being smaller and nocturnal. There are three species of kiwi which, unlike most birds, has nostrils at the tip of the bill that give it a

Right: the takahe summers in high mountain valleys and winters in beech forests lower down. It is the size of a large chicken.

Below: kiwis usually manage to stay well out of sight in their forest home, where they go about their business quietly and quickly at night. Like other flightless birds, the male kiwi incubates the eggs and cares for the chicks after they hatch.

good sense of smell. Kiwi's wings are mere tokens, so small that they are invisible under the plumage. Their feathers are long but narrow, which gives them the appearance of being short. Kiwis have powerful legs that enable them to run with great speed even though with a waddle. Their eggs, of which they usually lay only one, are disproportionately large – a quarter the size of the adult's body and as much as a seventh of its weight.

The takahé is a brightly colored bird that was long thought to be extinct until it was rediscovered on South Island in 1948 in Fjordland National Park. Sub-fossil remains indicate that this flightless bird was once widespread throughout both North and South Islands, but it is now found mainly in the Murchison Mountains. Having become rare, it is strictly pro-

Above: in adapting to life in New Zealand, the kakapo filled the role of deer by chewing ferns and eating grass. This adaptation became a disadvantage when deer were introduced on the island.
Below: first brought to New Zealand in 1861 to provide sport, red deer – and other species later – became a threat to the kakapo. Not only have deer competed with the kakapo for food, but by nibbling tree seedlings they also prevented forest regrowth.

tected by law.

The kakapo or owl-parrot is another bird that has only just escaped extinction, having been hunted for food by stoats and having had their habitats usurped by herds of deer. It is now one of New Zealand's rarest birds, living as a neighbor of the takahé in the beech forests of Fjordland in South Island. The kakapo is a parrot although its face looks like an owl's. It is moss green above and green-yellow below. Feeding on fruit, grass, and roots, it is nocturnal and retires into hollows or burrows scratched out among tree roots by day. Kakapos occasionally climb trees from which they do not fly but glide because, although their wings are well developed, their pectoral muscles are not strong enough to operate them efficiently.

The Island Regions: New Zealand

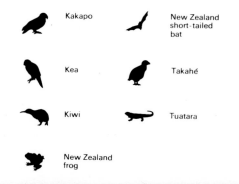

🦜	Kakapo	🦇	New Zealand short-tailed bat
🦜	Kea	🐦	Takahé
🐾	Kiwi	🦎	Tuatara
🐸	New Zealand frog		

Below: sheep grazing on a New Zealand farm. European settlers unleashed horrors on the native wildlife with the introduction of the animals they needed and wanted for the kind of life they were used to. Sheep farmers set the forests aflame as the easiest way to create pastures. With the trees and shrubs, the ground birds and feeble-winged quail went up in the furious fires. Baring the land produced soil erosion and flooding, all of which had an adverse effect on New Zealand's indigenous wild animals.

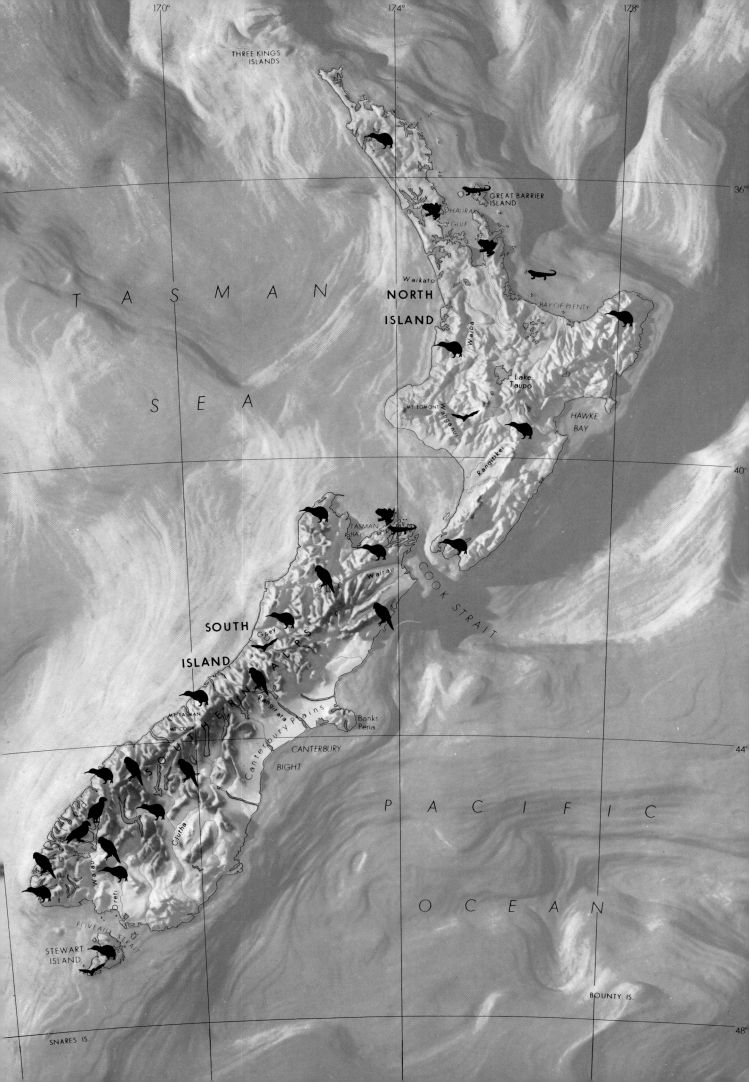

Animal Life of New Zealand

Of the many birds found in New Zealand, there are four indigenous species of parakeet. They are the red-crowned, yellow-crowned, orange-fronted, and the Antipodes Island parakeets. The red- and yellow-crowned species, which feed on seeds, buds, fruit, and leaves, suffered at the hands of the early European

large hollow trees and moves in small flocks of 10 or so. The Maoris used to eat its flesh and decorate themselves with its feathers, which they also used as currency. Although a harmless bird, the kaka has suffered persecution because of its similarity to its drabber cousin the kea. This bird is thought of as a sheep killer, and accordingly is hunted and killed itself. However, although the kea is known to feed on dead sheep and other carrion, its main diet is fruit, leaves, buds, and insects.

Other birds of flight in New Zealand include the swamp-dwelling pukeko, a close relative of the

Above: like all parrots, the kea has a strong hooked beak and is noisy, getting its name from the loud sound it makes in calling. It is a very hardy bird, sometimes living above the treeline on South Island, which is the only location it is to be found.

settlers who killed them in large numbers because they damaged crops and orchards. These two species are forest inhabitants. The orange-fronted parakeet lives in the high mountain districts and the Antipodes Island parakeet is confined to a group of small uninhabited islands southeast of New Zealand. The Antipodes are also the nesting ground of penguins with highly populated colonies for two thirds of the year.

Closely related to the parakeets are such parrots as the kaka and the kea. The kaka is fairly common throughout the forests of New Zealand. A vividly colored bird of crimson rump and abdomen, it shows scarlet underwings when it flies. The kaka breeds in

302

Left: falcons need stability in the air to enable them to dive quickly when they sight their prey, and for this they have long and pointed wings that sweep back in a V-wing style. It is the female, larger and bolder than the male, that is used in sport.

The tuatara lays between eight and 15 eggs at a time, which it buries in nests. These hatch without incubation or any other kind of attention, but take 15 months to do so. The tuatara's metabolism is the slowest of all living vertebrates, and the animal grows at a slow pace as well – about a half inch every eight years. It lives to a very old age, some authorities putting the maximum at over 100 years. This animal is now confined to some of the small isolated islands which are free of the rats that prey on their eggs. Tuataras are most active at night, but sometimes can be seen basking in the sun outside their burrows during the day.

The only amphibian in New Zealand is a primitive frog, of which there are three species. A fourth species related to it lives in North America. It is extremely rare, and is now protected. It lives in the mountains where the air is cold as well as moist. There is no tadpole stage, the eggs hatching straight into tiny tailed frogs. The tail disappears as the frogs become adult, but the muscles that worked it remain.

flightless takahé, and the bellbird and stitchbird. There are also several honeyeaters, among them the 11-inch-long tui or parson bird whose throat bears white feather tufts resembling a clerical collar. The tui is black with an iridescent bronze, green, and purple sheen. It is an excellent mimic and fine singer. New Zealand's birds of prey include the New Zealand falcon or kararea and the harrier or kahu, the second of which is often a roadside scavenger.

The 2-foot-long tuatara, which with its big head and ridge of spines down its back looks like a strange lizard, is the only reptile that is classed in an order and family on its own. It is in fact a survival from the ancient reptile group known as "beak heads," differing internally in several respects from modern lizards.

Right: the ancestors of the tuatara were wiped out by competition from more adaptable lizards, but this one survived on the islands that became New Zealand because they separated from the continental land mass before the competitors had arrived.

Left: a harrier and its chick. Harriers have soft plumage and a facial ruff like owls, but are not related. In searching for prey, they zigzag over the ground at a low level. Then they pounce suddenly to attack.

A Naturalist's Paradise

The Galápagos lie in the Pacific Ocean about 600 miles west of South America. Thirteen of this group of islands are fairly large. They include Isabela, Fernandina, Santa Cruz, San Salvador, and San Cristóbal. Many of the others are so small that they could more properly be called islets. The Galápagos were formed by volcanic action between 10 and 15 million years ago and have never been joined to any continent. When in 1535 the Bishop of Panama paid the islands a visit, he could find no water and had to quench his thirst by chewing cactus leaves. He said that it seemed that God had caused it to rain stones on these islands, a reference to its terrain of volcanic debris, cinder slopes, and lava fields. Charles Darwin, who made the name Galápagos almost synonymous with his theories of the origins of species and evolution, on his first visit likened the vista to that of the Black Country of the English midlands, an area full of slag heaps. Another naturalist as recently as 1938 found the place "monstrous," commenting critically on the landscape of "dense thorn scrub, cactus spines, loose sharp lava."

Right: giant Galápagos tortoises wallow in pools of rain water on the island of Isabela. *Galapago* is an old Spanish word for tortoise, and the name of the island group came from this animal that was once so numerous there. They are strictly plant eaters.
Below: cactus growing near the northern shore of Fernandina Island. This species takes root in lava fields that retain no moisture, thriving there where few other plants can even survive. Some Galápagos cacti even grow tall enough to resemble trees.

In spite of the way settlers look upon them as nearly inhabitable, the Galápagos islands are a naturalist's paradise. They not only provide a stop-off for many migratory birds, but are also the breeding ground for many unique animals. The most famous of the Galápagos wildlife are the finches, the giant tortoises, and the iguanas. The Galápagos tortoise is one of the world's largest land tortoises, weighing up to 553 pounds and measuring about 5 feet in length. This animal was nearly annihilated by whalers and passing seafarers who collected them to use as fresh meat on long voyages because they stayed alive for months on board the ships. Between 1811 and 1844, 15,000 of them suffered this fate.

The marine iguanas, which feed on seaweed, can reach a size of 4 feet in length although they are usually between 2.5 and 3 feet long. Their main

natural enemy is the shark. They themselves are seemingly benign creatures over which crabs crawl freely in search of ticks and parasites living in the folds of their skin. Marine iguanas can often be seen sunning themselves on rocks after foraging in the cold sea water for food. The land iguana feeds on almost any type of vegetation it can find, including cacti.

Left: a land iguana munching the fruit of a prickly pear. Land iguanas are larger than their marine cousins, reaching a length of 5 feet. One species of the land iguana that is considered a food delicacy is threatened with extinction, and only 300 remain.

Above: the Galápagos penguin lives farther north than any other penguin species. They can live on the equator as they do because the cool waters of the Humboldt Current sweeps past the region.
Below: unlike any other lizard, marine iguanas browse underwater to find the seaweed they like to feed on. They do not actually live in the water, but they are good swimmers.

They live in burrows underground, often using old lava tubes. Both marine and land iguanas have been the victims of once tame dogs that have gone wild and feed on their eggs and young.

Among the birdlife of the Galápagos are such seabirds as brown pelicans, blue-footed boobies, and frigates or man o' war birds. There are also flightless birds such as the cormorant and the small Galápagos penguin. These two birds often share the same habitat of offshore rocks. There are also several species of mockingbird which vary from island to island. Only one species lives on any one island.

The Galápagos fur seal has been reduced to only 1000, having been killed for its beautiful coat.

The Island Regions:
The Galapagos Group

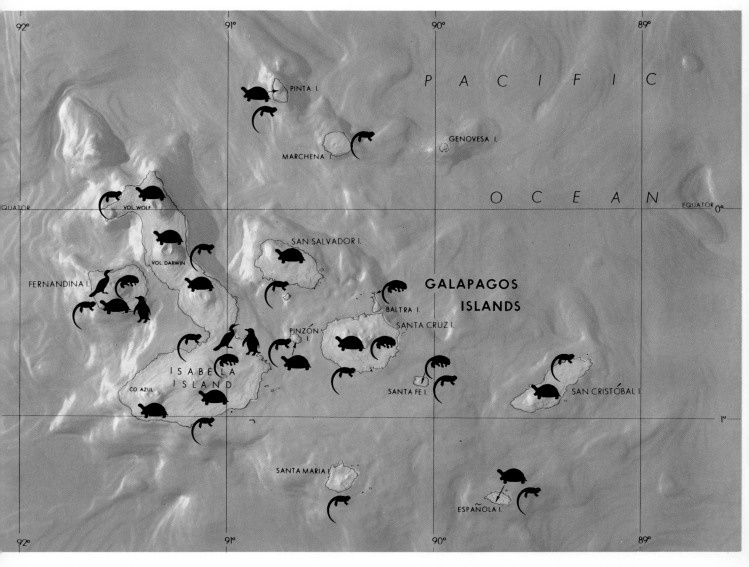

P A C I F I C

PINTA I.

MARCHENA I.

GENOVESA I.

O C E A N

EQUATOR 0°

VOL. WOLF

SAN SALVADOR I.

VOL. DARWIN

FERNANDINA I.

BALTRA I.

GALAPAGOS
ISLANDS

SANTA CRUZ I.

PINZÓN

ISABELA
ISLAND

CO. AZUL

SANTA FE I.

SAN CRISTÓBAL I.

SANTA MARIA I.

ESPAÑOLA I.

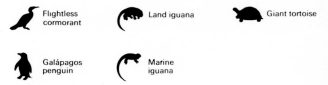

Flightless
cormorant

Land iguana

Giant tortoise

Galápagos
penguin

Marine
iguana

Left: the wings of the Galápagos cormorant have been reduced to stubs that serve for balancing rather than for flight. This species has not had need of flight because it has no enemies on the Galápagos. It and the penguin are the only flightless seabirds.

Right: this photograph of the shore on Fernandina Island in the Galápagos shows how certain animals occupy distinct horizontal zones. There are blue-footed boobies at the top level, marine iguanas in the middle zone, and red crabs at the bottom.

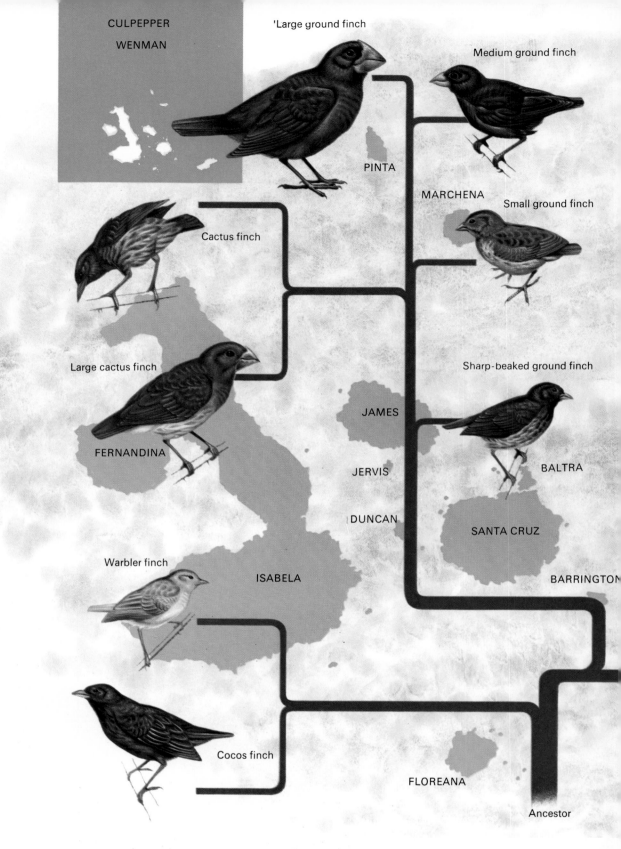

'Large ground finch

Medium ground finch

PINTA

MARCHENA

Small ground finch

Cactus finch

Large cactus finch

JAMES

Sharp-beaked ground finch

JERVIS

FERNANDINA

DUNCAN

BALTRA

SANTA CRUZ

Warbler finch

ISABELA

BARRINGTON

Cocos finch

FLOREANA

Ancestor

Darwin's Finches

The descendants of animals that breed after arriving by accident on oceanic islands such as the Galápagos can move into a large number of habitats unclaimed by other animals. By adapting to the varying condi-

tions, one species may evolve into a number of species, each occupying a different ecological niche – a phenomenon known as adaptive radiation. This is one of the reasons why islands have such a large number of unique animals, and it is demonstrated perfectly in the islands making up the Galápagos.

When Charles Darwin landed in the Galápagos in 1835 he was puzzled to find that the birds differed not only from the South American species but also from each other. For example, the mockingbirds of Chat-

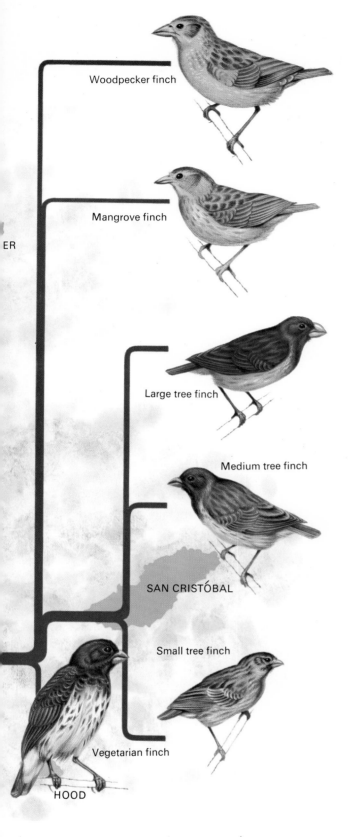

Woodpecker finch

Mangrove finch

Large tree finch

Medium tree finch

SAN CRISTÓBAL

Small tree finch

Vegetarian finch

HOOD

ER

Above: the 13 species of finch found on the Galápagos Islands all came from a common ancestor, as did the Cocos finch that lives 600 miles to the northeast. Over the years these finches sought out new feeding grounds and then adapted to them. Each of the species evolved its own beak shape and size to deal with a different diet. This is an example of the phenomenon of adaptive radiation by which many species evolve from a common one.

ham, Hood, and Charles Islands were each different enough to be classified as different species, even though less than 60 miles separated these islands. There was also a large variety of small finches scat-

tered throughout the islands, all slightly different if similar.

On his return to England Darwin completed his studies of the Galápagos finches, now usually known as Darwin's finches, and wrote: "Seeing this gradation and diversity of structure in one small, intimately related group of birds, one might really fancy that from an original paucity of birds in this archipelago, one species has been taken and modified for different ends."

It seems likely that the ancestor of these finches were small South American birds that were blown from their native home and managed to survive in the new environment many centuries ago. Over the years they colonized the other islands, each time finding a habitat that differed slightly. With no competition from other birds and no predators to contend with, they were able to change and adapt slowly over the generations. As a result, today there are 13 kinds of finches living in the Galápagos group.

These birds have similar dull dark coloring, build the same kind of roofed nests, and lay similar eggs that are white spotted with pink. However, it is the differences between them rather than the similarities that so excited Darwin and have continued to interest zoologists ever since. There are six species of ground finches that feed on seeds and fruit, as did their South American ancestors. The beaks of these birds are of various sizes and designed to deal with the different fruits and seeds they eat. The biggest beak is on the finch eating the toughest seeds, the thinnest on the one mixing its seed with insects. Most of the time, therefore, they do not compete for food, and four of these species live together on most of the islands.

There are also six tree finches, five of them feeding on insects and possessing the thin bill typical of an insect eater. The sixth has a beak like a parrot's and feeds on fruit and buds. One of these arboreal finches is a tool user, one of the few in the avian world. This variety is the woodpecker finch, which feeds on the larvae of wood-boring insects. Lacking the long beak and tongue of the woodpecker, it prizes its prey from under the bark of trees with a cactus spine, trimming the spine for the purpose.

In addition to adaptive radiation, two other phenomena are often demonstrated on islands. One of these is a form of gigantism, seen in the giant tortoises of the Galápagos, Aldabra Island, Tonga, and the Seychelles. The other is the loss of wings in normally winged creatures. The best known example of this is the extinct dodo of Mauritius, and the Galápagos islands have an example of this in the flightless cormorant. This phenomenon is usually seen in insects, however, such as the flightless grasshopper of the Galápagos, the strap-winged fly of Tristan da Cunha, and the wingless fly and moth of Gough Island. Winglessness may be an actual advantage to small insects living on windswept islands because they are less likely to get blown out to sea.

Wildlife of the West Indies

The group of islands known collectively as the West Indies has probably never been connected to the mainland. For example, Cuba, the most westerly of the West Indies, is close to Mexico but there is a surprisingly wide difference between its wildlife and that of the nearby land mass. Of the many islands constituting the West Indies, those most significant for the naturalist are the four biggest, which are Cuba, Jamaica, Hispaniola – politically divided into Haiti and the Dominican Republic – and Puerto Rico.

In countries so limited in space and so heavily populated, it is to be expected that animal life has suffered severely, and this is the case in the West Indies. In fact, the Caribs as precursors of the European settlers, had already wiped out four species of ground sloth. Once agriculture and urban expansion increased, the process of wiping out the indigenous wildlife accelerated. Mammals including several species of shrew, bat, rice rat, hutia, and spiny rat, are now extinct. So are several varieties of parrots and macaws. The list of endangered animals is long and includes the solenodons, other species of hutia, the Cuban crocodile, and owls.

There are two species of solenodon, which are 1-foot-long primitive insectivores similar to shrews. One, sometimes called the almique, inhabits Cuba and the other, the agouta, lives in Haiti. Both are

Below: the solenodon belongs to a family of insectivores that was widespread in North America some 30 million years ago. It was killed off by competition everywhere except in Cuba and Haiti. There are few of them either in the wild or in captivity.

endangered. The solenodons were first discovered by Europeans in 1833. They belong to a family all to themselves although superficially they resemble the tenrecs of Madagascar to which they are related. Unlike tenrecs, they have tails as long as their bodies. Solenodons are nocturnal. Like some of the shrews, their hunting ability is enhanced by the venomous saliva they secrete. A curious feature of the solenodons is that the females' pair of nipples is situated on the buttocks – perhaps because the chest and groin contain musk glands that give off a goatlike scent.

Below: Jamaican trapdoor spiders dig burrows with the aid of comblike spines on the margin of their jaw. They coat the burrow with earth and saliva and line it with the silk they spin.

Formerly free of enemies in their habitat, these animals are now preyed on by dogs, cats, and mongooses introduced by humans.

One of the animals unique to the islands is the hutia, a primitive rodent. Small cousins of the coypus, the hutias resemble the African hyraxes. Most of the 20 species that formerly lived on Cuba, Haiti, Jamaica, and the Bahamas are extinct today.

Hispaniola is the home of the rhinoceros iguana, a large primitive member of its family and distantly related to the iguanas of the Galápagos. Cuba is the habitat of the extremely rare Cuban crocodile, which number about 500 at the most.

Two different types of anolid lizards have come to the West Indies, one from Central America and the other from South America. The Central American varieties settled in Jamaica, while the South American species favored Hispaniola, Puerto Rico, and the more southeastern small islands.

Each parrot species of the West Indies is confined to one island only except for one species that occurs both in the Bahamas and Cuba.

Above: the lesser Indian mongoose was introduced into the West Indies, especially Jamaica, to help get rid of the vipers that infested the islands. They became a pest in turn, and are one of the threats to the solenodon.

Right: an anole eating a bush cricket. Anoles eat both insects and fruit, changing according to their availability by season. Anoles are abundant in all of the West Indies.

The Island Regions: The West Indies

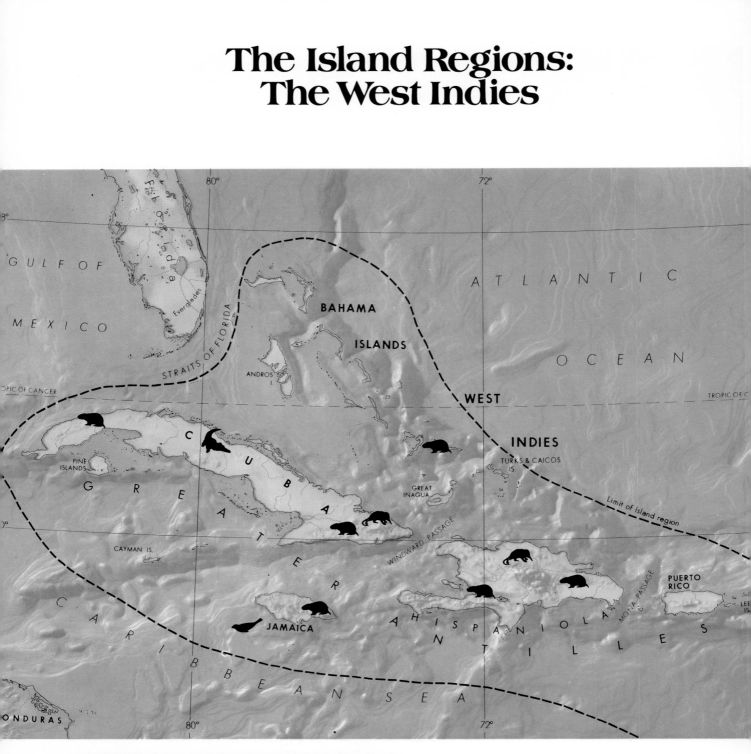

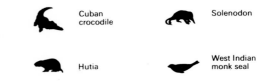

Cuban crocodile

Solenodon

Hutia

West Indian monk seal

Left: the hutia is unknown outside of the West Indies, where there are several species. Those found on Jamaica and Little Swan Island are smaller than the four species that live on Cuba. They have long been a food animal for the local inhabitants, who hunt them with dogs, and since the introduction of the mongoose to the islands, they have had another formidable enemy.
Right: a Cuban crocodile emerging from the water. Like others of its family, this species usually walks with its body held well clear of the ground and its legs moving stiffly directly under the body. When entering the water, however, it will slide on its belly and paddle with its legs. Having been commercially exploited for many years, it is in danger of extinction at the present.

Island Variety

Among the many islands whose wildlife, like that of Madagascar or the Galápagos, differs greatly from the nearest mainland, some occur in groups and others in remote isolation. For instance, in the Indian Ocean there are the island groups of the Maldives, Aldabras, and Seychelles, and the single island of Mauritius. In the Bay of Bengal are the Andaman and Nicobar island groups. In the Atlantic Ocean there are the Azores, the Canary, and the Cape Verde island groups and, further south, such lonely outposts as Ascension Island, St. Helena, and the Tristan da Cunha group. Tiny Gough Island, which is part of Tristan da Cunha but separated from the rest of the group, has such different types of terrain on its small surface that there is never a season when it is not occupied by some kind of migratory bird: petrels, albatrosses, terns, shearwaters, and skuas among them. It also provides a home for the rockhopper penguins that nest there in large communities, laying their eggs in holes in the rocky ground.

Left: a pair of albatrosses courting. It is believed that albatrosses remain with the same mate for life. They breed in large colonies on remote islands, mostly in the southern hemisphere.
Below: the Hawaiian honeycreeper has a long curved beak with which it probes flowers for insects and nectar. Like Darwin's finches, each of the different species of honeycreeper has a bill that is specialized to deal with the kind of food it eats.

Even farther afield from any great land mass are some of the atolls and volcanic islands of the Pacific Ocean such as the Hawaiian group, the Society Islands, and Tahiti.

The same phenomenon of adaptive radiation that Darwin observed on the Galápagos with the finches and tortoises and that is seen with the parrots and lizards of the West Indies is also to be found in Hawaii with its honeycreepers. There are nine different kinds of honeycreepers, all of which evolved from a common ancestor akin to the tanager. Both Hawaii and the Society Islands demonstrate the same diversity of form in their land snails. Hawaii has had a mixture of influences, having been colonized by birds mainly of American origin, and by insects and plants of chiefly Oriental origin.

Aldabra, one of the Indian Ocean islands, supports a huge population of about 80 thousand giant tortoises that have the same kind of association with the white-throated rail that exists between the carmine bee eater and the kori bustard in Africa. As the giant tortoise crawls along, the flightless white-throated rail follows slowly in its wake, devouring the insects disturbed by the enormous reptile's progress.

Mauritius and the Seychelles, also in the Indian Ocean, have some particularly interesting birdlife. There are three very rare birds still to be found on Mauritius. They are the Mauritius kestrel, the rarest falcon in the world, the pink pigeon, and a species of parakeet. The indigenous birds of the Seychelles include the Scops owl on Mahé Island, the paradise flycatcher on La Digue, and the Seychelles fodi, a species of weaverbird, on Cousin, Cousine, and Frigate Islands.

The Canary Islands have the most abundant wildlife of all the Atlantic islands, including the rare monk seal on its coasts. As their name implies, these islands are especially rich in birdlife – not only the canary itself, but also Trocaz and canary pigeons and the very rare laurel pigeon. This last species feeds on laurel berries and nests in deep inaccessible gorges, laying only a single egg per clutch unlike most pigeons. Another indigenous bird is Berthelot's pipit, a species that prefers the ground to the trees and runs rather than hops. The mother pipit is a model of loving care and protection: should her fledglings be threatened she will act as a decoy, luring the enemy away from her brood by chirping and writhing as if she had been injured.

Such lizards as have survived the early settlers' guns include Gallot's lizard, which lives in most habitats from sea level to altitudes of over 10,000 feet. This lizard is not very popular with farmers because of its liking for tomatoes and other fruits, which it adds to its diet of insects, small vertebrates, and carrion on occasion. The small number of Simony's lizards still living in the Canaries have suffered the ironical fate of being nearly exterminated by zoologists in their search for study specimens and zoo stock.

Below: the day gecko, which inhabits the Seychelles, is about 30 percent smaller than its relatives on neighboring Madagascar. Geckos make sounds more often than any other lizard.

Wildlife Endangered

Numerous animals have become extinct throughout the ages, and the process of extinction is known to be speeding up today. There is no doubt that modern civilization has contributed heavily to this endangerment of animal species. The fact is, however, that the process of wildlife extinction was under way well before humans came onto the scene. Zoologists point out that most species of animals that ever lived are now extinct. It is after all a natural process. Extinction is the natural fate of any animal that has specialized too much to change when its environment changes, or of any animal that meets with a better adapted competitor.

There are two kinds of extinction for which humans are to blame. The first is by direct assault; the second is by indirect interference with an animal's habitat. Food, furs, feathers, financial gain, fear, and even fun – all these motives have led mankind to endanger such animals as the American passenger pigeon, the buffalo, the big whales, and the giant turtles by outright killing. All the animals illustrated on these pages are today endangered by human appetites and

Above: there are probably no more than 500 snow leopards left in the Himalayan part of their range, and they are still hunted for their beautiful soft coat in other areas. Their pelts go to the luxury fur trade at very high prices where imports are allowed.

Above: alligators are the last of their kind – the great reptiles related to the prehistoric dinosaurs and also to the remote ancestors of birds. They are killed at a great rate for use of their skins in the leather trade and musk glands in perfumery.
Left: a prospective buyer in a warehouse in Nairobi, Kenya, examines a huge array of zebra, leopard, and antelope skins. The sale of such skins is a good source of revenue for this country.
Below: air is pumped into a dead whale to keep it afloat as it is towed alongside a fishing boat. Technology has triumphed over even the blue whale, largest of all mammals and a giant compared to humans. It is helpless against modern killing methods.

greed. But a large proportion of the wildlife that is in danger of extinction is threatened almost by default. The spread of human industry, urbanization, and agriculture is inevitable if the world's population is to be clothed, fed, and sheltered. In the wake, many of the world's animals could suffer and become extinct as they have before, especially the last 300 years.

What can be done? The setting up of the World Wildlife Fund in 1961 is one outstanding post-World War II effort to save the world's wildlife. There are now more than 600 wildlife parks, reservations, and sanctuaries scattered around the world, and the work they do in animal conservation is extensive. About 200 leading ones are indicated on the next two pages.

Left: unfortunately for the future of the harp seal, it is the pup that is in most demand on the market – both the white-coated baby under 10 days old and the young "beater." Newfoundland herds have been reduced by nearly half in the last 10 years.

317

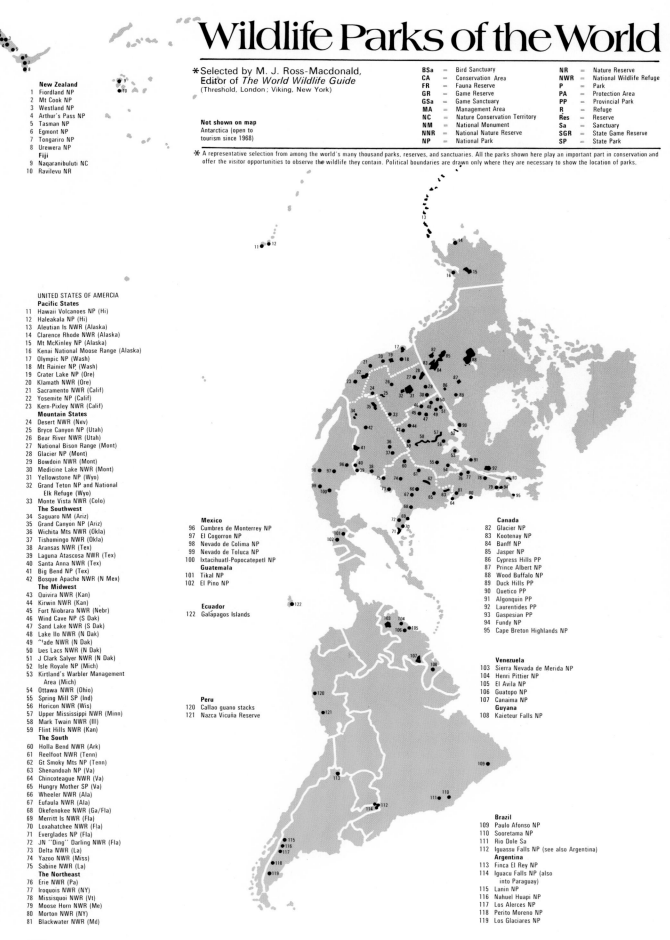

Wildlife Parks of the World

＊Selected by M. J. Ross-Macdonald,
Editor of *The World Wildlife Guide*
(Threshold, London ; Viking, New York)

Not shown on map
Antarctica (open to
tourism since 1968)

BSa	=	Bird Sanctuary	NR	=	Nature Reserve
CA	=	Conservation Area	NWR	=	National Wildlife Refuge
FR	=	Fauna Reserve	P	=	Park
GR	=	Game Reserve	PA	=	Protection Area
GSa	=	Game Sanctuary	PP	=	Provincial Park
MA	=	Management Area	R	=	Refuge
NC	=	Nature Conservation Territory	Res	=	Reserve
NM	=	National Monument	Sa	=	Sanctuary
NNR	=	National Nature Reserve	SGR	=	State Game Reserve
NP	=	National Park	SP	=	State Park

＊ A representative selection from among the world's many thousand parks, reserves, and sanctuaries. All the parks shown here play an important part in conservation and offer the visitor opportunities to observe the wildlife they contain. Political boundaries are drawn only where they are necessary to show the location of parks.

New Zealand
1 Fiordland NP
2 Mt Cook NP
3 Westland NP
4 Arthur's Pass NP
5 Tasman NP
6 Egmont NP
7 Tongariro NP
8 Urewera NP
Fiji
9 Naqaranibuluti NC
10 Ravilevu NR

UNITED STATES OF AMERCIA
Pacific States
11 Hawaii Volcanoes NP (Hi)
12 Haleakala NP (Hi)
13 Aleutian Is NWR (Alaska)
14 Clarence Rhode NWR (Alaska)
15 Mt McKinley NP (Alaska)
16 Kenai National Moose Range (Alaska)
17 Olympic NP (Wash)
18 Mt Rainier NP (Wash)
19 Crater Lake NP (Ore)
20 Klamath NWR (Ore)
21 Sacramento NWR (Calif)
22 Yosemite NP (Calif)
23 Kern-Pixley NWR (Calif)
Mountain States
24 Desert NWR (Nev)
25 Bryce Canyon NP (Utah)
26 Bear River NWR (Utah)
27 National Bison Range (Mont)
28 Glacier NP (Mont)
29 Bowdoin NWR (Mont)
30 Medicine Lake NWR (Mont)
31 Yellowstone NP (Wyo)
32 Grand Teton NP and National
    Elk Refuge (Wyo)
33 Monte Vista NWR (Colo)
The Southwest
34 Saguaro NM (Ariz)
35 Grand Canyon NP (Ariz)
36 Wichita Mts NWR (Okla)
37 Tishomingo NWR (Okla)
38 Aransas NWR (Tex)
39 Laguna Atascosa NWR (Tex)
40 Santa Anna NWR (Tex)
41 Big Bend NP (Tex)
42 Bosque Apache NWR (N Mex)
The Midwest
43 Quivira NWR (Kan)
44 Kirwin NWR (Kan)
45 Fort Niobrara NWR (Nebr)
46 Wind Cave NP (S Dak)
47 Sand Lake NWR (S Dak)
48 Lake Ilo NWR (N Dak)
49 ~lade NWR (N Dak)
50 Des Lacs NWR (N Dak)
51 J Clark Salyer NWR (N Dak)
52 Isle Royale NP (Mich)
53 Kirtland's Warbler Management
    Area (Mich)
54 Ottawa NWR (Ohio)
55 Spring Mill SP (Ind)
56 Horicon NWR (Wis)
57 Upper Mississippi NWR (Minn)
58 Mark Twain NWR (Ill)
59 Flint Hills NWR (Kan)
The South
60 Holla Bend NWR (Ark)
61 Reelfoot NWR (Tenn)
62 Gt Smoky Mts NP (Tenn)
63 Shenandoah NP (Va)
64 Chincoteague NWR (Va)
65 Hungry Mother SP (Va)
66 Wheeler NWR (Ala)
67 Eufaula NWR (Ala)
68 Okefenokee NWR (Ga/Fla)
69 Merritt Is NWR (Fla)
70 Loxahatchee NWR (Fla)
71 Everglades NP (Fla)
72 JN "Ding" Darling NWR (Fla)
73 Delta NWR (La)
74 Yazoo NWR (Miss)
75 Sabine NWR (La)
The Northeast
76 Erie NWR (Pa)
77 Iroquois NWR (NY)
78 Missisquoi NWR (Vt)
79 Moose Horn NWR (Me)
80 Morton NWR (NY)
81 Blackwater NWR (Md)

Mexico
96 Cumbres de Monterrey NP
97 El Cogorron NP
98 Nevado de Colima NP
99 Nevado de Toluca NP
100 Ixtacihuatl-Popocatepetl NP
Guatemala
101 Tikal NP
102 El Pino NP

Ecuador
122 Galápagos Islands

Peru
120 Callao guano stacks
121 Nazca Vicuña Reserve

Canada
82 Glacier NP
83 Kootenay NP
84 Banff NP
85 Jasper NP
86 Cypress Hills PP
87 Prince Albert NP
88 Wood Buffalo NP
89 Duck Hills PP
90 Quetico PP
91 Algonquin PP
92 Laurentides PP
93 Gaspesian PP
94 Fundy NP
95 Cape Breton Highlands NP

Venezuela
103 Sierra Nevada de Merida NP
104 Henri Pittier NP
105 El Avila NP
106 Guatopo NP
107 Canaima NP
Guyana
108 Kaieteur Falls NP

Brazil
109 Paulo Afonso NP
110 Sooretama NP
111 Rio Dole Sa
112 Iguassu Falls NP (see also Argentina)
Argentina
113 Finca El Rey NP
114 Iguacu Falls NP (also
      into Paraguay)
115 Lanin NP
116 Nahuel Huapi NP
117 Los Alerces NP
118 Perito Moreno NP
119 Los Glaciares NP

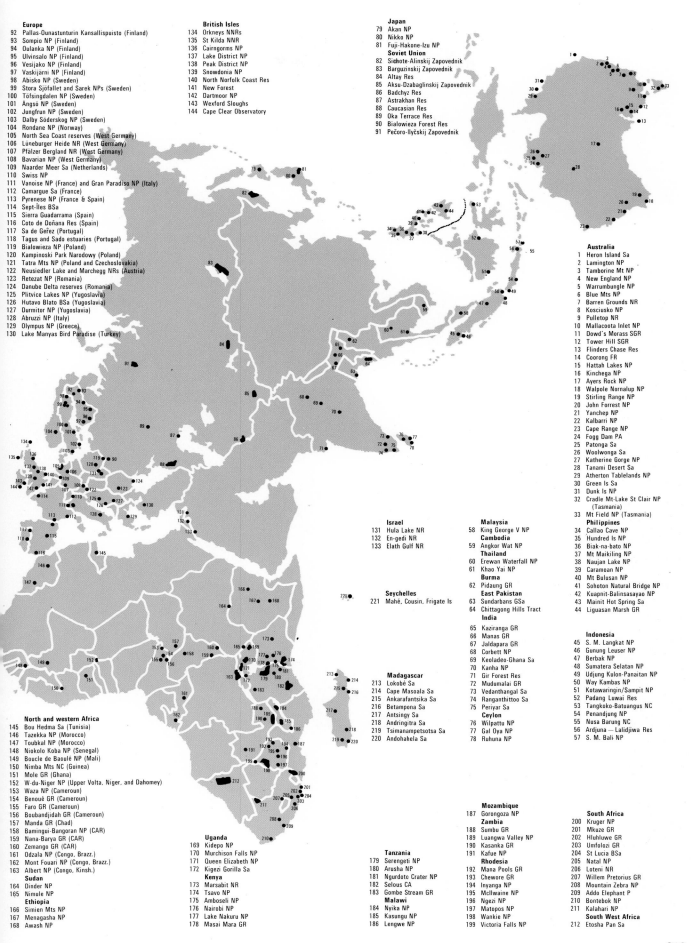

Europe
92 Pallas-Ounastunturin Kansallispuisto (Finland)
93 Sompio NP (Finland)
94 Oulanka NP (Finland)
95 Ulvinsalo NP (Finland)
96 Vesijako NP (Finland)
97 Vaskijarni NP (Finland)
98 Abisko NP (Sweden)
99 Stora Sjöfallet and Sarek NPs (Sweden)
100 Töfsingdalen NP (Sweden)
101 Ångsö NP (Sweden)
102 Jungfrun NP (Sweden)
103 Dalby Söderskog NP (Sweden)
104 Rondane NP (Norway)
105 North Sea Coast reserves (West Germany)
106 Lüneburger Heide NR (West Germany)
107 Pfälzer Bergland NR (West Germany)
108 Bavarian NP (West Germany)
109 Naarder Meer Sa (Netherlands)
110 Swiss NP
111 Vanoise NP (France) and Gran Paradiso NP (Italy)
112 Camargue Sa (France)
113 Pyrenese NP (France & Spain)
114 Sept-Îles BSa
115 Sierra Guadarrama (Spain)
116 Coto de Doñana Res (Spain)
117 Sa de Gerêz (Portugal)
118 Tagus and Sado estuaries (Portugal)
119 Bialowieza NP (Poland)
120 Kampinoski Park Narodowy (Poland)
121 Tatra Mts NP (Poland and Czechoslovakia)
122 Neusiedler Lake and Marchegg NRs (Austria)
123 Retezat NP (Romania)
124 Danube Delta reserves (Romania)
125 Plitvice Lakes NP (Yugoslavia)
126 Hutavo Blato BSa (Yugoslavia)
127 Durmitor NP (Yugoslavia)
128 Abruzzi NP (Italy)
129 Olympus NP (Greece)
130 Lake Manyas Bird Paradise (Turkey)

British Isles
134 Orkneys NNRs
135 St Kilda NNR
136 Cairngorms NP
137 Lake District NP
138 Peak District NP
139 Snowdonia NP
140 North Norfolk Coast Res
141 New Forest
142 Dartmoor NP
143 Wexford Sloughs
144 Cape Clear Observatory

Japan
79 Akan NP
80 Nikko NP
81 Fuji-Hakone-Izu NP

Soviet Union
82 Sichote-Alinskij Zapovednik
83 Barguzinskij Zapovednik
84 Altay Res
85 Aksu-Dzabaglinskij Zapovednik
86 Badchyz Res
87 Astrakhan Res
88 Caucasian Res
89 Oka Terrace Res
90 Bialowieza Forest Res
91 Pečoro-Ilyčskij Zapovednik

Israel
131 Hula Lake NR
132 En-gedi NR
133 Elath Gulf NR

Seychelles
221 Mahé, Cousin, Frigate Is

Malaysia
58 King George V NP
Cambodia
59 Angkor Wat NP
Thailand
60 Erewan Waterfall NP
61 Khao Yai NP
Burma
62 Pidaung GR
East Pakistan
63 Sundarbans GSa
64 Chittagong Hills Tract
India
65 Kaziranga GR
66 Manas GR
67 Jaldapara GR
68 Corbett NP
69 Keoladeo-Ghana Sa
70 Kanha NP
71 Gir Forest Res
72 Mudumalai GR
73 Vedanthangal Sa
74 Ranganthittoo Sa
75 Periyar Sa
Ceylon
76 Wilpattu NP
77 Gal Oya NP
78 Ruhuna NP

Madagascar
213 Lokobé Sa
214 Cape Masoala Sa
215 Ankarafantsika Sa
216 Betampona Sa
217 Antsingy Sa
218 Andringitra Sa
219 Tsimanampetsotsa Sa
220 Andohahela Sa

Australia
1 Heron Island Sa
2 Lamington NP
3 Tamborine Mt NP
4 New England NP
5 Warrumbungle NP
6 Blue Mts NP
7 Barren Grounds NR
8 Kosciusko NP
9 Pulletop NR
10 Mallacoota Inlet NP
11 Dowd's Morass SGR
12 Tower Hill SGR
13 Flinders Chase Res
14 Coorong FR
15 Hattah Lakes NP
16 Kinchega NP
17 Ayers Rock NP
18 Walpole Nornalup NP
19 Stirling Range NP
20 John Forrest NP
21 Yanchep NP
22 Kalbarri NP
23 Cape Range NP
24 Fogg Dam PA
25 Patonga NP
26 Woolwonga Sa
27 Katherine Gorge NP
28 Tanami Desert Sa
29 Atherton Tablelands NP
30 Green Is Sa
31 Dunk Is NP
32 Cradle Mt-Lake St Clair NP (Tasmania)
33 Mt Field NP (Tasmania)

Philippines
34 Callao Cave NP
35 Hundred Is NP
36 Biak-na-bato NP
37 Mt Maikiling NP
38 Naujan Lake NP
39 Caramoan NP
40 Mt Bulusan NP
41 Sohoton Natural Bridge NP
42 Kuapnit-Balinsasayao NP
43 Mainit Hot Spring Sa
44 Liguasan Marsh GR

Indonesia
45 S. M. Langkat NP
46 Gunung Leuser NP
47 Berbak NP
48 Sumatera Selatan NP
49 Udjung Kulon-Panaitan NP
50 Way Kambas NP
51 Kotawaringin/Sampit NP
52 Padang Luwai NP
53 Tangkoko-Batuangus NC
54 Penandjung NP
55 Nusa Barung NC
56 Ardjuna — Lalidjiwa Res
57 S. M. Bali NP

North and western Africa
145 Bou Hedma Sa (Tunisia)
146 Tazekka NP (Morocco)
147 Toubkal NP (Morocco)
148 Niokolo Koba NP (Senegal)
149 Boucle de Baoulé NP (Mali)
150 Nimba Mts NC (Guinea)
151 Mole GR (Ghana)
152 W-du-Niger NP (Upper Volta, Niger, and Dahomey)
153 Waza NP (Cameroun)
154 Benoué GR (Cameroun)
155 Faro GR (Cameroun)
156 Boubandjidah GR (Cameroun)
157 Manda GR (Chad)
158 Bamingui-Bangoran NP (CAR)
159 Nana-Barya GR (CAR)
160 Zemango GR (CAR)
161 Odzala NP (Congo, Brazz.)
162 Mont Fouari NP (Congo, Brazz.)
163 Albert NP (Congo, Kinsh.)
Sudan
164 Dinder NP
165 Nimule NP
Ethiopia
166 Simien Mts NP
167 Menagasha NP
168 Awash NP

Uganda
169 Kidepo NP
170 Murchison Falls NP
171 Queen Elizabeth NP
172 Kigezi Gorilla Sa
Kenya
173 Marsabit NR
174 Tsavo NP
175 Amboseli NP
176 Nairobi NP
177 Lake Nakuru NP
178 Masai Mara GR

Tanzania
179 Serengeti NP
180 Arusha NP
181 Ngurdoto Crater NP
182 Selous CA
183 Gombe Stream GR
Malawi
184 Nyika NP
185 Kasungu NP
186 Lengwe NP

Mozambique
187 Gorongoza NP
Zambia
188 Sumbu GR
189 Luangwa Valley NP
190 Kasanka GR
191 Kafue NP
Rhodesia
192 Mana Pools GR
193 Chewore GR
194 Inyanga NP
195 McIlwaine NP
196 Ngezi NP
197 Matopos NP
198 Wankie NP
199 Victoria Falls NP

South Africa
200 Kruger NP
201 Mkuze GR
202 Hluhluwe GR
203 Umfolozi GR
204 St Lucia BSa
205 Natal NP
206 Loteni NR
207 Willem Pretorius GR
208 Mountain Zebra NP
209 Addo Elephant P
210 Bontebok NP
211 Kalahari NP
South West Africa
212 Etosha Pan Sa

319

Index

The end of the day for an African fish
eagle in the Okavango swamps of
Botswana. This smallest of the sea
eagles has a range covering all of Africa
south of the Sahara, living near rivers,
lakes, the ocean, and sometimes swamps.
Fish eagles often choose a favorite
perch and use it regularly as a lookout
post for sighting their prey.

322

Picture Credits

226(B)	Gerald Cubitt/Bruce Coleman Ltd.
227(T)	Peter Jackson/Bruce Coleman Ltd.
227(B)	C. B. Frith/Bruce Coleman Ltd.
228	Jane Burton/Bruce Coleman Ltd.
229(TL)	Jane Burton/Bruce Coleman Ltd.
229(TR)	Bruce Coleman Ltd.
229(C)	Göetz D. Plage/Bruce Coleman Ltd.
229(B)	Sullivan & Rogers/Bruce Coleman Ltd.
230(L)	Frank W. Lane
230(TR)	Taneka Kojo/Animals Animals © 1973
230(BR)	M. P. L. Fogden/Bruce Coleman Ltd.
231	Bruce Coleman Ltd.
232(T)	Norman Tomalin/Bruce Coleman Inc.
232(B)	Tom McHugh/Photo Researchers Inc.
233	Grzimek/Okapia
234	C. B. & D. W. Frith/Bruce Coleman Ltd.
235(T)	H. A. E. Lucas/Spectrum Colour Library
235(B)	C. B. & D. W. Frith/Bruce Coleman Ltd.
236	De Klemm/Jacana
237	A. Rainon/Pitch
238	J. Brownlie/Bruce Coleman Ltd.
240(L)	Jane Burton/Bruce Coleman Ltd.
241(T)	D. Fröbisch/ZEFA
241(B)	Aldus Archives
242(T)	Janet Finch/Frank W. Lane
242(BL)	Bruce Coleman Ltd.
242(R)	S. C. Bisserot/Bruce Coleman Ltd.
243(T)	John Wallis/Bruce Coleman Ltd.
243(B)	Frederic/Jacana
244–245	© Aldus Books
246	John Markham/Bruce Coleman Ltd.
247(T)	Douglas Baglin Photography Pty. Ltd./NHPA
247(B)	Bruce Coleman Ltd.
248(L)	Leonard Lee Rue III/Bruce Coleman Ltd.
249(T)	J. R. Brownlie/Bruce Coleman Ltd.
249(B)	G. R. Roberts, Nelson, New Zealand
250(T)	Graham Pizzey/Bruce Coleman Ltd.
250(B)	Jack Fields/Photo Researchers Inc.
251	Graham Pizzey/Bruce Coleman Ltd.
252(L)	A. Eddy/National Science Photos
252(R)	J. R. Brownlie/Bruce Coleman Ltd.
253(T)	Bruce Coleman Ltd.
253(B)	Francisco Erize/Bruce Coleman Ltd.
254	G. R. Roberts, Nelson, New Zealand
255(T)	G. R. Roberts, Nelson, New Zealand
255(B)	J. R. Brownlie/Bruce Coleman Ltd.
256(T)	Bruce Coleman Ltd.
256(B)	J. R. Brownlie/Bruce Coleman Ltd.
257(T)	Francisco Erize/Bruce Coleman Ltd.
257(B)	Bruce Coleman Ltd.
258	Jane Burton/Bruce Coleman Ltd.
259(T)	G. R. Roberts, Nelson, New Zealand
259(B)	Janet Finch/Frank W. Lane
260	Bruce Coleman Ltd.
261(R)	Graham Pizzey/Bruce Coleman Ltd.
262(L)	John Wallis/Bruce Coleman Ltd.
262(R)	Bill Angove/Colorific!
263(T)	John Wallis/Bruce Coleman Ltd.
263(B)	Graham Pizzey/Bruce Coleman Ltd.
264	Donald Trounson/The Photographic Library of Australia
265(T)	F. Park/ZEFA
265(BL)	Bruce Coleman Ltd.
265(BR)	Graham Pizzey/Bruce Coleman Ltd.
266(T)	John W. Brownlie/Bruce Coleman Inc.
266(B)	Eric Crichton/Bruce Coleman Ltd.
267(L)	Bruce Coleman Ltd.
267(R)	R. W. Burton/Bruce Coleman Ltd.
268(L)	V. Serventy/Bruce Coleman Inc.
269(T)	Bruce Coleman Ltd.
269(B)	J. R. Brownlie/Bruce Coleman Ltd.
270	Picturepoint, London
271(TL)	Al Giddings/Bruce Coleman Inc.
271(TR)	Cyril Laubscher/Bruce Coleman Ltd.
271(B)	K. W. Pink/Bruce Coleman Inc.
272	Bruce Coleman Ltd.
273(T)	Bruce Coleman Ltd.
273(B)	Tom Myers/Tom Stack & Associates
274	Alain Compost/Bruce Coleman Ltd.
275(TR) (B)	Brian Coates/Bruce Coleman Ltd.
276	Jen & Des Bartlett/Bruce Coleman Ltd.
278(T)	Andrew Clarke/British Antarctic Survey
278(B)	D. & K. Urry/Bruce Coleman Ltd.
279	J. Prevost/Jacana
280	© Aldus Books
281	Clem Haagner/Ardea, London
282	Francisco Erize/Bruce Coleman Ltd.
283(L)	Mario Fantin/Photo Researchers Inc.
283(R)	Carleton Ray/Photo Researchers Inc.
284	G. Williamson/Bruce Coleman Inc.
285	Institute of Oceanographic Sciences
286	Bruce Coleman Ltd.
288	Mats Wibe Lund
289(TL)	Mats Wibe Lund
289(R)	Heather Angel
290(L)	Heather Angel
290(R)	Peter Johnson/NHPA
291(T)	Eric Hosking
291(B)	Fritz/Jacana
292(L)	C. B. Frith/Bruce Coleman Ltd.
292(R)	G. D. Plage/Bruce Coleman Ltd.
293(T)	Masud Quraishy/Bruce Coleman Ltd.
293(B)	Gerald Cubitt
294	© Aldus Books
295	Norman Myers/Bruce Coleman Ltd.
296(L)	Gerald Cubitt
296(R)	A. Jolly/Photo Researchers Inc.
297(TR)	R. D. Martin/Bruce Coleman Ltd.
297(BR)	Norman Myers/Bruce Coleman Ltd.
298	Photo Centre Ltd./NHPA
299(TR)	M. F. Soper/Bruce Coleman Ltd.
299(L) (BR)	G. R. Roberts, Nelson, New Zealand
300	Bill N. Kleeman/Tom Stack & Associates
301	© Aldus Books
302(T)	Frank W. Lane
302(B)	M. F. Soper/Bruce Coleman Ltd.
303(T)	M. F. Soper/Bruce Coleman Ltd.
303(BR)	John Markham/Bruce Coleman Ltd.
304(L)	Adrian Warren/Ardea, London
304(R)	Heather Angel
305(TRL) (TR)	Heather Angel
305(BR)	Philippa Scott/NHPA
306(T)	© Aldus Books
306(B)	Heather Angel
307	Heather Angel
308–309	David Nockels © Aldus Books
310(T)	Oxford Scientific Films/Bruce Coleman Inc.
310(B)	Bert/Jacana
311(T)	Jane Burton/Bruce Coleman Ltd.
311(B)	David Hughes/Bruce Coleman Ltd.
312(T)	© Aldus Books
312(B)	Norman Tomalin/Bruce Coleman Ltd.
313	M. Timothy O'Keefe/Bruce Coleman Ltd.
314	Sven Gillsäter/Tiofoto
315(T)	J. A. Hancock/Bruce Coleman Ltd.
315(B)	Marilyn Silverstone/Magnum
316(T)	ZEFA
316(B)	Bruce Coleman Ltd.
317(T)	James Simon/Bruce Coleman Ltd.
317(BL)	ZEFA
317(BR)	Peter Poole © Aldus Books
318–319	© Aldus Books
320	Göetz D. Plage/Bruce Coleman Ltd.